IMAGES
of America

CRETE

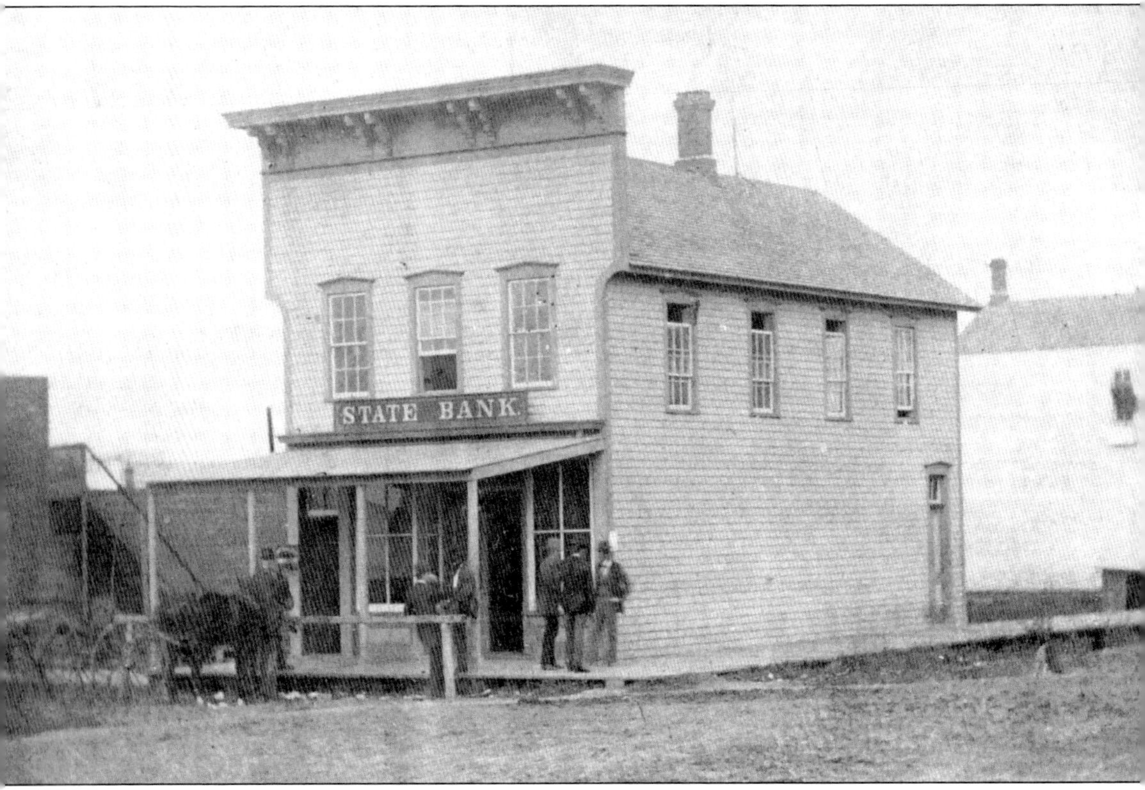

In the beginning . . . this photograph shows the northeast corner of Thirteenth Street and Maine Avenue in the 1870s. The State Bank of Nebraska, organized by Col. Thomas Doane, John R. Clark, and John Fitzgerald, was built there in 1872. In 1879, this frame structure was replaced by a brick building, which appears several times in this book. This barren scene is a reminder of just how far Crete has come. (Saline County Historical Society.)

On the Cover: In May 1888, downtown Crete displayed an impressive collection of new brick business buildings. In this view, looking southwest from the Thirteenth Street and Maine Avenue intersection, a group of boys gathers near 20-year-old Harry Buchanan, who is seated on his nickel-plated bicycle, in front of the First National Bank. (Author's collection.)

IMAGES
of America

CRETE

Janet L. Jeffries

ARCADIA
PUBLISHING

ISBN 978-0-7385-9392-0

Published by Arcadia Publishing
Charleston, South Carolina

Printed in the United States of America

Library of Congress Control Number: 2012932363

For all general information, please contact Arcadia Publishing:
Telephone 843-853-2070
Fax 843-853-0044
E-mail sales@arcadiapublishing.com
For customer service and orders:
Toll-Free 1-888-313-2665

Visit us on the Internet at www.arcadiapublishing.com

This book is dedicated to these historians, now deceased, who spent much of their lives researching, recording, and sharing Crete and Doane College history:

Sandra Jones Breitkreutz
Dr. Annadora Foss Gregory
Alice Sebek Kalkwarf
M. David Osterhout
Lloyd K. Reeves
Dr. Donald J. Ziegler

Contents

Acknowledgments

I have long been absorbed in family and local history. Senior family members, particularly my great-grandfather, Fred W. Ball, often talked of the "old days" in Crete and Nebraska. My mother, Bernice, a schoolteacher, and my father, Donald, a lineman, part-time farmer, and horseman, regularly had the family engaged in re-creating activities of the past, such as farming with horse-drawn equipment, churning butter, grinding wheat, and quilting. I rode sidesaddle in theme parades and carried the mailbag during the reenactment of the statewide pony express run during Nebraska's 1967 centennial.

I am fortunate that my work has required activity in local and state history. My time as historian/architectural historian at the Nebraska State Historical Society and Berggren Architects, my role as Doane College historian and archivist, and my duties with the Crete Heritage Society have further allowed me to research and share area history with a wide constituency.

Several people generously loaned photographs for this book. I am particularly thankful to Judy Rada of the Saline County Historical Society, who shared an amazing collection of historic Crete photographs. Photographs are credited as follows: Saline County Historical Society (SCHS), Crete Heritage Society (CHS), Doane College Archives (DCA), and United Church of Christ, First Congregational (UCC). Others who loaned photographs are acknowledged on the pages where their images appear.

I appreciate the support of my friends at the *Crete News*, particularly Barbara Nigg and Jennifer Lampila, who helped uncover missing pieces of information and allowed me free reign of their archives. Other townspeople kindly gave me specifics when I called to verify facts and jar memories.

Scott Kuncl and my husband, Ted Beauvais, provided advice and assistance when it was time to sort photographs and double-check facts, and my family was patient when I neglected them to work on the book.

I am pleased that Arcadia Publishing and my editor, Winnie Rodgers, gave me the opportunity to introduce Crete to a larger audience.

I am especially grateful to my sister, Joyce C. Jeffries, who spent countless hours proofreading various drafts of this work and was a sounding board during this project.

—Janet L. Jeffries
2012

INTRODUCTION

Crete is situated on the east bank of the Big Blue River, 25 miles southwest of Lincoln, Nebraska's capitol city. Although not the county seat, Crete is the largest town in Saline County, currently boasting a population of more than 6,000 residents.

Settlers first arrived at the Crete townsite in the early 1860s and included Jesse Bickle and his wife, Elizabeth, who are credited as the town's first permanent residents. They homesteaded on the river about 1863 and built a log cabin that still stands today as part of a larger frame house, now a house museum owned by the Crete Heritage Society. The Bickles were from Crete, Illinois, and they named the post office they operated in their log house Crete, after their former home.

Land speculation began soon after it was announced that the Burlington Missouri River Railroad (BMRR) would build a line through northern Saline County. Jesse Bickle platted a townsite, called Blue River City, on the southeast portion of his homestead and became very involved with town building. Although Bickle is generally recognized as the official founder of Crete, many other people, including BMRR civil engineer Col. Thomas Doane and other Doane College founders were also deeply involved in Crete's early development.

When Thomas Doane built the rail line through this part of the state, he named several towns alphabetically from east to west, beginning with Asylum in Lancaster County and ending with Lowell in Kearney County. Many of these communities were named for towns in Doane's native Massachusetts. The BMRR Townsite Company platted a town adjacent to Blue River City, and conflict developed over the situation. After much discussion, a compromise was reached and Bickle's Crete post office name was allowed to prevail because Doane needed a "C" town at this location.

The two infant towns were officially combined as Crete on March 7, 1871, and began to thrive as a regional agricultural trade center. When a bridge was completed over the Big Blue River that same year, the town served as an outfitting point for settlers moving west by wagon.

Colonel Doane chose Crete as the location for a congregational college and convinced the railroad company to donate 600 acres adjacent to the new townsite for this purpose. The college was incorporated on July 11, 1872.

Crete developed more rapidly than most small Nebraska towns, even without the advantages of being a county seat. The town's early commercial boosters, including homesteaders like the Bickles, were soon joined by a group of cultivated New Englanders working to establish the college. The influence of the Doane College founders gave an element of refinement to the community, and during the 1870s and 1880s, the cultural climate in Crete was quite genteel for the time. Doane College brought many economic and social advantages to the city.

Several interesting examples of cultural activity took place in the young frontier town. In 1879, city fathers chose a parklike design for Riverside Cemetery in the spirit of Mount Auburn Cemetery in Massachusetts, resulting in a landscape style unusual to the frontier at that time.

In 1882, Doane College officials and other influential Nebraska religious leaders organized the state's first Chautauqua assembly. An elaborate Chautauqua park was platted adjacent to Riverside Cemetery on the western edge of Crete to accommodate the annual event. Pleasure boating on the Big Blue River, the broad entertainment fare offered at Band's Opera House, and the events available to the public at the college formed a unique cultural combination for the rural community. The residential architecture still extant in the College Hill and Prospect Hill neighborhoods also alludes to the genteel lifestyles of the late-19th-century residents.

Crete's original north-south street names indicate the influence of the New England town builders. The seven avenues west of Boswell, which fronts the college campus, were originally named for New England states like Connecticut, Rhode Island, and New Hampshire. The main commercial street was called Maine Avenue, after the state of Maine. The streets were renamed after trees in the 1920s.

The Crete Mills is the oldest industry in the community. It dates to 1869, when it opened as a water-powered sawmill in the south part of town under the name Mapleton Mills. By 1870, a gristmill was also in operation there. The mill went through several name changes and one location change in its first 20 years and became well known regionally and nationally. As early as 1878, goods were being shipped as far away as Scotland. The mill is still in operation today as a division of Bunge Milling and processes corn used in a variety of food products for national and international markets.

Crete was home to two-term Nebraska governor James W. Dawes, a pioneer lawyer who served as governor from 1883 to 1887. His 1880s house still stands in the College Hill Historic District.

Arbor Day founder J. Sterling Morton of Nebraska City was a friend of several Crete residents, including Thomas Doane and local nurseryman E.F. Stephens. Stephens and Doane were both intrigued by the idea of tree planting on the prairie. On the advice of Morton, experimentation in growing species of trees and plants on the prairie was carried out in the landscaping of Thomas Doane's BMRR grades and on the Doane College campus. Many of these original trees remain part of the campus landscape.

Crete's population in the late 19th century was comprised of several ethnic groups, primarily Bohemians and Germans. Though the German population was substantial, immigrants from the Czech lands have left the most significant mark on the historic and contemporary ethnic landscape in the Crete and Saline County area. Crete's ethnic mix continues to evolve and has changed significantly in the last several years. The current immigrant population is now represented by a substantial number of Hispanic and Asian families.

Crete vied for the Saline County seat twice and lost. In 1877, a movement was launched to move the courthouse to Crete from nearby Pleasant Hill, since that town had not yet attracted a railroad. A countywide election was held, allowing citizens to vote between Crete, Pleasant Hill, and Wilber. Wilber received the greatest number of votes. In 1927, the question of county seat location again surfaced, this time fueled by a deteriorating courthouse building. The 1870s courthouse in Wilber needed to be replaced, so the county considered building a new courthouse in Crete. Wilber again won the election, and the new courthouse was built on the site of the old one. Since the early 20th century, however, Crete has hosted the Saline County Fair on the former Chautauqua grounds, now called Tuxedo Park.

Crete has made steady economic progress and experienced continual population growth throughout its 140-year history. The town is recognized as a progressive community that maintains its hometown charm and historical character. Several vintage homes and college buildings are listed in the National Register of Historic Places within the College Hill Historic District, the Doane College Historic District, and in individual nominations. The photographs presented in the following pages provide the reader with a captivating look at Crete's past.

One

A Vital Downtown

After Crete and Blue River City combined in 1871, town builders developed the area south of the Burlington Missouri River Railroad (BMRR) tracks as the commercial district. The town was designed in grid form by the BMRR's townsite company and was established primarily on the adjacent homesteads of Mary George and Jesse Bickle. Crete grew as a T-town, with the tracks and the main commercial street running perpendicular to one another. Crete's 19th-century business district emerged along Maine Avenue between Ninth Street and the railroad tracks that cross Maine Avenue near Fifteenth Street. Early businesses were also located on Thirteenth Street, the major east-west thoroughfare through town, as well as on and near Illinois and New Hampshire Avenues near the tracks (later named Norman and Linden Avenues respectively). The BMRR railroad line dissected the plat on a northeast/southwest diagonal with the majority of the town south of the tracks. A second rail line was built by the Missouri Pacific in 1888 and came into Crete from the southeast, crossing Maine Avenue just north of Ninth Street.

Although Crete had a municipal block, Central Park, that housed the city hall and the jail, not all community activities took place there. The intersection of Maine Avenue and Thirteenth Street, outfitted with a moveable bandstand, often became the nucleus of town in lieu of the typical town squares that defined many Nebraska town plans.

Maine Avenue was spelled with an "e" until 1922, when the names of the north-south streets in Crete were changed from states to trees. In this book, the historic spelling of Maine Avenue is used.

By 1872, Crete boasted 83 diverse commercial and industrial establishments and several professional services such as attorneys and physicians. Crete's first newspaper, the *Saline County Post,* was publishing by 1871. Many early operations evolved into long-term businesses.

The first downtown buildings were generally frame, but during the later 19th and early 20th centuries, most were replaced by brick and concrete block structures. The following photographs of downtown street scenes offer insight into commercial life in Crete through the middle of the 20th century.

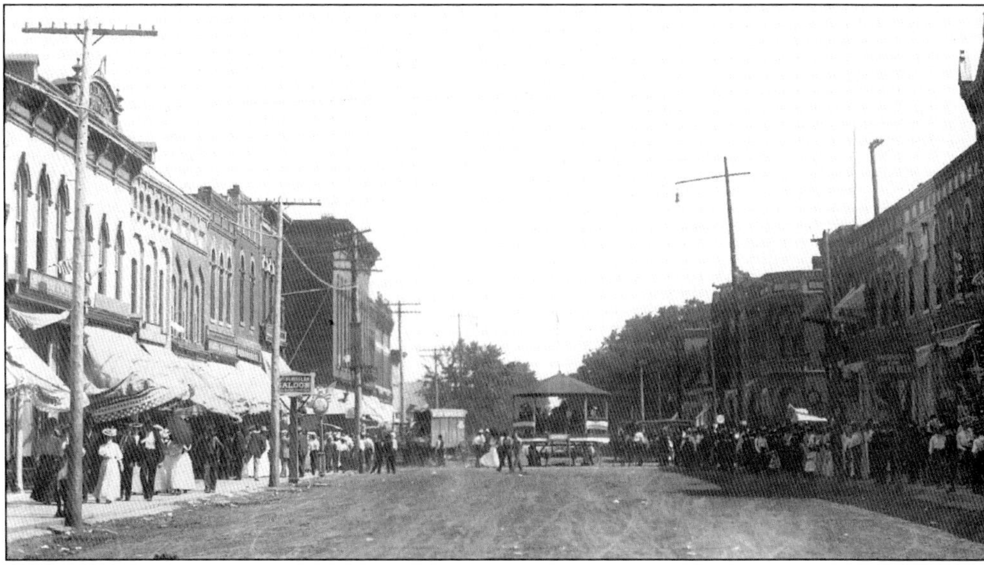

This 1900 photograph, looking north from the 1200 block, shows the bandstand in the Thirteenth Street and Maine Avenue intersection where people gathered for a community event. The extended awnings on the west side indicate that the photograph was taken in the morning. (Robert Sykes collection.)

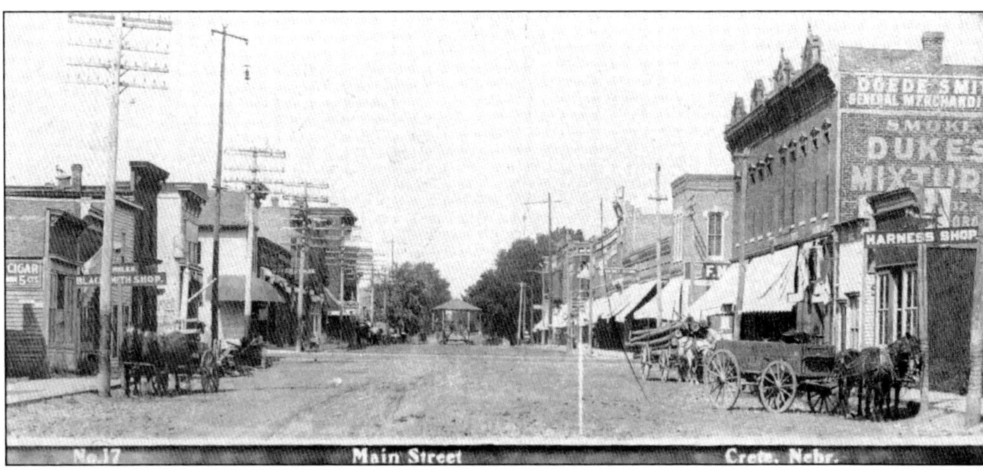

This view looking north on Maine Avenue in the late 1880s also shows a bandstand at Thirteenth Street and Maine Avenue. On the right, or the east side of the street, is Doede Smith's general store, which still stands on the southeast corner of Twelfth Street and Maine Avenue, although it has been stripped of its architectural details. Several small frame store buildings are still extant at this time. (Robert Sykes collection.)

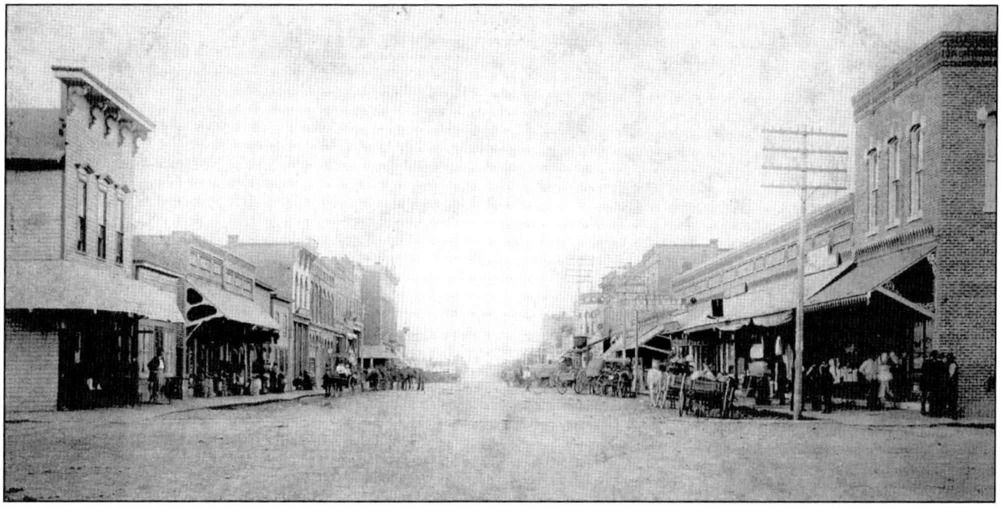

This 1890s view of Maine Avenue looks north from Twelfth Street. The frame false-front building on the left is Fred Boekel's IXL Meat Market. That corner later became the site of City National Bank. The brick building on the right is Frank Nedela's saloon and drugstore. North of Nedela's store are the buildings that once housed Ben Franklin and are now home to K.H.'s Sport Shop and Crete Floral and Gifts. (*Crete News* collection.)

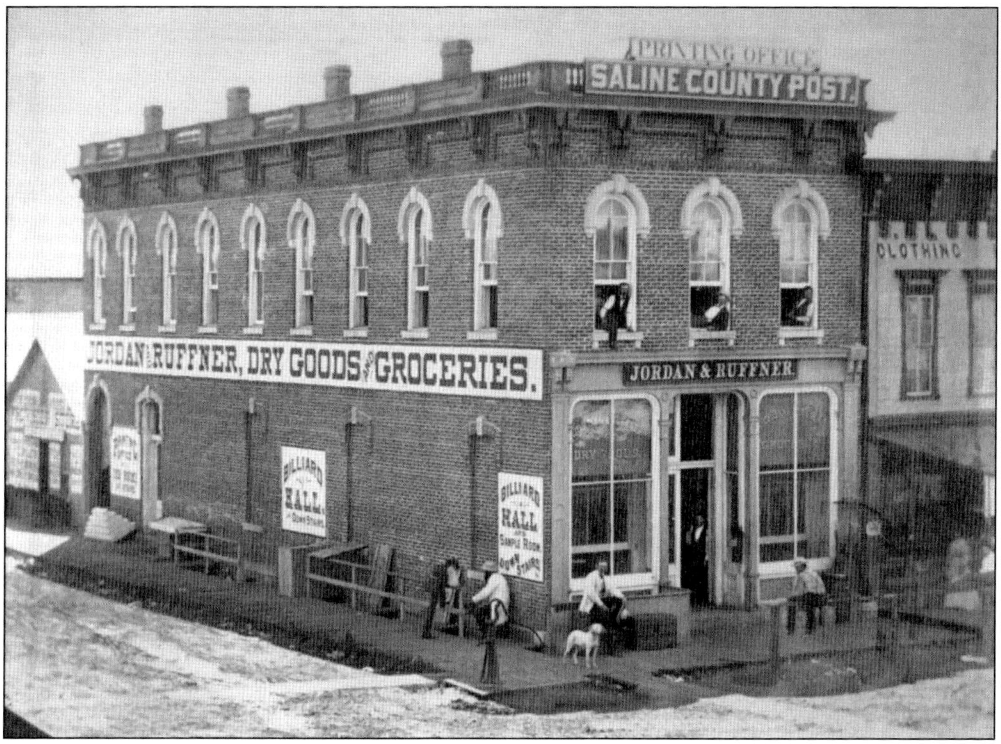

This building, at the southeast corner of Thirteenth Street and Maine Avenue, was built by T.H. Miller, who rented it out for commercial use. This corner is still the town's major intersection. In the 1870s and early 1880s, the building was home to the Jordan and Ruffner store. The *Saline County Post* newspaper, founded in 1871, operated from the second story. Later, Steidl Drug occupied the site. (Author's collection.)

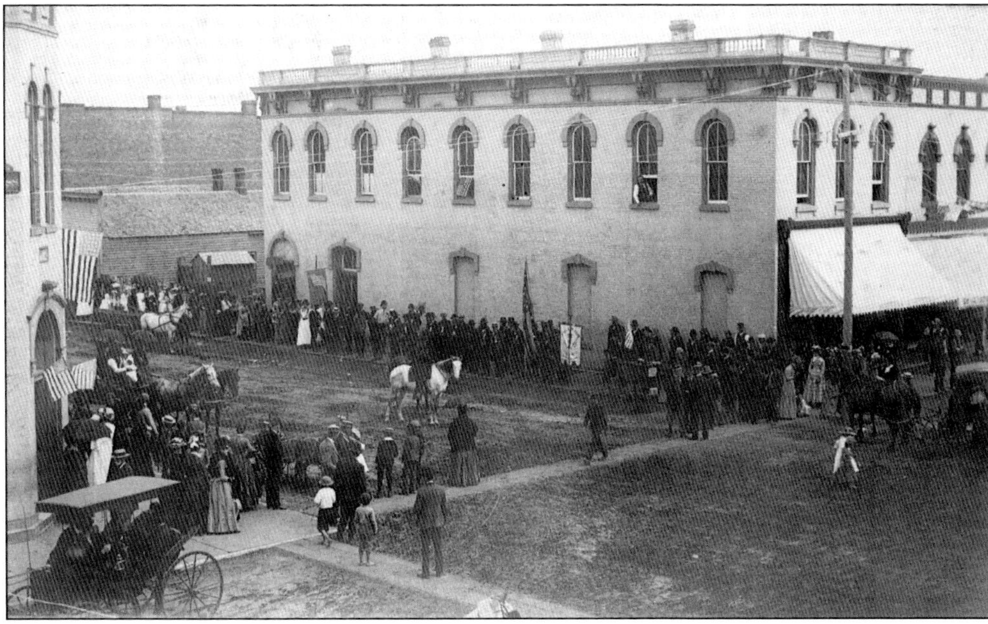

This 1883 view looks southeast toward the intersection of Thirteenth Street and Maine Avenue, probably from the upper level of Band's Opera House. The white GAR banner is seen against the building housing Steidl Drug—formerly the Jordan and Ruffner store location—suggesting this was a political event. The State Bank of Nebraska's corner entrance is at the far left. (CHS.)

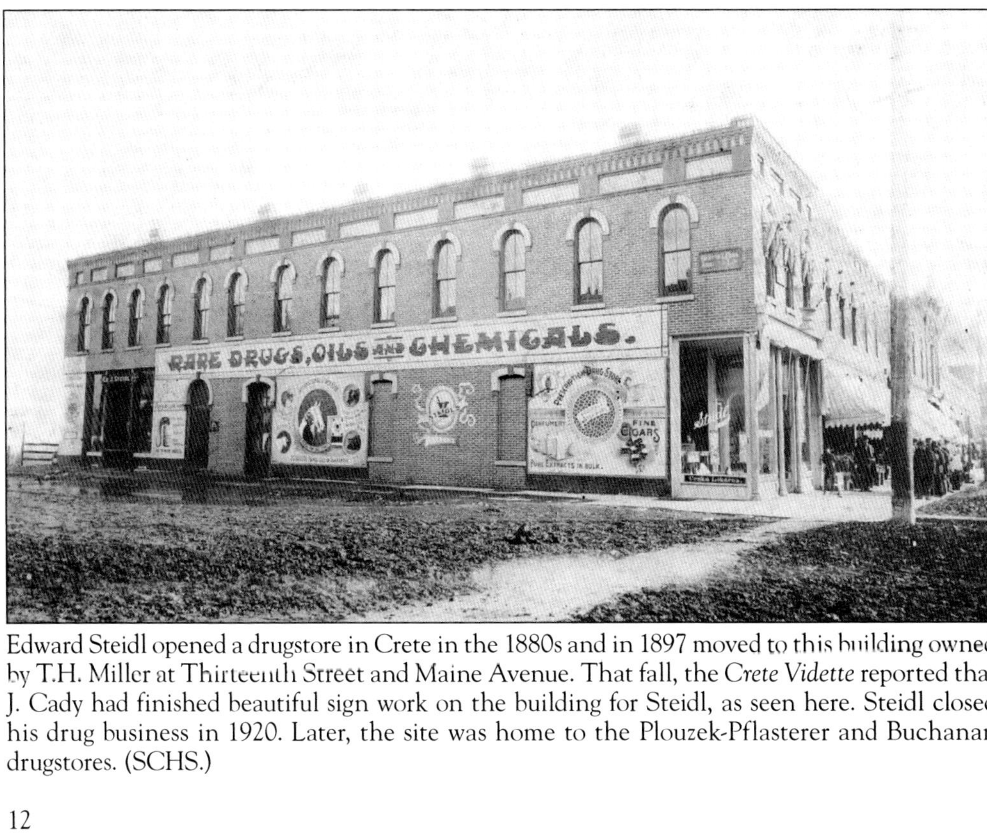

Edward Steidl opened a drugstore in Crete in the 1880s and in 1897 moved to this building owned by T.H. Miller at Thirteenth Street and Maine Avenue. That fall, the *Crete Vidette* reported that J. Cady had finished beautiful sign work on the building for Steidl, as seen here. Steidl closed his drug business in 1920. Later, the site was home to the Plouzek-Pflasterer and Buchanan drugstores. (SCHS.)

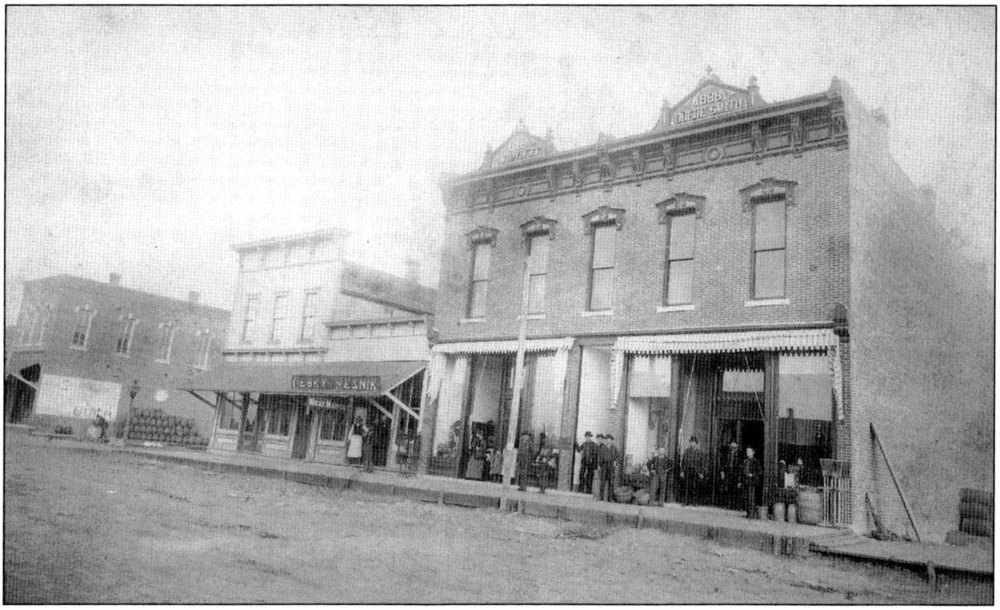

This view, taken about 1890, shows the east side of Maine Avenue in the 1100 block. The brick building on the far left is Frank Nedela's saloon and drugstore at Twelfth Street and Maine Avenue. The double brick building was constructed by jeweler C.W. Havlicek and implement dealer Doede Smith. The frame buildings on the corner are gone, but the brick structures remain. (*Crete News* collection.)

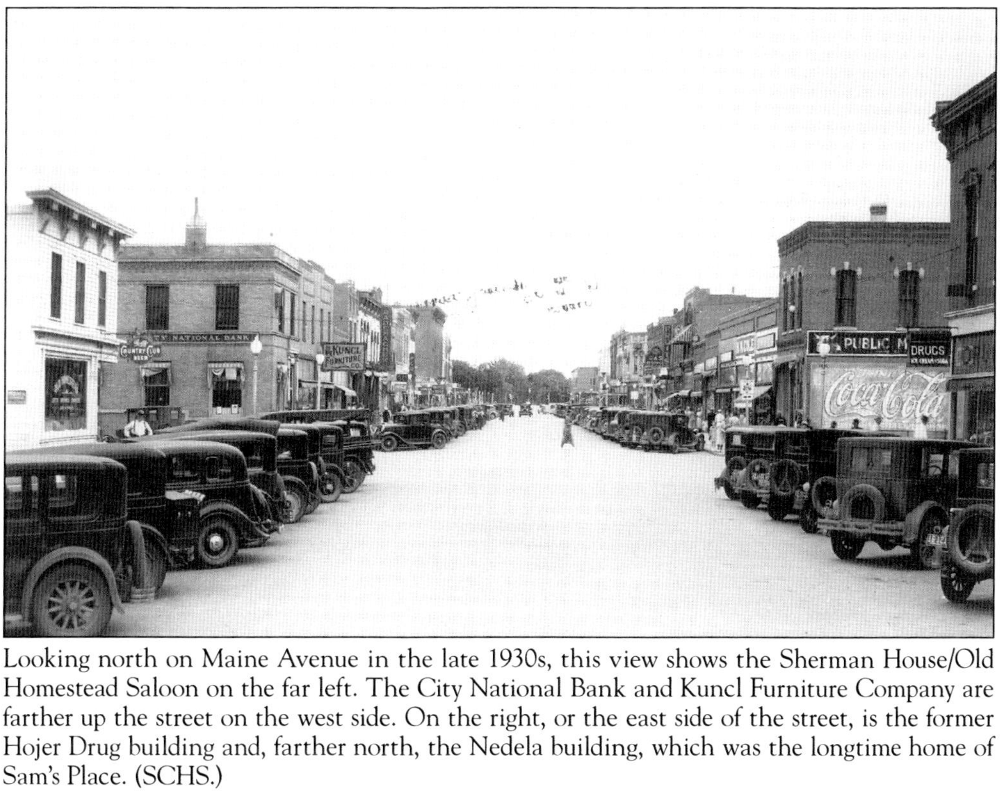

Looking north on Maine Avenue in the late 1930s, this view shows the Sherman House/Old Homestead Saloon on the far left. The City National Bank and Kuncl Furniture Company are farther up the street on the west side. On the right, or the east side of the street, is the former Hojer Drug building and, farther north, the Nedela building, which was the longtime home of Sam's Place. (SCHS.)

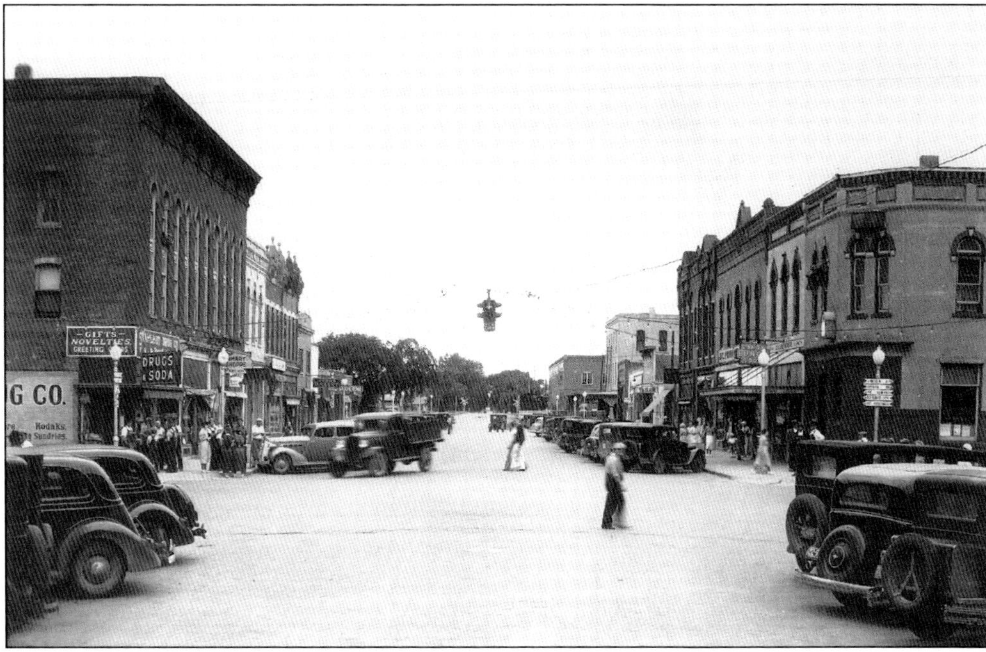

In this 1930s view of Maine Avenue looking north from Thirteenth Street, Band's Opera House is on the left and the former Crete State Bank building is on the right. Stalhut Drug is in the lower level of the opera house. North of the bank, on the east side, is the J.C. Penney store with the Cosmopolitan Hotel and Fairmont Creamery in the distance behind it. (SCHS.)

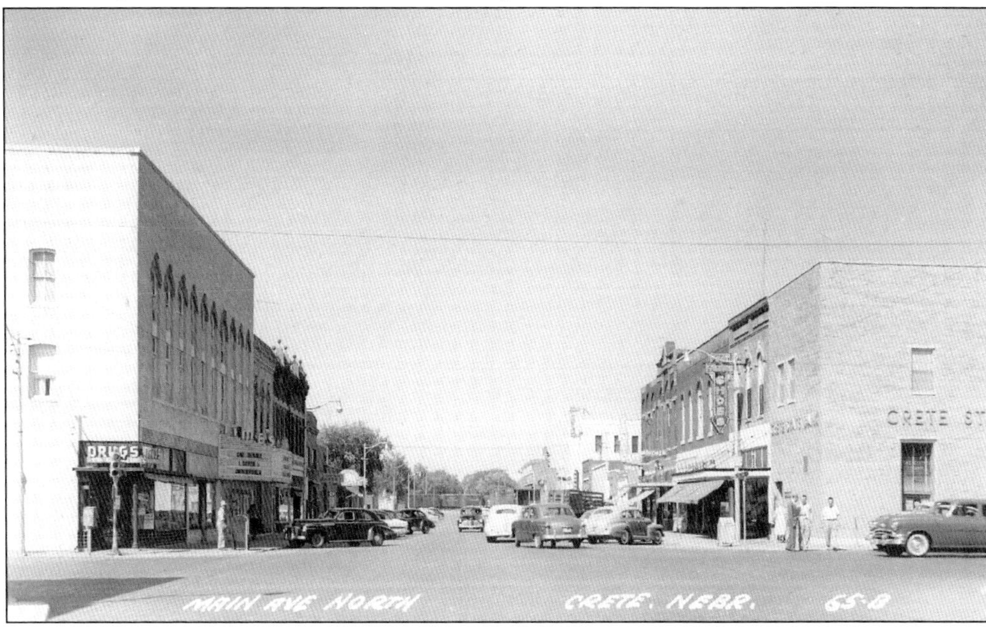

This 1950s view of Maine Avenue looking north shows Band's Opera House on the left and the Crete State Bank building on the right. Both buildings had been remodeled by this time. The opera house brick was plastered over, and the Times Theatre became part of the building in 1938. The bank's main entrance was changed, all architectural features were removed, and the building was faced with new brick. (Kuncl family collection.)

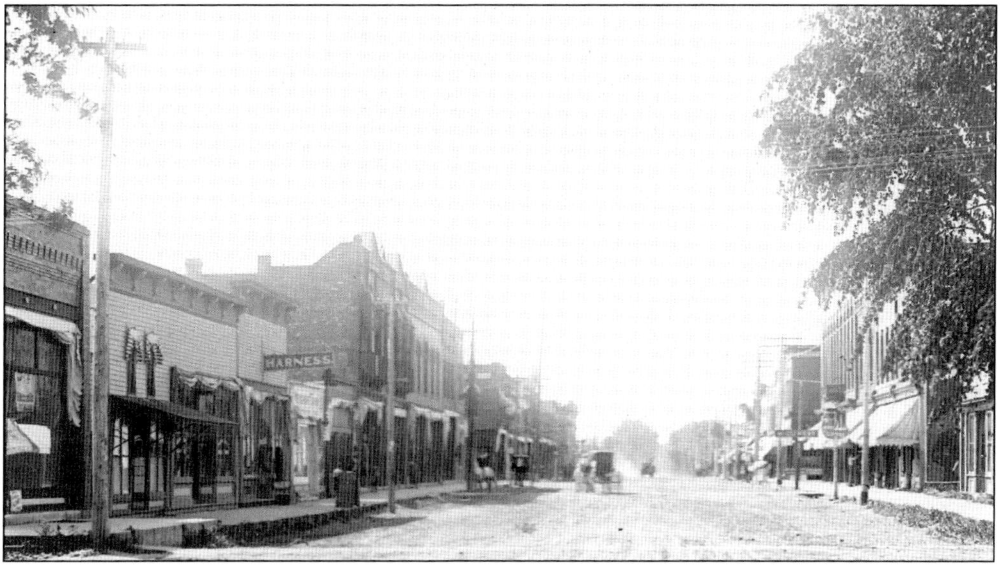

In the 1880s, Maine Avenue still had several frame buildings like those on the left, or east side of the street. This view looks south from Fourteenth Street, and the horse-drawn buggy is just about to Thirteenth Street. Bespalec Heating and Plumbing is at the far left, and the smallest frame building, beyond the harness shop, is presently Katherine's Kurl Shop, one of Crete's oldest commercial structures. (Marti Ator Williams collection.)

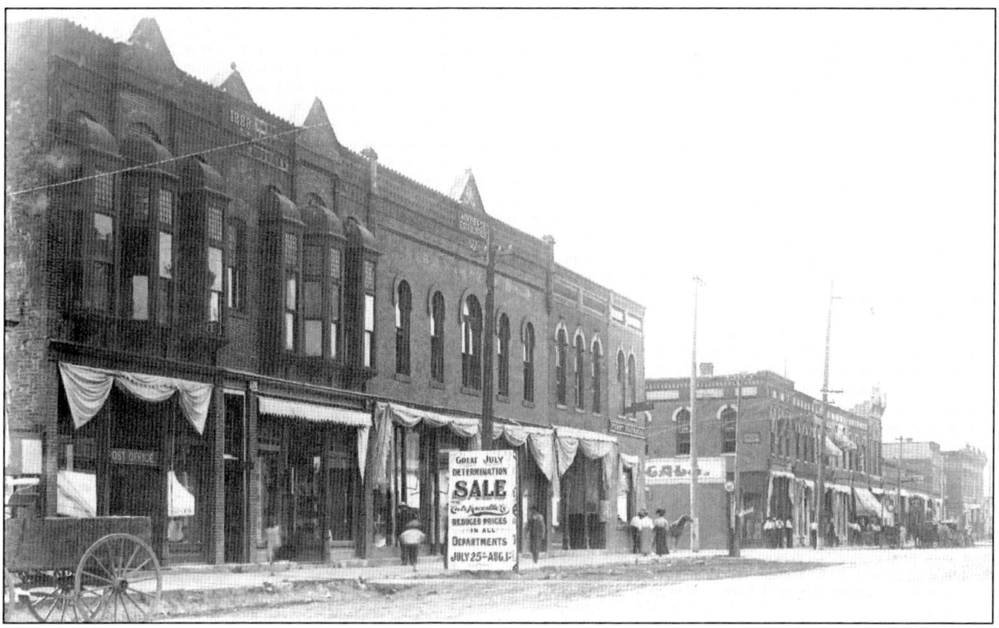

This 1890s view of Maine Avenue looking south toward Thirteenth Street shows the Crete Mercantile Company having a big summer sale. Crete Mercantile was located in what was later the J.C. Penney store. Owner M.E. Haight offered customers a variety of goods and services, including clothing, housewares, furniture, and undertaking. Joseph Kuncl, founder of Kuncl Funeral Home, worked here in the furniture department for many years. (CHS.)

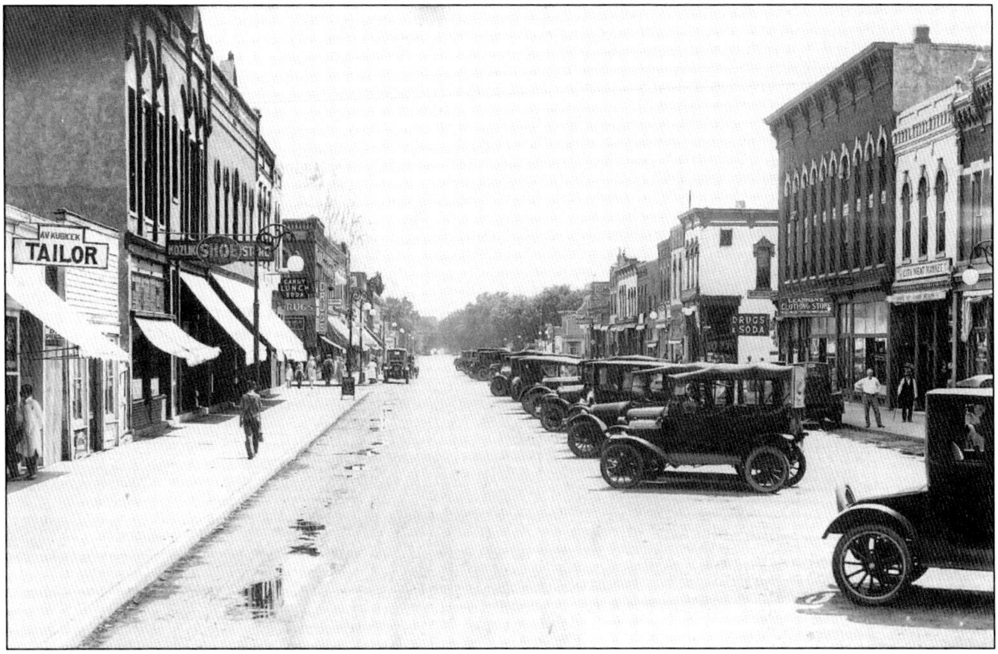

This 1920s photograph of Maine Avenue looking south from near Fourteenth Street shows an interesting parking arrangement. Band's Opera House, at the northwest corner of Thirteenth Street and Maine Avenue, is the tall building on the right. (Kuncl family collection.)

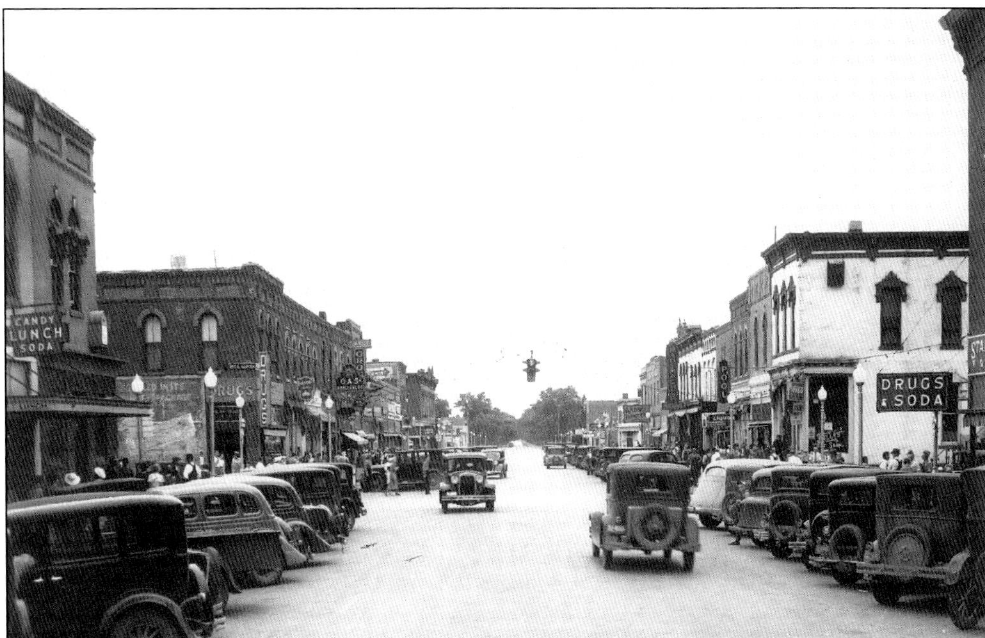

These two cars approach the intersection of Thirteenth Street and Maine Avenue in this photograph looking south on Maine Avenue in 1941. The pool hall is on the right, or west side of the street. The old, tall streetlight poles have been replaced by shorter ones topped with globes, and a stoplight now hangs over the intersection. (SCHS.)

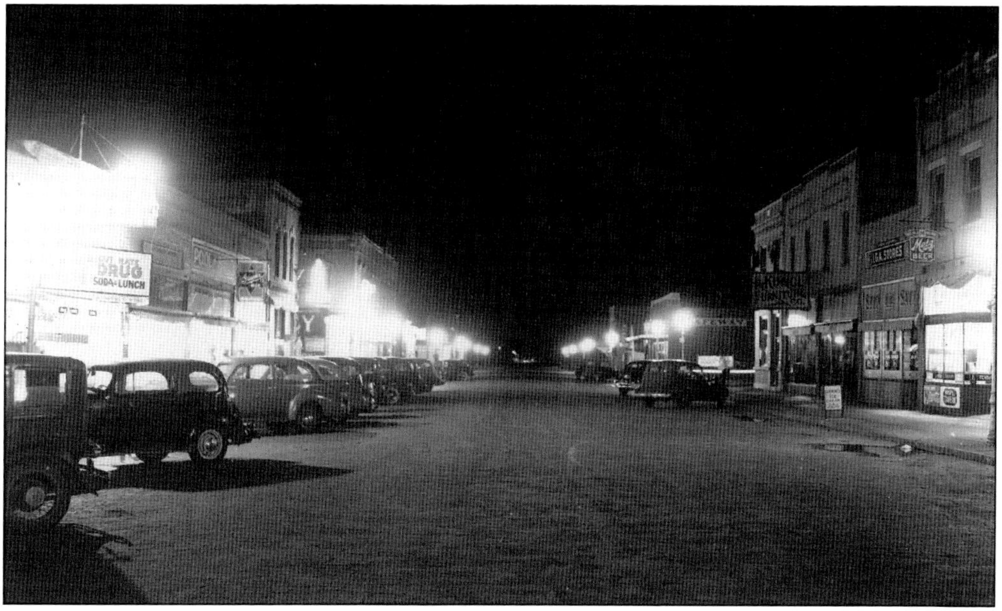

The May 29, 1941, *Crete News* announced plans for new downtown streetlights. New traffic lights with three colors—instead of just red and green like the previous lights—were also installed at Thirteenth Street and Maine Avenue. This nighttime photograph, dated 1941, looks south on Maine Avenue from Thirteenth Street and was probably taken to celebrate the new lights. IGA grocery, Kuncl Furniture Company, and Safeway grocery are on the right. (SCHS.)

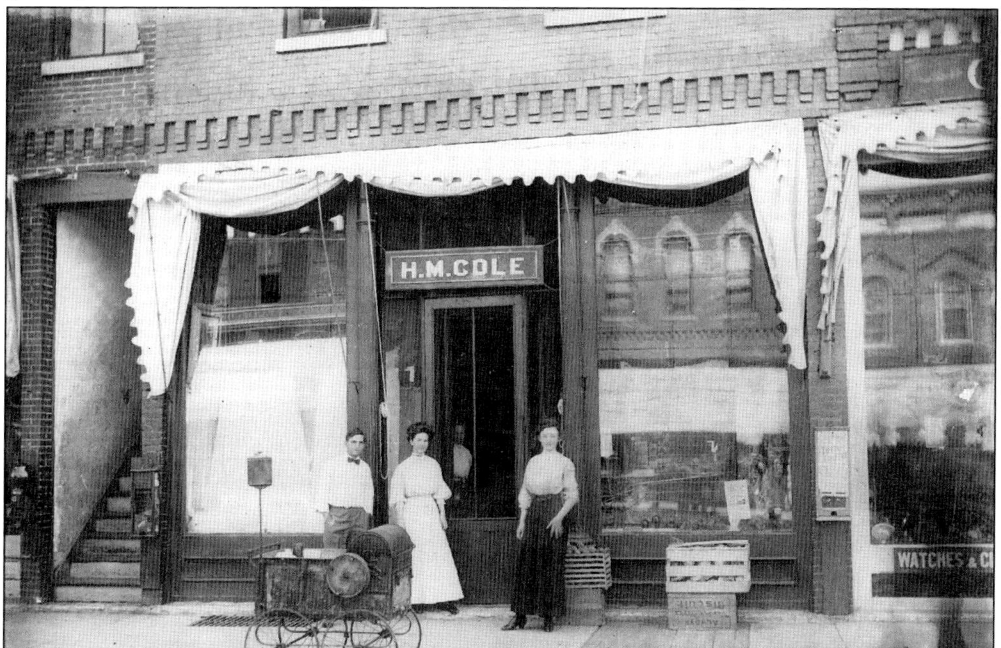

Henry M. Cole brought his family to Crete in 1885 and opened a general store at 1238 Maine Avenue. Posing in front of the store about 1905 are, from left to right, Monroe "Roe" Cole, May Cole, and Lilly Kolarik Kolouch. The apparatus on the cart in front of the store is a peanut roaster. The building served as a jewelry store for many years and is now a restaurant. (CHS.)

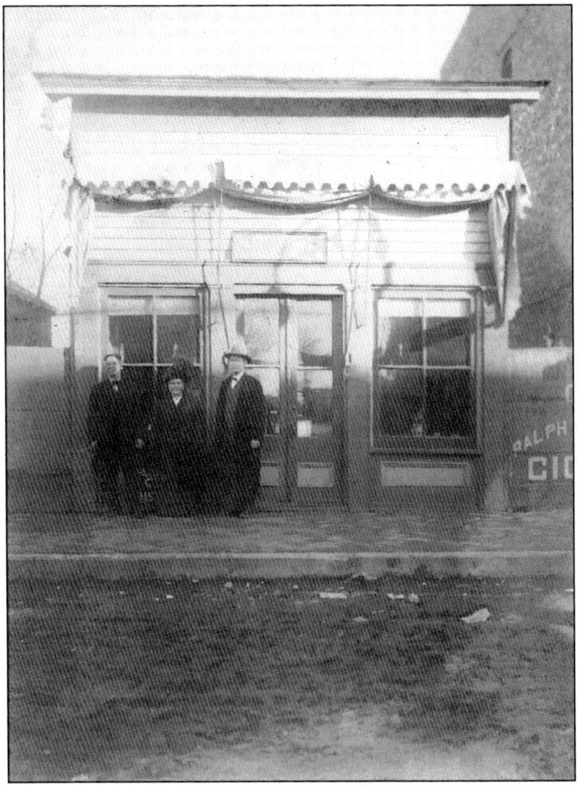

This frame structure at 1328 Maine Avenue is the oldest commercial building in downtown Crete. Constructed about 1870, the building has housed several businesses, including a carpenter shop, a cigar shop, and now Kathryn's Kurl Shop. Before any school buildings were completed, Charles Bowlby taught here in the store during the winter of 1870–1871. This 1916 photograph shows Bowlby on the right and two of his former students, Barbara Papik and Ernest Francl. (CHS.)

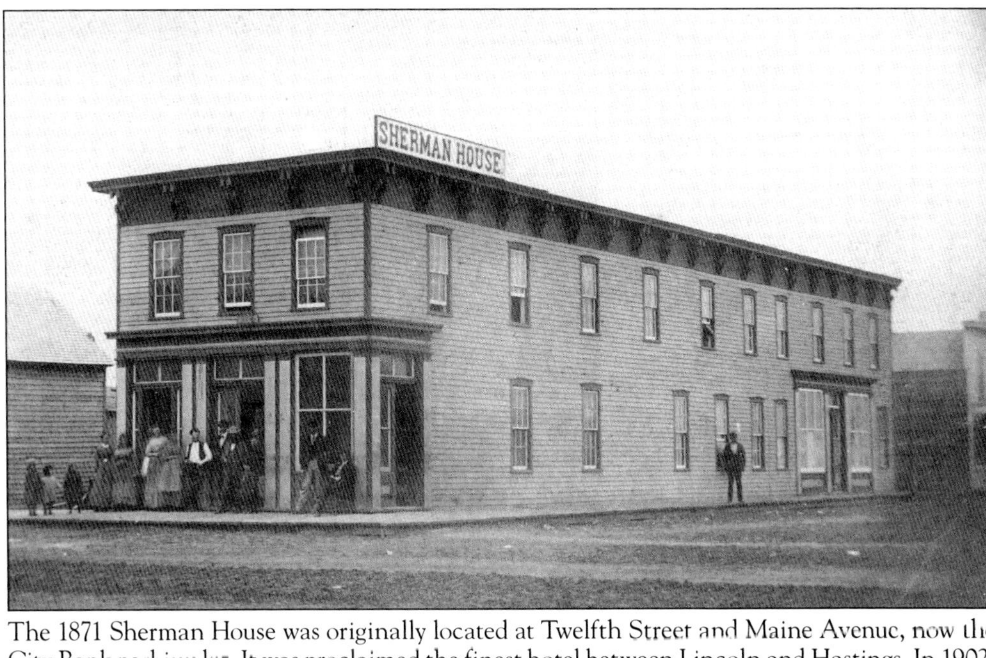

The 1871 Sherman House was originally located at Twelfth Street and Maine Avenue, now the City Bank parking lot. It was proclaimed the finest hotel between Lincoln and Hastings. In 1902, it became a saloon called Old Homestead. It was moved to the present Pamida/Shopko block in 1940 and became an apartment house. In 1976, when the Gibson/Pamida store was built, it was moved to 820 Juniper Avenue, where it continues to serve as an apartment house. (SCHS.)

The first newspaper in Crete was the *Saline County Post*, founded in 1871. The *Post* evolved into other newspapers, including the *Saline County Union*, *State Vidette*, and the current *Crete News*, whose first issue appeared in 1908. Originally published from the opera house basement, the *Crete News* was housed in this building at 136 East Thirteenth Street for 35 years. In 1964, the business moved to 1201 Linden Avenue. (CHS.)

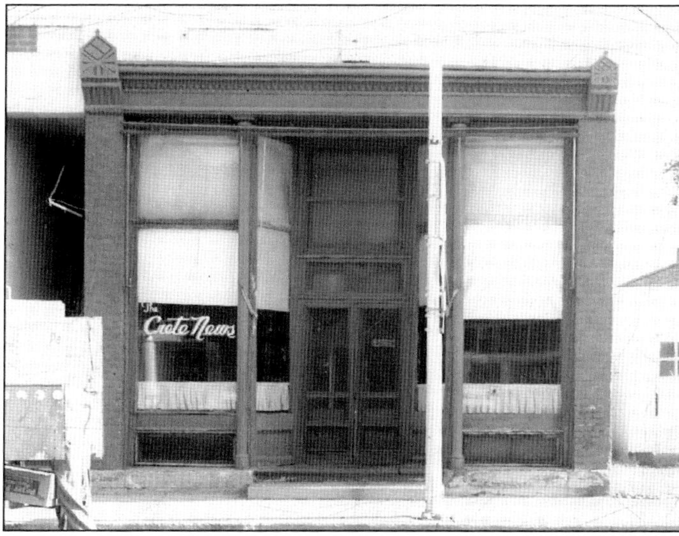

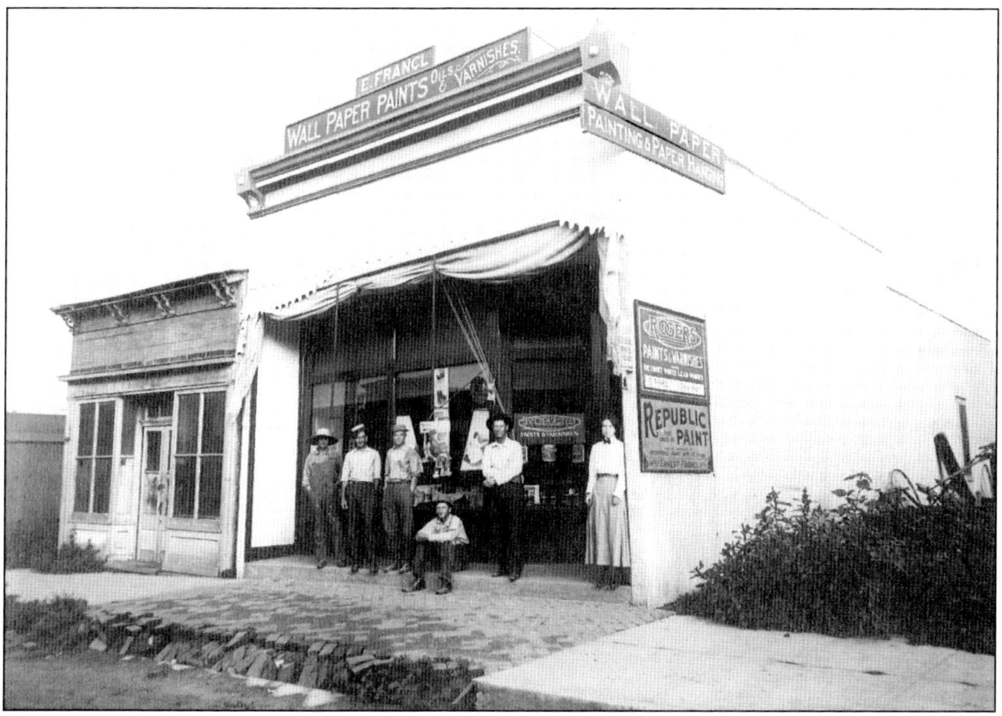

Ernest Francl had a paint and home improvement store on Maine Avenue, near Twelfth Street, that often made the news. The company's creative design in Crete homes and business buildings was noteworthy. In addition to basic painting and wallpapering, the Francls did artistic work with stenciling and decorative painting. The original sign on the side of the building is now displayed at the Benne Memorial Museum. (CHS, Krebs collection.)

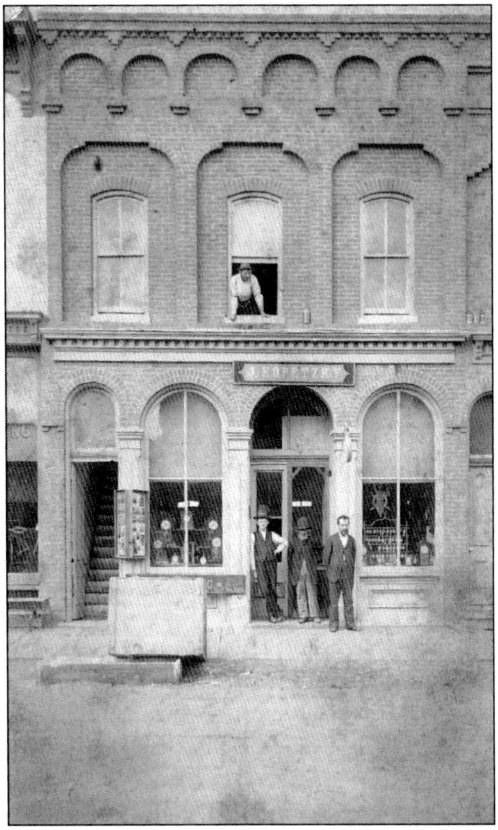

Kopetsky's Jewelry Store was at 1229 Maine Avenue, the site of the present Quality Dry Cleaners. Bohemian immigrant Joseph Kopetsky learned the jeweler's trade in Austria and came to Nebraska in 1864, where he homesteaded south of what is now Crete. At the same time, he worked as a jeweler in area settlements. He opened a store in Crete in 1871 and constructed this brick building in 1888. (CHS.)

The Crete Mercantile Store, seen here about 1910, was a large department store at 1312–1314 Maine Avenue, in what later became the J.C. Penney store. Leaning on the counter is Joseph Kuncl, the manager of the furniture and undertaking department. Owner M.E. Haight added the undertaking department in 1907, and when Haight retired, Kuncl established his own furniture store and mortuary, launching what is now a fourth-generation family business. (Kuncl family collection.)

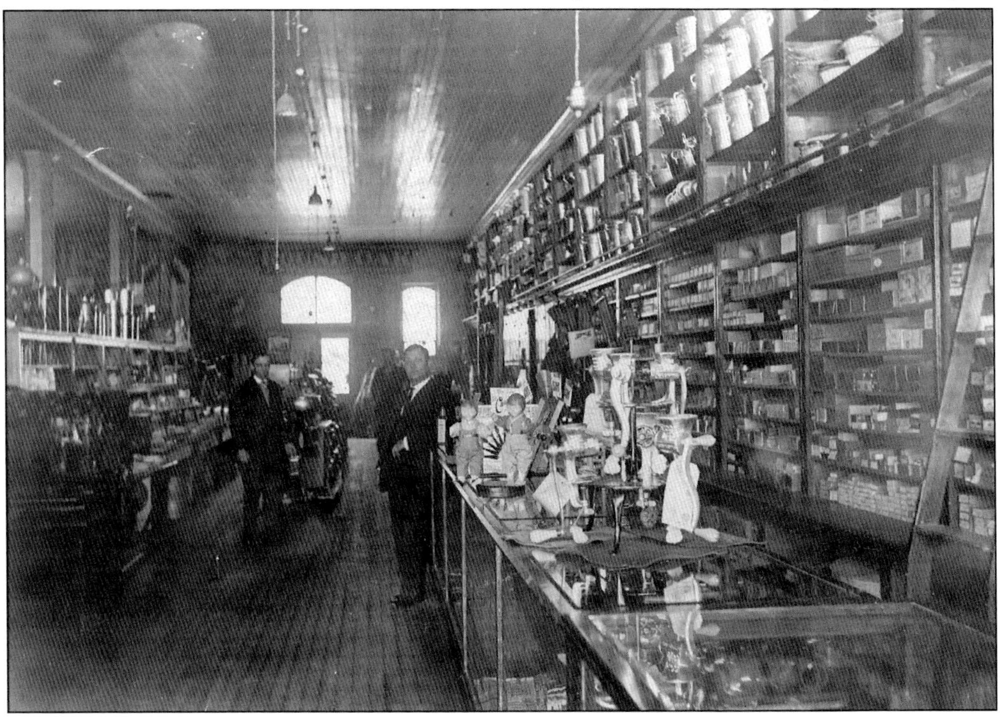

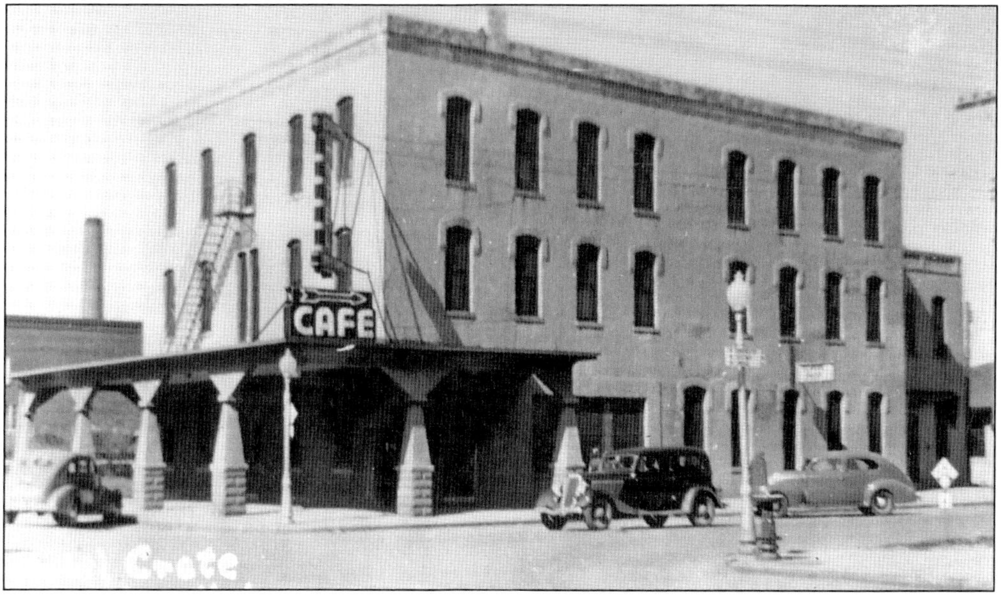

The Cosmopolitan Hotel was built in 1879. According to the June 20, 1879, *Saline County Union*, the brick hotel, located on the northeast corner of Fourteenth Street and Maine Avenue, was to be completed in September at a cost of $8,000. By 1882, proprietor Henry Code reported that about 15 commercial men per day registered there. It later became the Crete Hotel and was covered with stucco. (SCHS.)

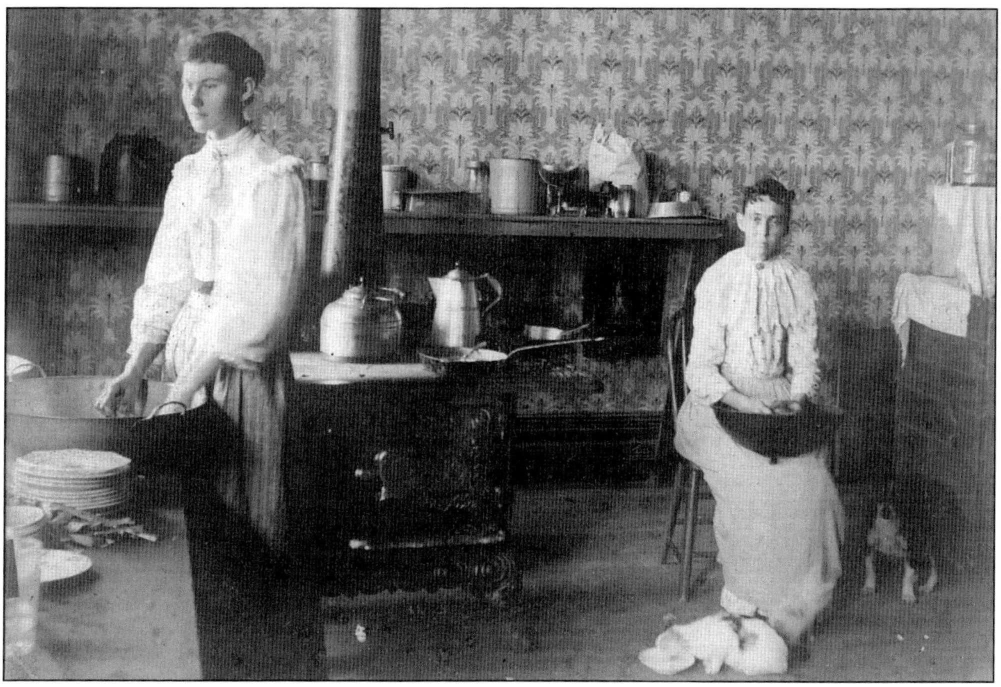

This photograph shows the Crete Hotel kitchen in 1897. The hotel's location near the Burlington railroad line made it a popular place for casual diners as well as longtime boarders. The hotel went out of business in the 1960s and was eventually razed after serving for many years as a storage facility for Skala OK Tires. (SCHS.)

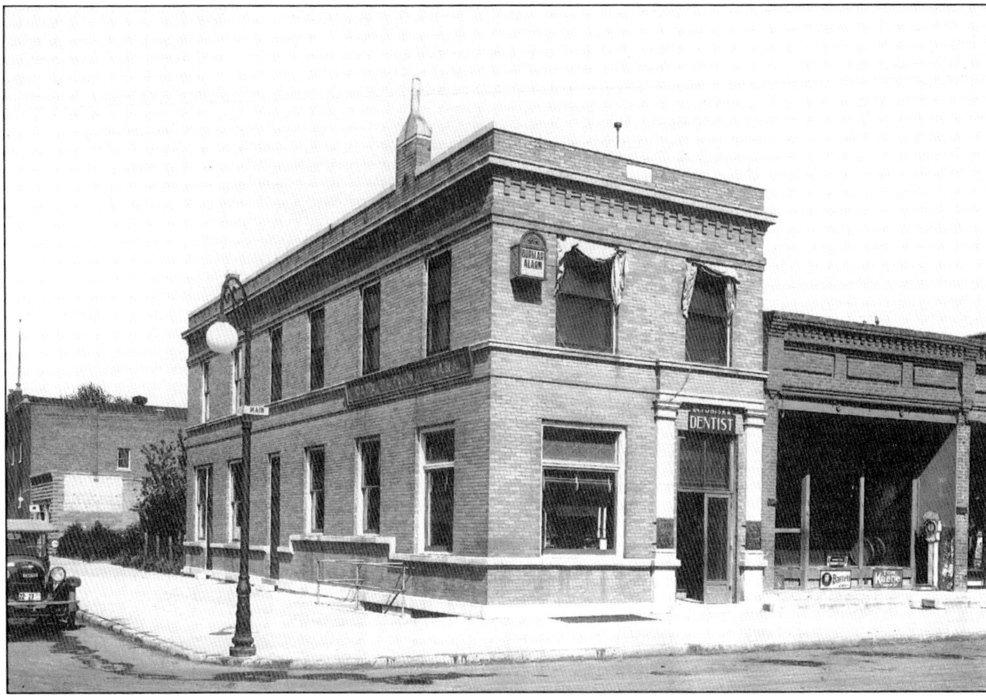

This 1922 photograph shows the City National Bank, built by C.M. Marcelino and established in 1910 at 1201 Maine Avenue. A 1912 advertisement stated that the bank had $25,000 in capital, a fire- and burglar-proof vault, and after being open two years had deposits totaling $235,945. H.S. Fuller was president at the time, and other officers were Charles W. Weckbach, Ralph D. Brown, and F.A. Novak. Dr. Charles Tobiska's dental office occupied the second floor. (CHS.)

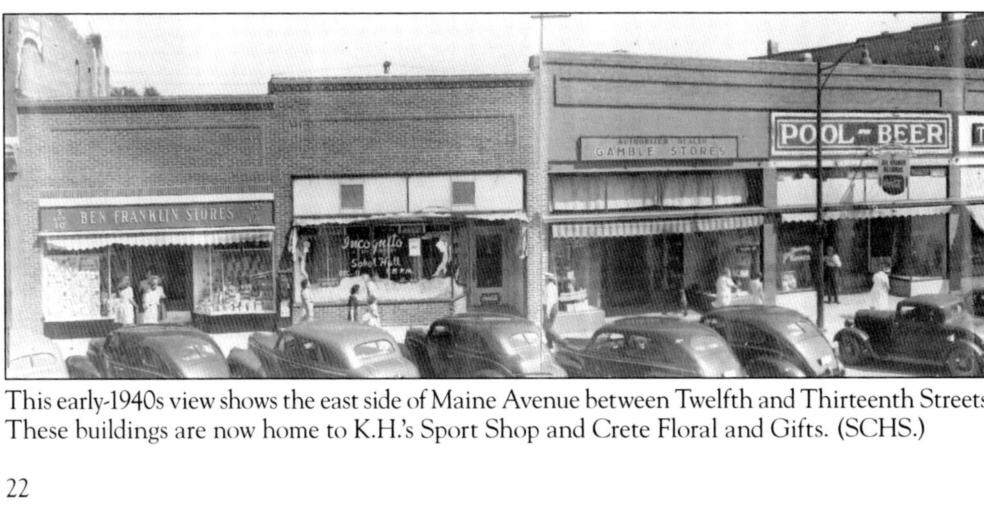

This early-1940s view shows the east side of Maine Avenue between Twelfth and Thirteenth Streets. These buildings are now home to K.H.'s Sport Shop and Crete Floral and Gifts. (SCHS.)

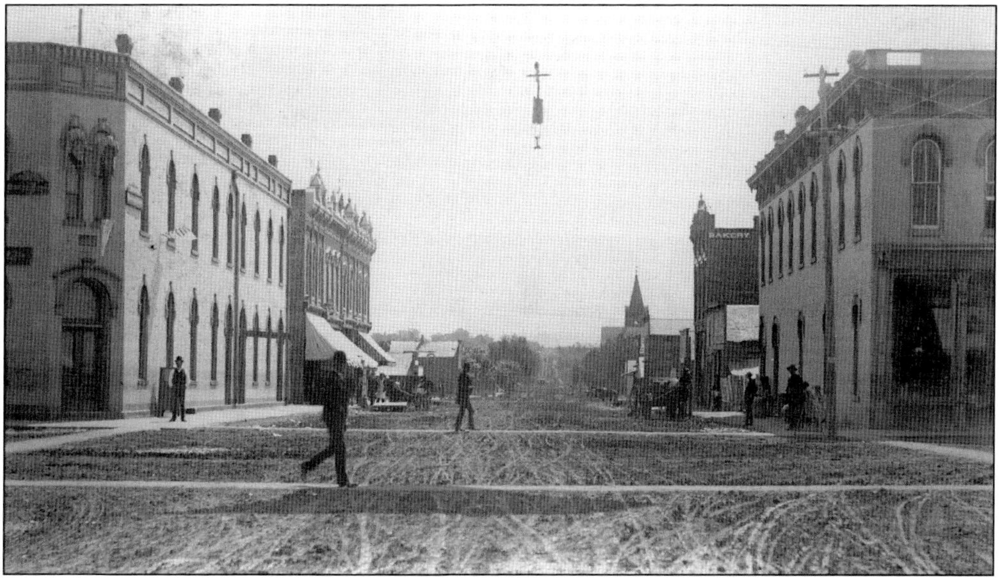

The intersection of Thirteenth Street and Maine Avenue is seen here about 1890. On the left is the State Bank of Nebraska, and on the right is the building that would become Steidl Drug in 1897. The spire of Grace Methodist Church is seen in the distance. (CHS, Jennie Chapman Stevens collection.)

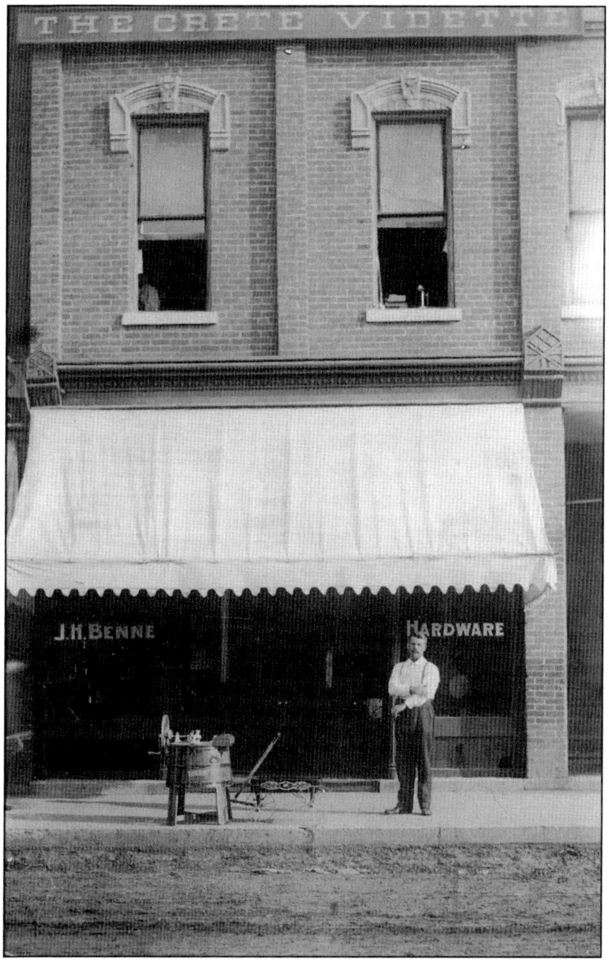

J.H. Benne ran a hardware store on Thirteenth Street, selling a variety of tools, paint, stoves, washing machines, and cutlery. Here, Benne stands outside the store with a washing machine. The *Crete Vidette* newspaper office was upstairs. Dr. Howard Doty's dental office, at 130 East Thirteenth Street, is now in this building, which has been extensively remodeled. (CHS.)

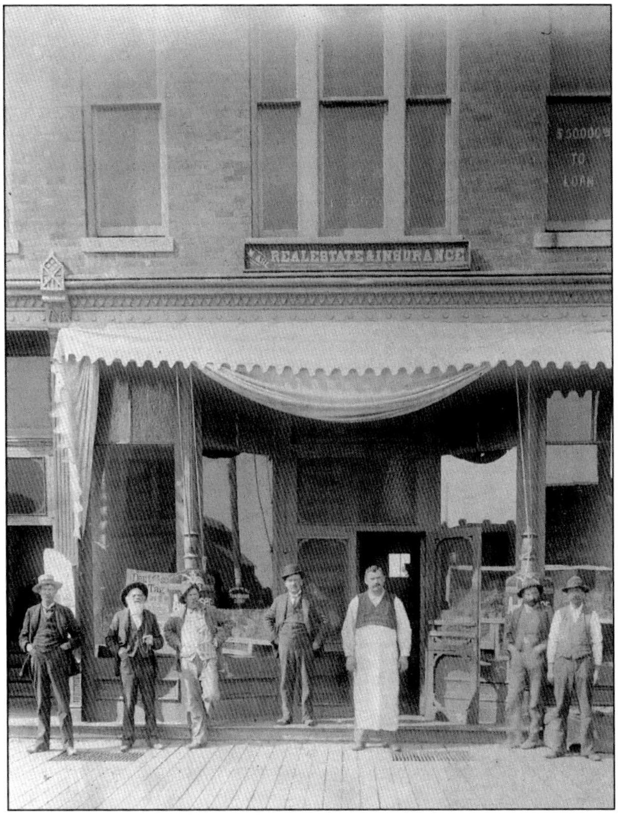

William Kersenbrock (in apron) ran a saloon on East Thirteenth Street and was also the town constable. On January 1, 1889, Kersenbrock charged Buffalo Bill Cody with drunkenness after he spent a wild New Year's Eve in the saloon. Records show that Buffalo Bill was fined $1 plus court costs of $4.60 for the infraction. (Kersenbrock family collection.)

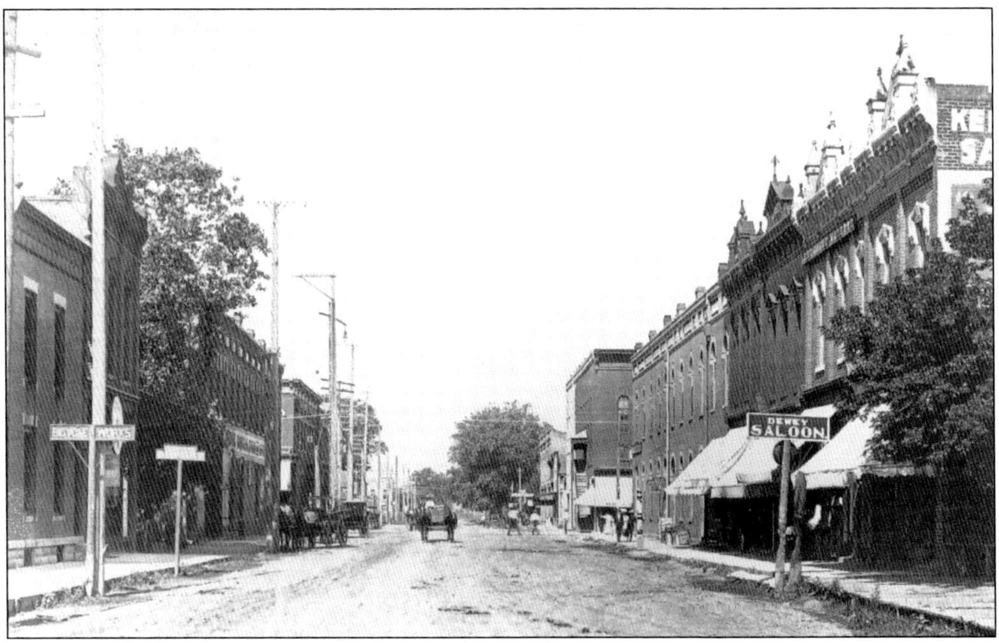

This 1880s view shows Thirteenth Street looking west from Linden Avenue toward Maine Avenue. Most of these buildings still stand, although they have been substantially altered. In the upper right, a painted sign on the building appears to say Kersenbrock Sample Room. (UCC.)

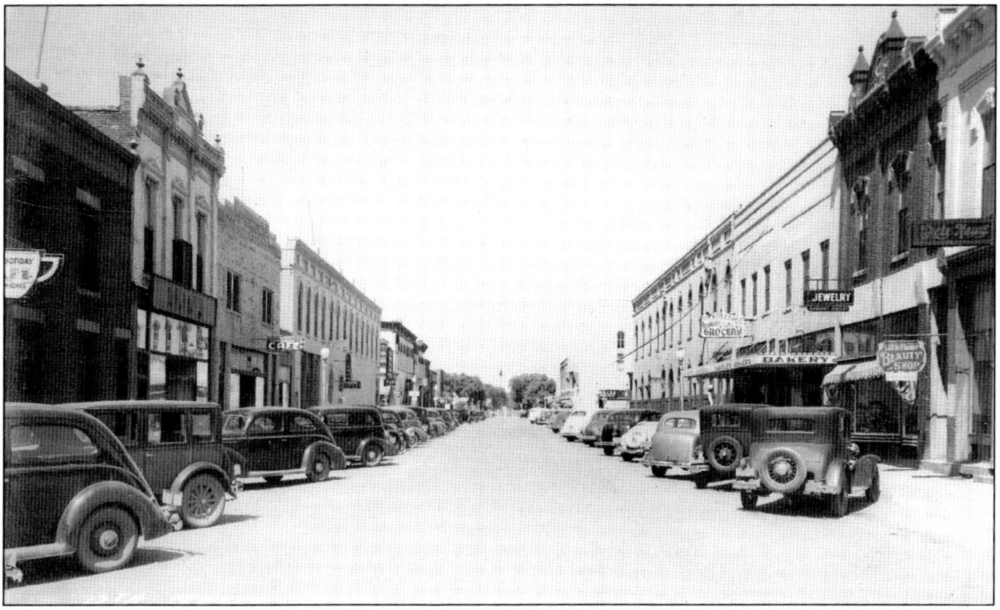

This early-1940s view of Thirteenth Street looks west from Linden Avenue. On the left, or south side of the street, is the Coffee Cup, a café operated by Bill Sonday in the 1930s and early 1940s. The *Crete News* building is on the far right, and Kindles Bakery was down the street. (Robert Sykes collection.)

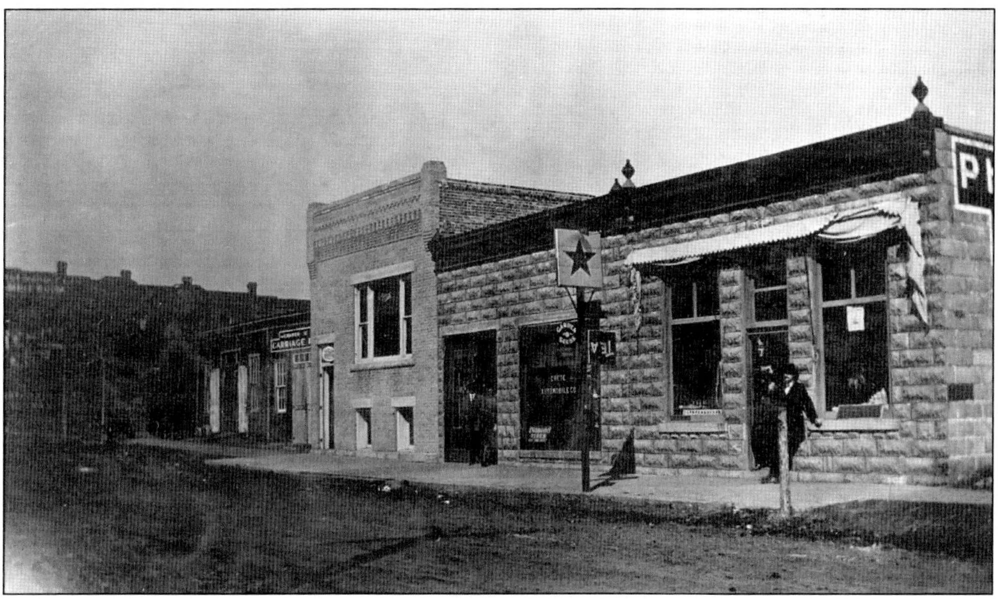

This photograph shows the north side of East Thirteenth Street between Kingwood and Linden Avenues. The tall building housed the telephone company and a shoe repair shop for many years. The building to the right of the phone company, now the location of Crete Chiropractic Center, was home to the Crete Plumbing and Heating Company in the early 1900s. (CHS.)

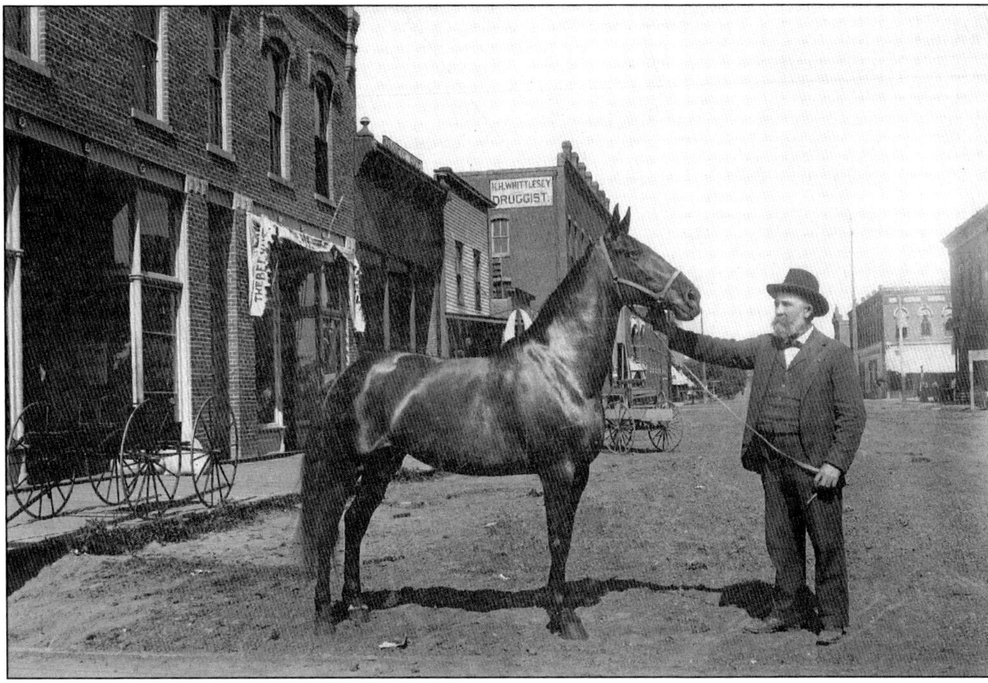

Implement dealer Hugh McCargar posed with his horse in front of his store at 142 West Thirteenth Street in the 1890s. Behind him is the intersection of Thirteenth Street and Maine Avenue. McCargar sold farm equipment, carriages, and farm wagons in his brick building (left). He was also a two-term state senator, a breeder of Jersey cattle, and an avid horseman. Crete's AIA Martial Arts Academy now occupies the remodeled building. (CHS, Gladys Rahe collection.)

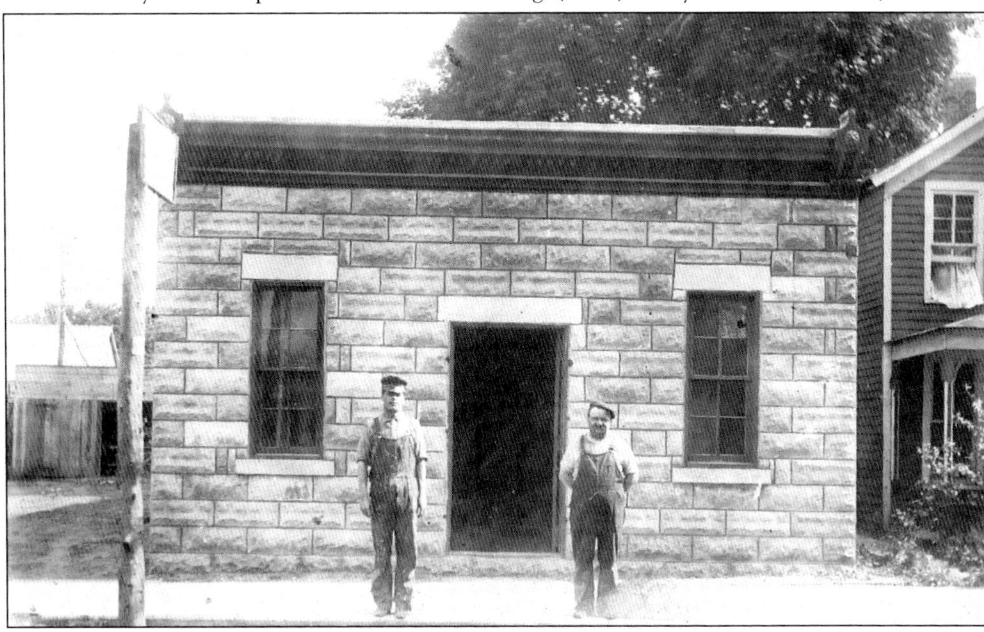

The Yunko Blacksmith Shop, at 225 West Thirteenth Street, was run by Ignatz Yunko and his son Joe. This photograph from about 1920 most likely shows the Yunkos in front of their shop. The property is now home to Basic Body Works. (CHS.)

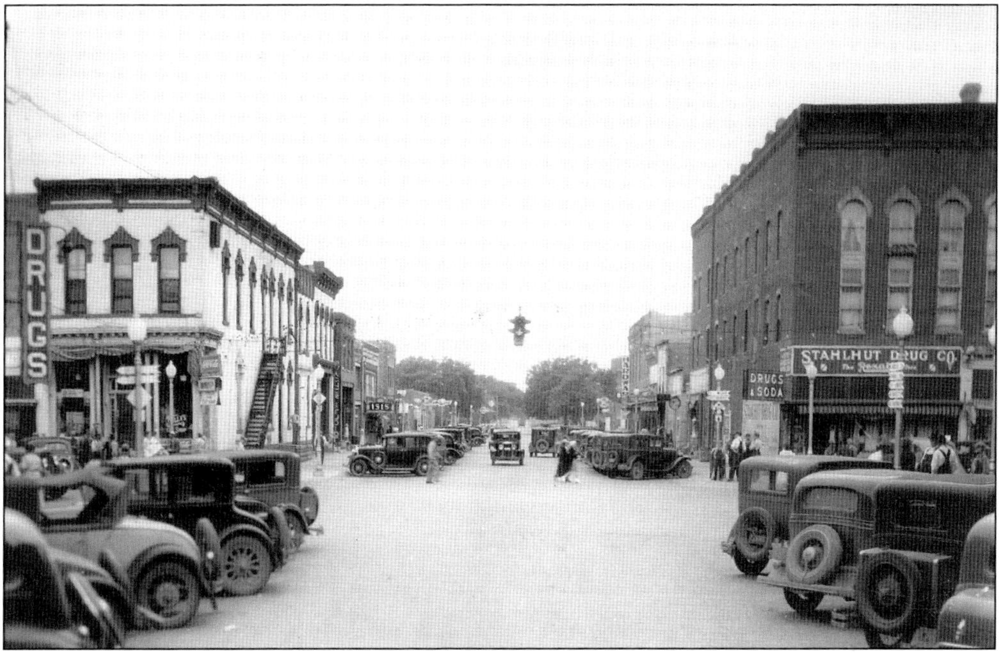

This late-1920s view of Thirteenth Street looking west shows Band's Opera House on the right and the First National Bank building on the left. The Isis Theatre is down the street on the left. Stahlhut Drug, on the right, was a longtime tenant in the opera house block. (SCHS.)

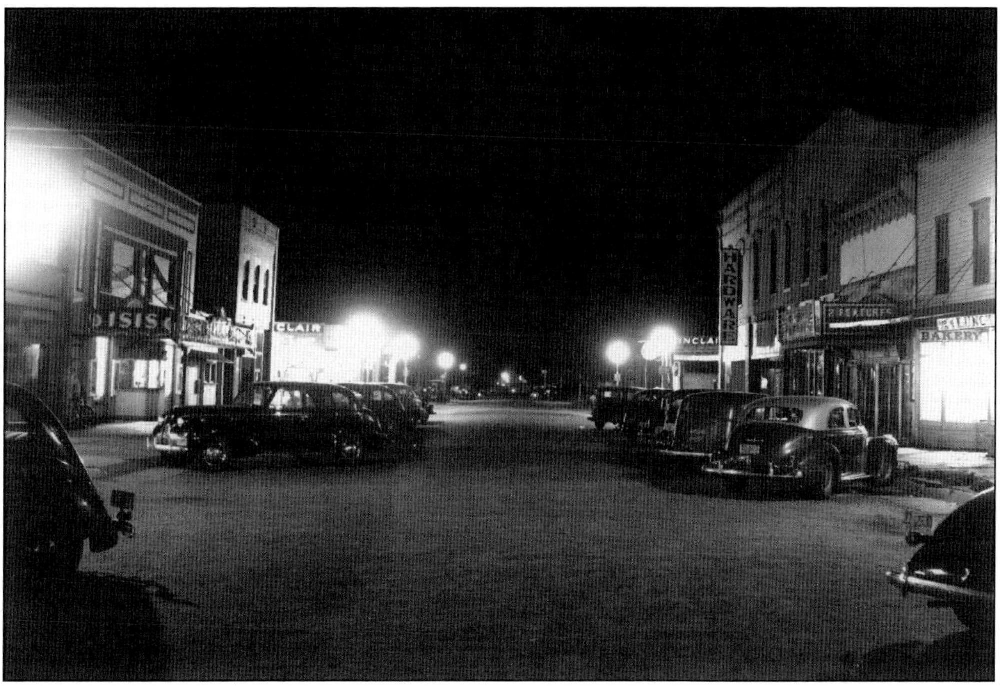

This nighttime photograph is dated 1941 and was probably taken to show off the new city streetlights. This is a good view of the Isis Theatre on the left and the older Lyric Theatre on the right. Beyond the theaters are the Sinclair filling station on the right and the Sinclair garage on the left. (SCHS.)

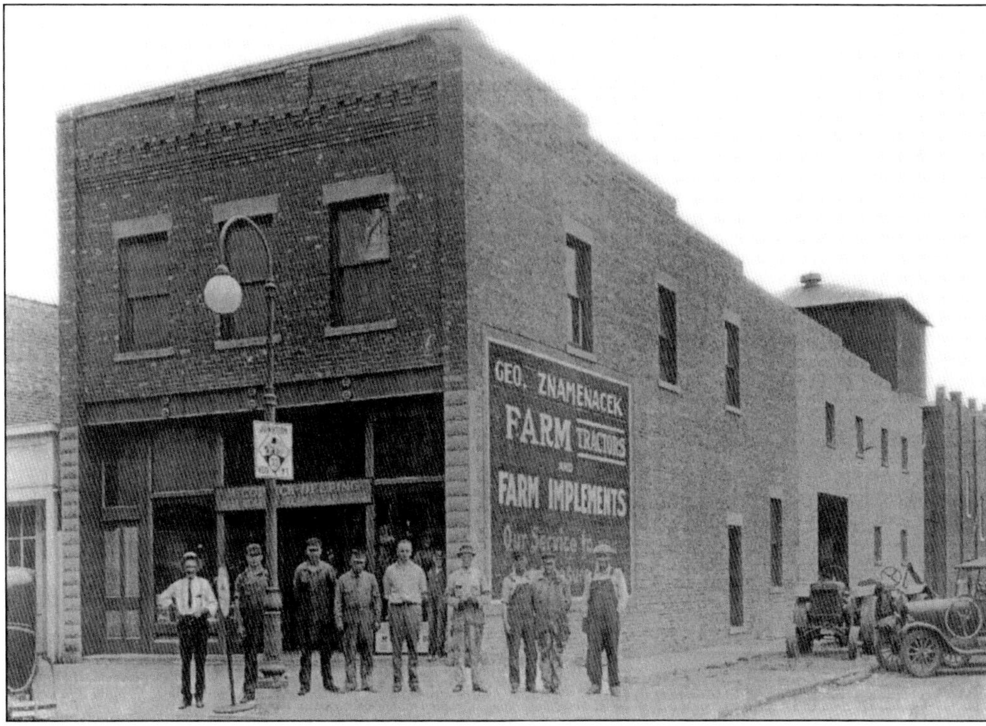

This photograph shows the Znamenacek implement store around 1930. Located on the southeast corner of Thirteenth Street and Norman Avenue, the building was home to Booth's Seed House and Malone's CPA business. Booth's Seed House was not just a retail store, seed was also processed and packaged there. (Marilyn Feeken Reiss collection.)

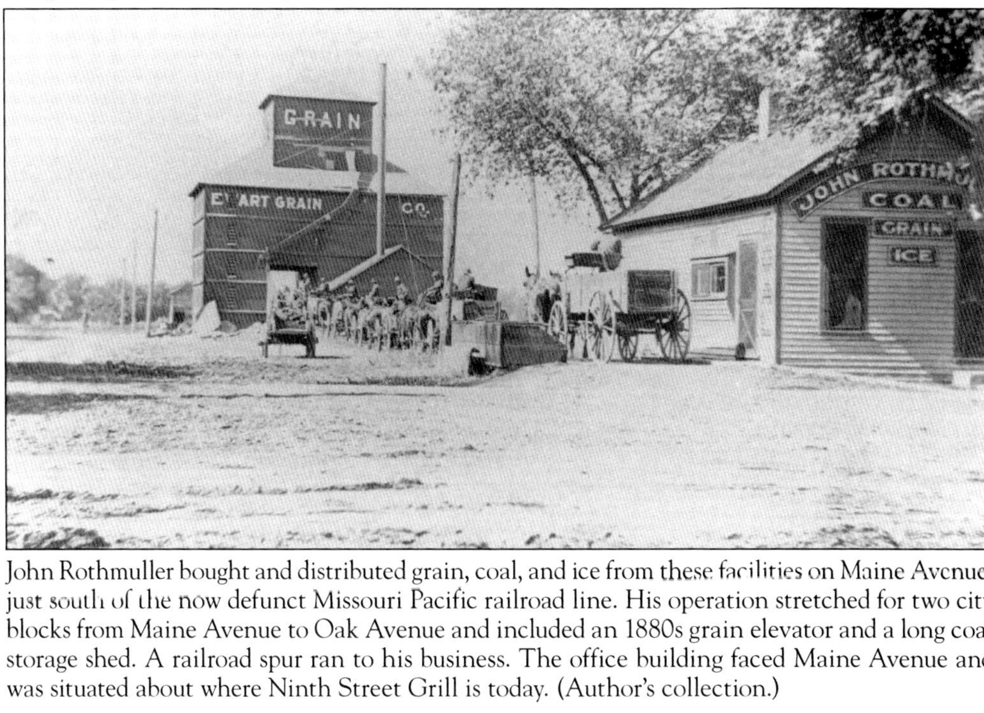

John Rothmuller bought and distributed grain, coal, and ice from these facilities on Maine Avenue, just south of the now defunct Missouri Pacific railroad line. His operation stretched for two city blocks from Maine Avenue to Oak Avenue and included an 1880s grain elevator and a long coal storage shed. A railroad spur ran to his business. The office building faced Maine Avenue and was situated about where Ninth Street Grill is today. (Author's collection.)

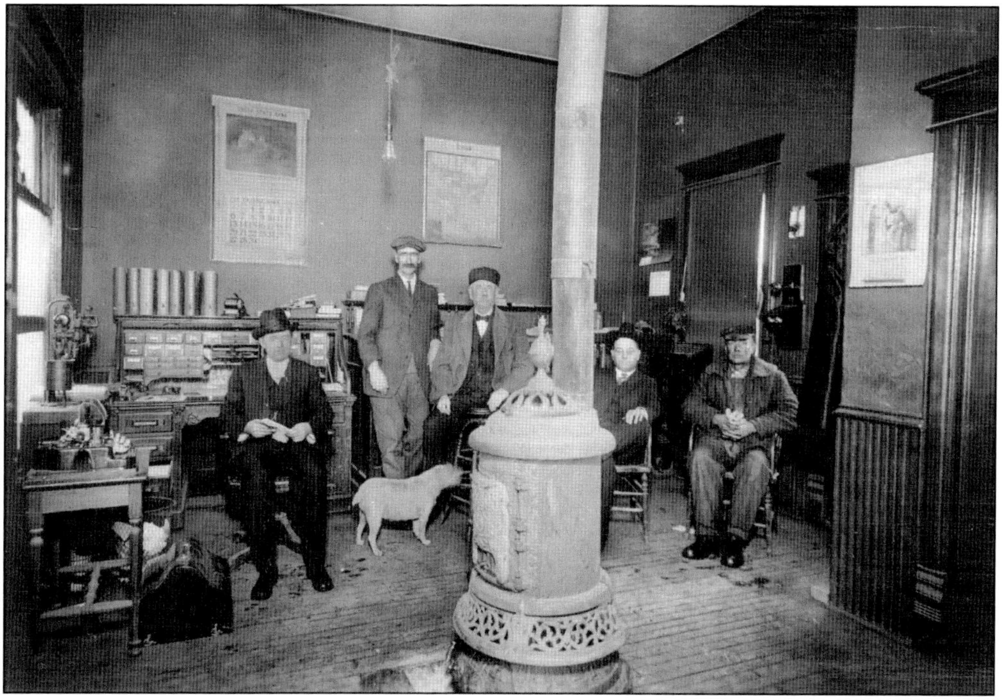

Sack Lumber Company was founded in Sutton, Nebraska, in 1899 by Philipp Sack Sr. and sons. The Crete yard, at Maine Avenue and Eleventh Street, was purchased in 1916, and Philipp's son Jacob became manager. Today, the company, managed by Philipp's great-grandson Ronald Sack, includes 11 yards. Pictured in the Crete yard office in 1916 are, from left to right, Jacob Sack, former manager L.E. Pugh, Judge Eckert, Harry Price, and an unidentified man. (Sack Lumber Company collection.)

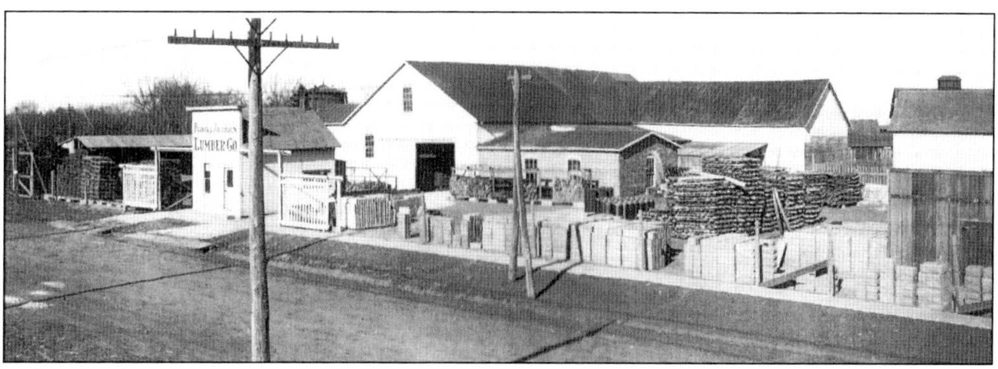

Parker Lumber Company was founded in 1908 as Parker and Jacobsen Lumber and Coal Company by Edmund Parker and Richard Jacobsen. It was located on the north side of West Thirteenth Street between Oak and Pine Avenues. After Jacobsen died in 1932, it became Parker Lumber Company. In 1967, the company moved west of Crete. Edmund Parker's son Paul managed the business until 1973, when it was sold and became Crete Lumber Company. (Tom Parker collection.)

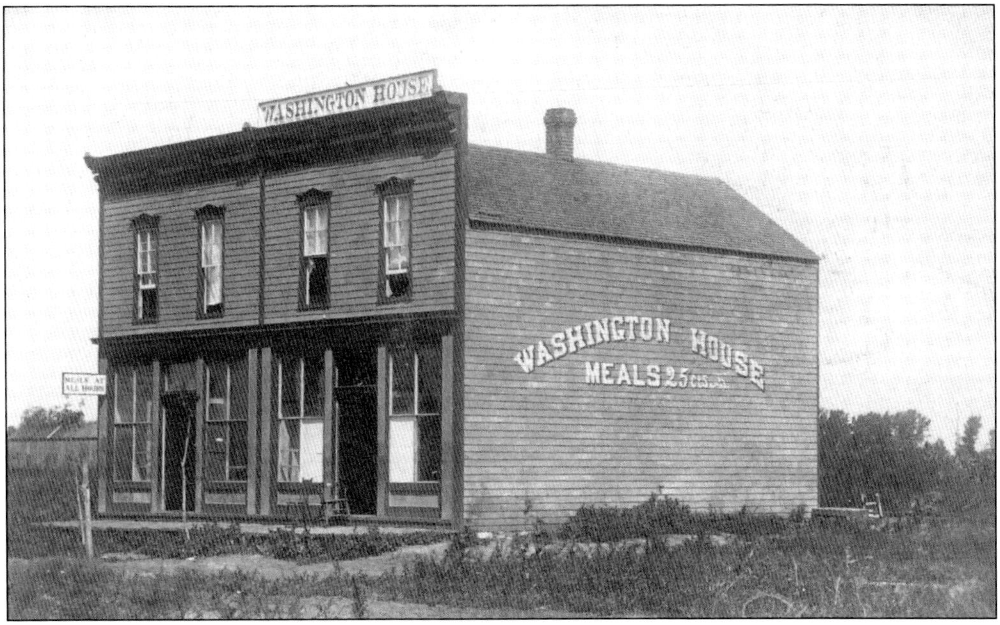

These two hotels were built in the early 1870s during Crete's early settlement period, a time when new arrivals, travelers moving west, and railroad workers needed lodging. The Washington House (above) was on West Thirteenth Street, most likely at the northeast corner of Thirteenth Street and Redwood Avenue. The National Hotel (below), run by a Mr. Lowe, was situated on Maine Avenue just north of Fourteenth Street, later the site of the Cosmopolitan Hotel. (Both, SCHS.)

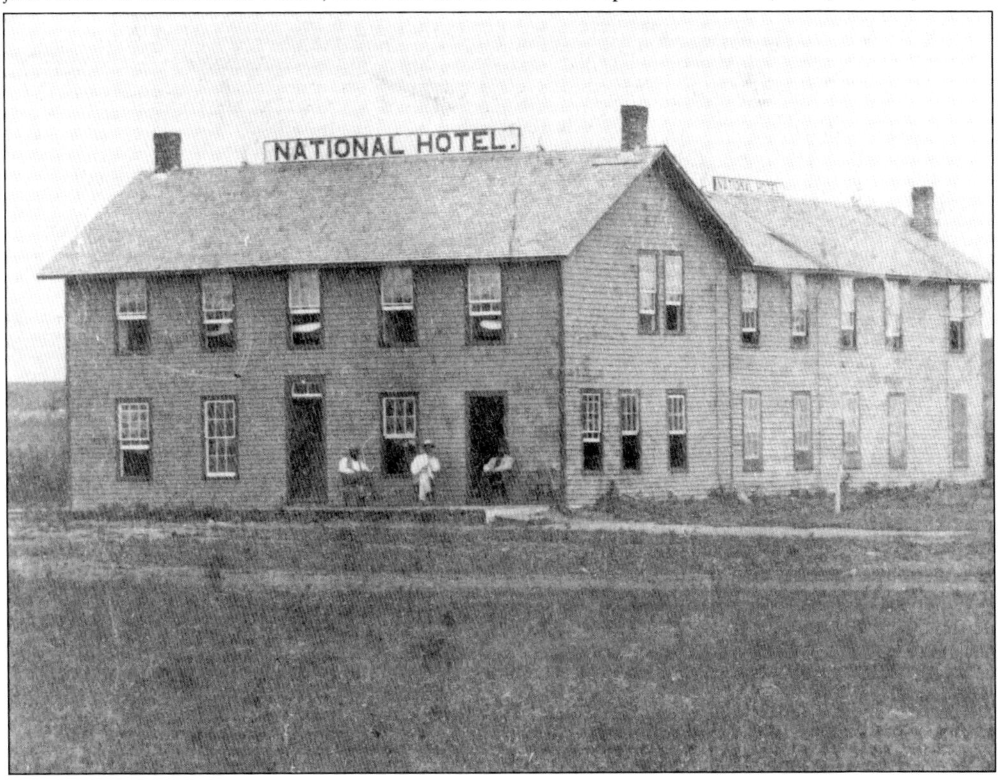

Two

The Progressive City

As Crete moved out of the settlement period, the town began to show signs of urban refinement and community organization. Although still primarily an agricultural trade center, the town saw numerous civic improvements, expanded commercial endeavors, and gained a maturity that defined the prosperous end of the 19th century. The city infrastructure grew during the town's first 20 years, keeping pace with Lincoln and Omaha and other larger Midwestern cities.

Crete's utility system developed in the 1880s and 1890s, and electricity became available just a few years after Thomas Edison invented the lightbulb. Crete also had a waterworks operation and an early telephone system.

Substantial industries, including breweries, a bottling works, the Crete Mills, the Fairmont Creamery, and several manufacturing plants were flourishing by 1900. Service businesses multiplied in the first few decades to keep up with the growing population and its needs. These included blacksmiths, buggy makers, lumberyards, auto repair shops, gasoline stations, and laundries. Retail businesses also flourished.

In 1912, with Crete's population at about 2,500 people, several enterprising town leaders founded the Crete Commercial Club. This forerunner of the chamber of commerce worked for the economic advancement of the town and prepared public relations information to attract people to town.

Good relationships developed between industry and the commercial district. The Crete Mills provided power to the city for a time, and the Fairmont Creamery provided hot water for a swimming pool, supported by the Crete Commercial Club. In addition, the creamery also provided steam heat to several businesses.

The residential neighborhoods also showed signs of expansion and improvement. Many citizens built new homes, and housing continued to move up the hill toward the college.

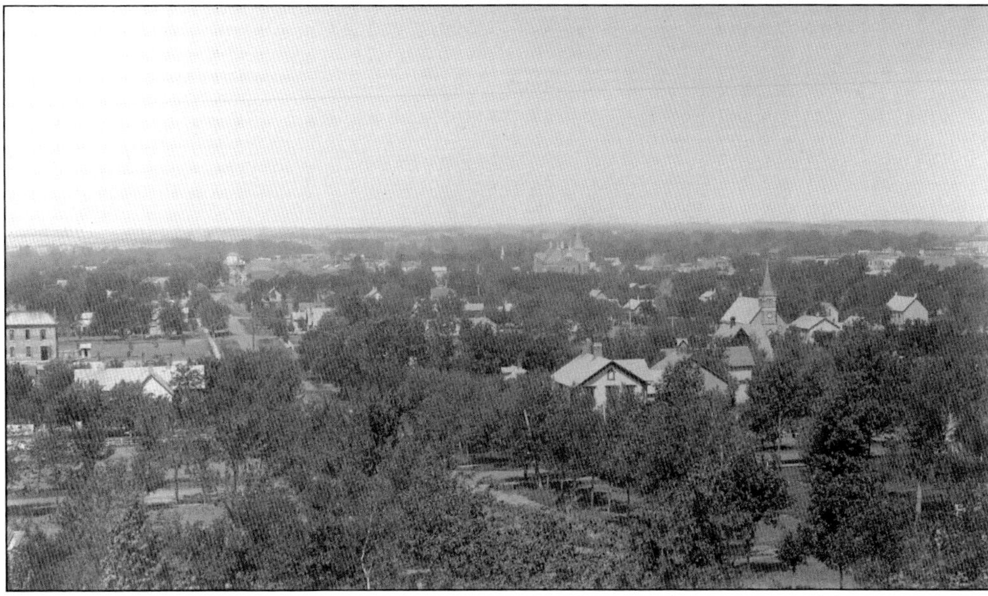

This 1890s view looks west at the College Hill neighborhood and the 20-year-old expanding city from Gaylord Hall on Boswell Avenue. The river and commercial district are in the distance. Tree-lined streets separate a variety of housing. St. Ludmilla's Catholic Church is on the right, and "Old '88" high school is in the distance. East Ward School is on the left, and the Eyster home on Forest Avenue is in the foreground. (CHS, Jennie Chapman Stevens collection.)

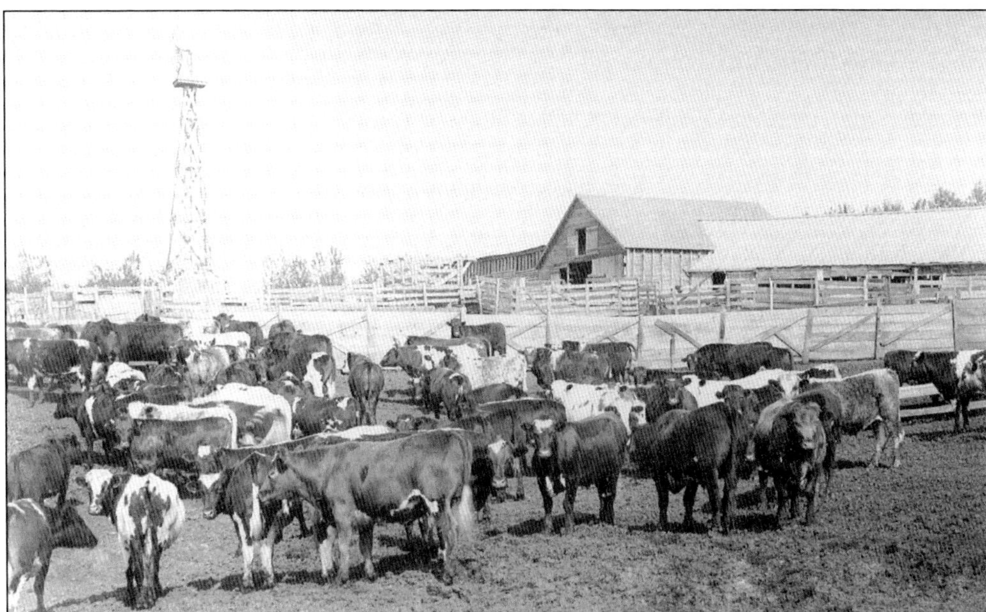

This large stockyard was west of Crete near Riverside Cemetery. Owned by J.R. Johnston, F.I. Foss, and George Stevens, the company raised cattle, horses, sheep, and hogs for local customers and to ship elsewhere. In 1883, the firm, operating as Johnston, Foss, and Stevens, had more than 1,000 animals. (CHS, Jennie Chapman Stevens collection.)

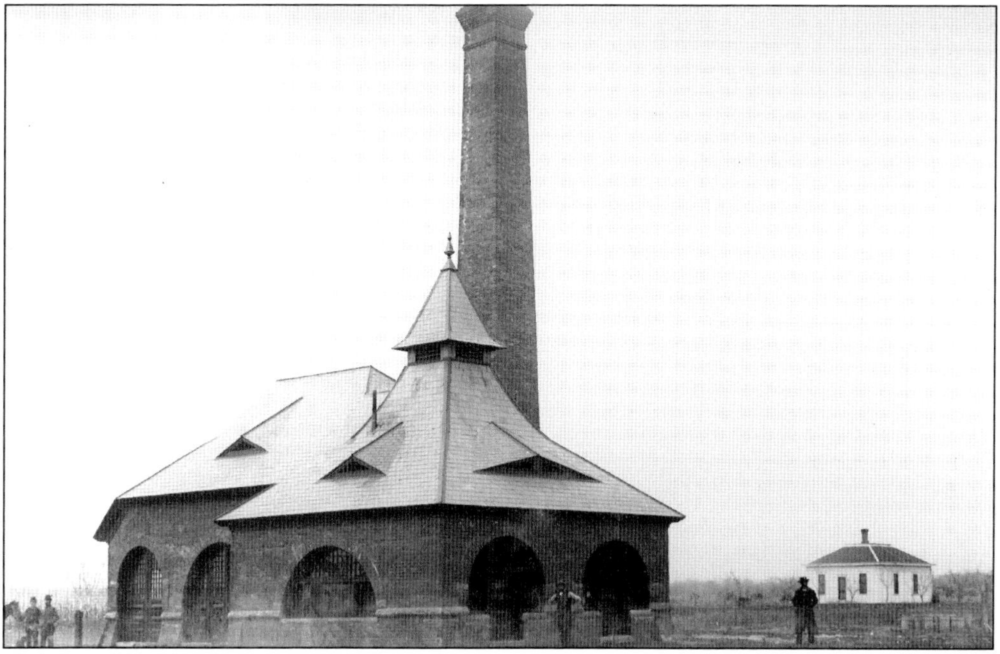

Built in 1889 by J.R. Johnston and George Stevens, this structure was Crete's first utility plant and the pump house for the city waterworks, a fire prevention system. Electricity was also generated here. Located at Eighteenth Street and Kingwood Avenue, the building was connected to a large reservoir on College Hill via pipes, which also ran to hydrants in downtown Crete. The structure was razed in 1981. (CHS, Jennie Chapman Stevens collection.)

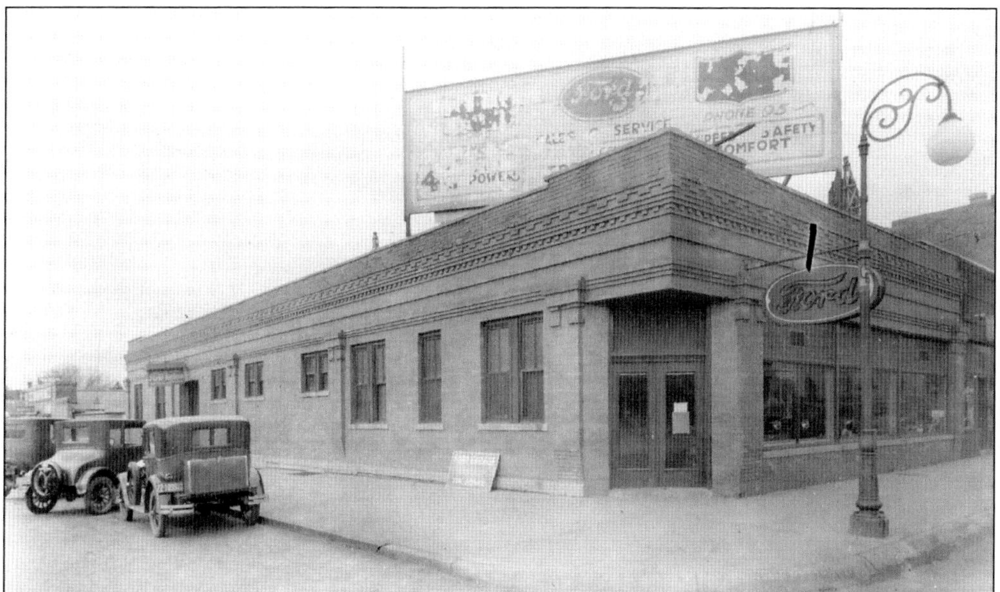

This Ford dealership, owned by John Kabley, was in the former Universal Auto Company building. Charles Algermission established Universal in 1909 and sold some of the first cars in Crete. In the 1920s, he sold the building to Kabley, who ran a Ford showroom and garage. The building, at Thirteenth Street and Linden Avenue, now houses Pinnacle Bank. (CHS, Kerst collection.)

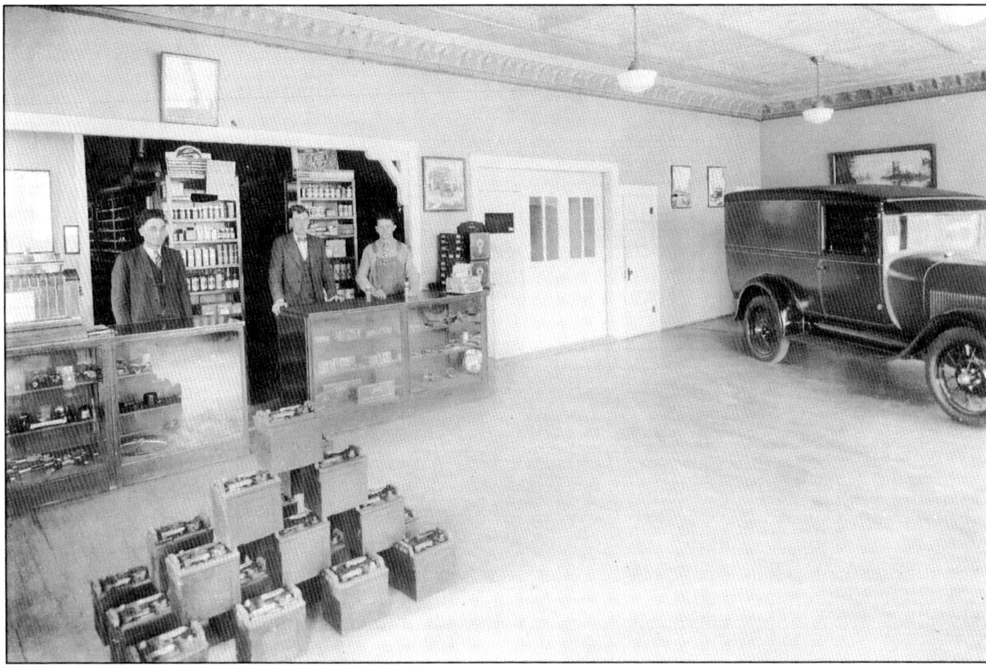

The coming of the automobile brought major lifestyle changes. By the 1910s, cars were seen on the streets of Crete alongside horse-drawn vehicles. This view shows the Kabley parts department and automobile showroom around 1929. Behind the counter are, from left to right, owner John Kabley, bookkeeper Fred Kerst, and parts man Fred Fahrenbruch. (CHS, Kerst collection.)

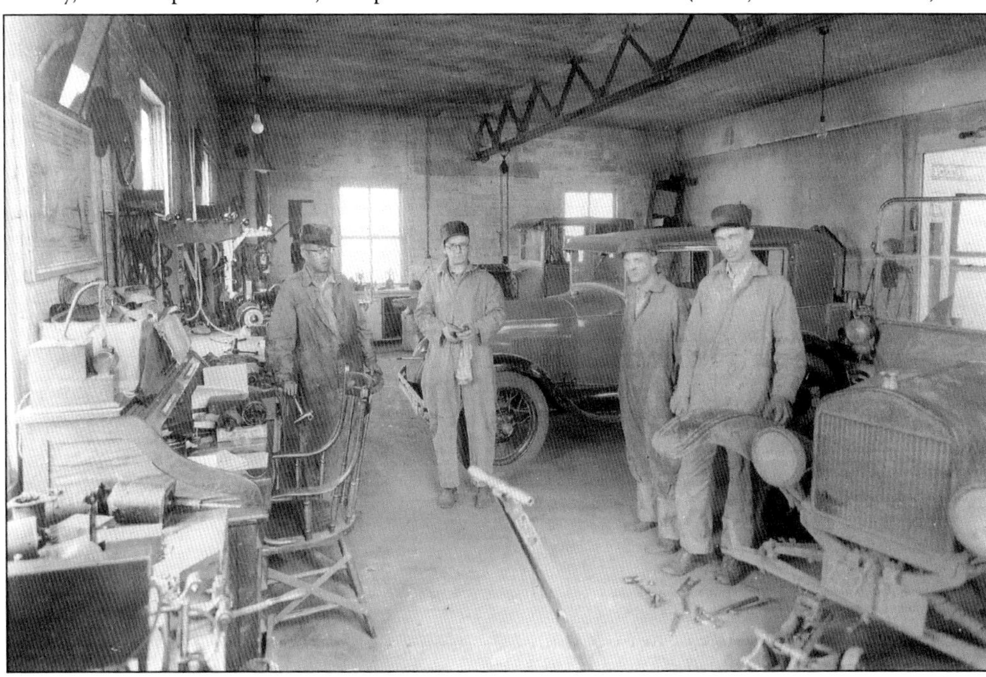

As people purchased automobiles, garages slowly replaced blacksmith and carriage repair shops. The Kabley garage, in the rear of the building, was fully equipped to handle all Ford repairs. Here, mechanics pause in their work to pose for this photograph. (CHS, Kerst collection.)

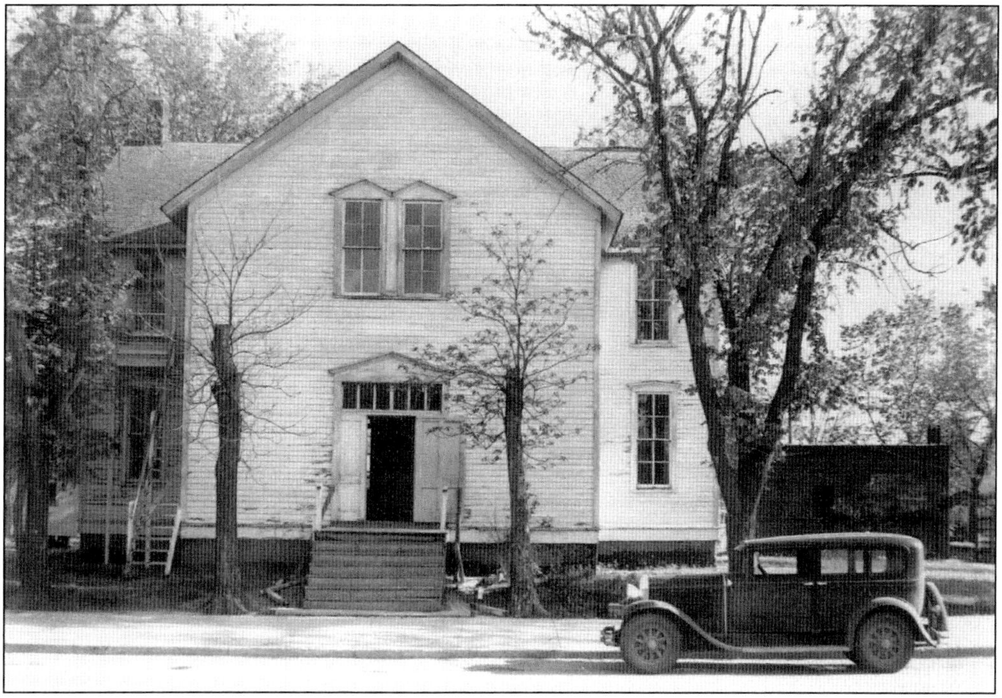

This frame building was Crete's first city hall. It was originally built as the town high school in 1882 on Block 158 for $3,174, and served the school district until about 1890, when a new brick high school was completed. This building was then moved to Thirteenth Street, facing north, to house city government. The brick jail is at right in this 1920s photograph. (Author's collection.)

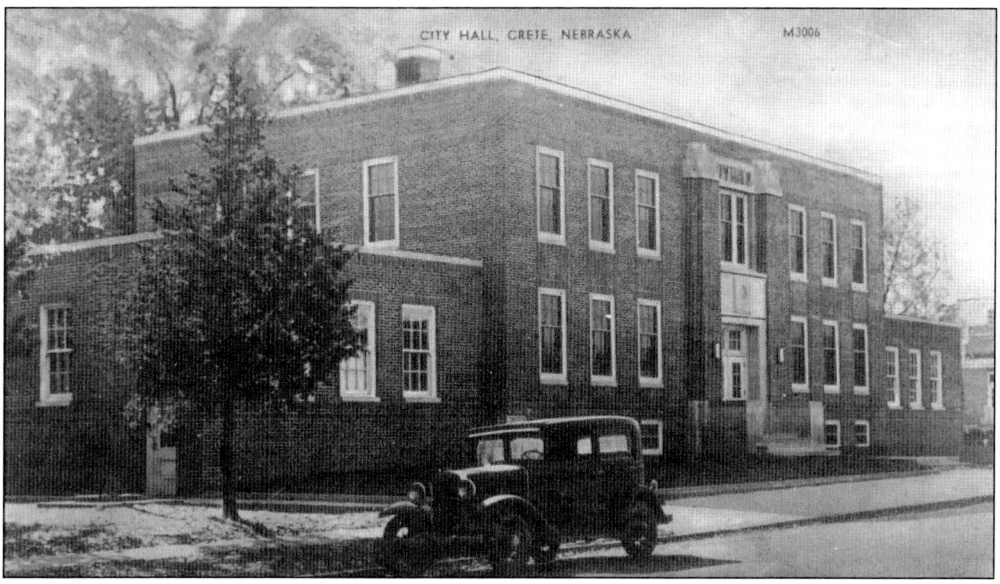

City hall was built in 1939 with a Works Progress Administration (WPA) grant. The building committee met with representatives from community organizations to finalize plans that included garages and workshops for fire department and city vehicles, offices for city departments, community meeting spaces, a kitchen, storage vaults, and a jail. City offices moved to temporary quarters so the frame city hall could be razed prior to construction. (Marti Ator Williams collection.)

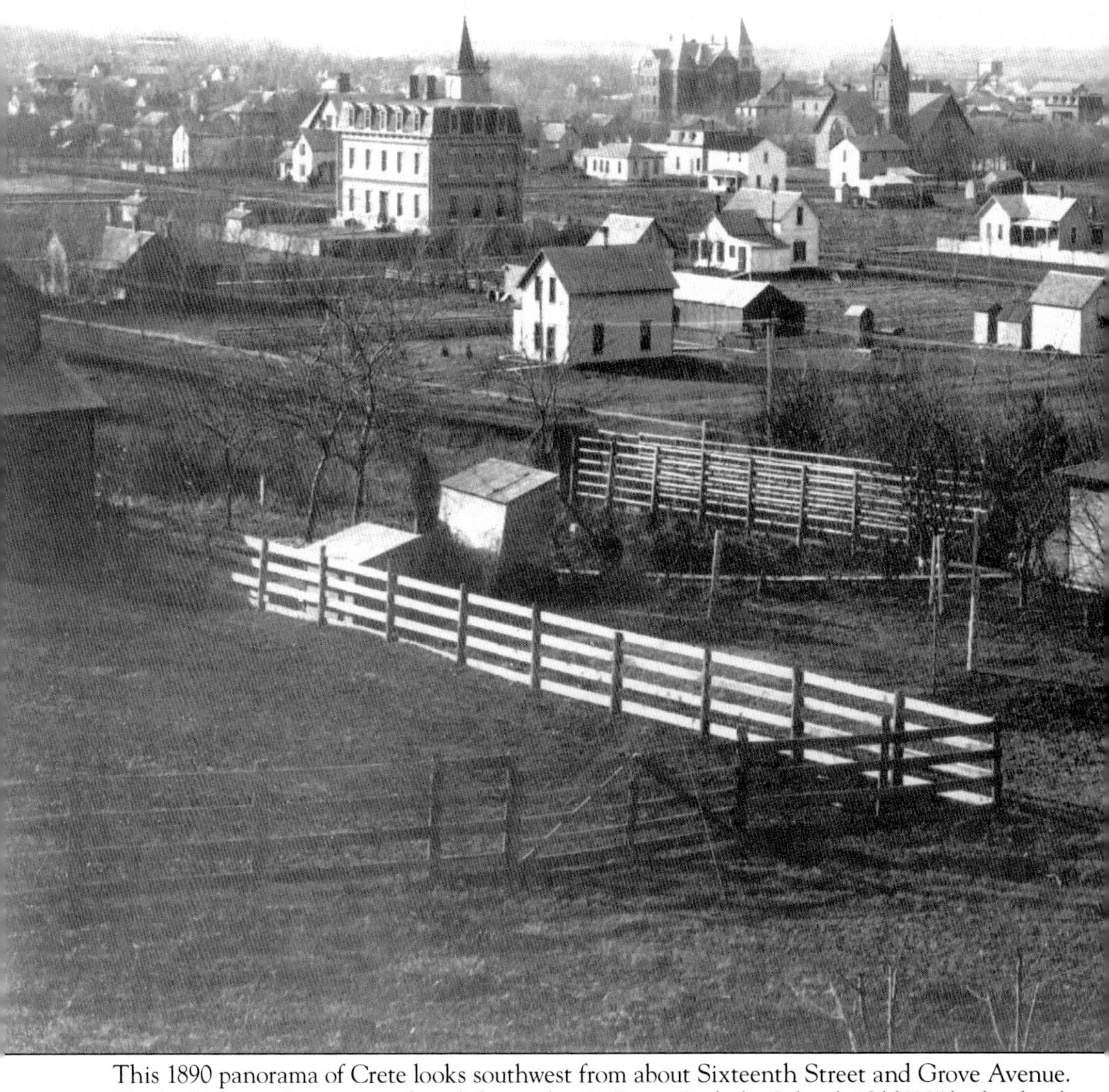

This 1890 panorama of Crete looks southwest from about Sixteenth Street and Grove Avenue. The buildings with spires are, from left to right, St. James Catholic School, "Old '88" high school,

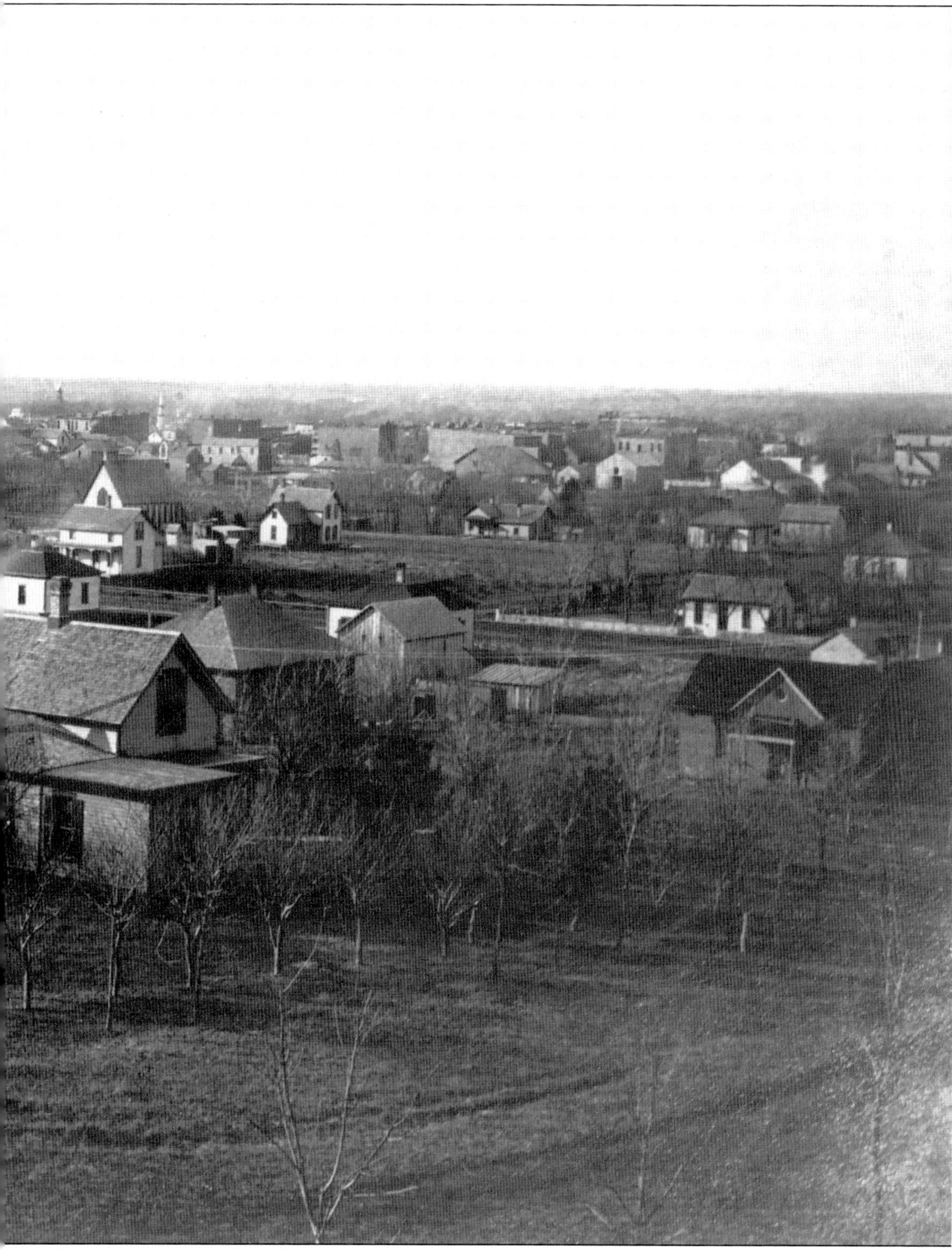

and the Grace Methodist Church. Trinity Memorial Episcopal Church is to the right of the Methodist church and the commercial district is in the distance. (CHS.)

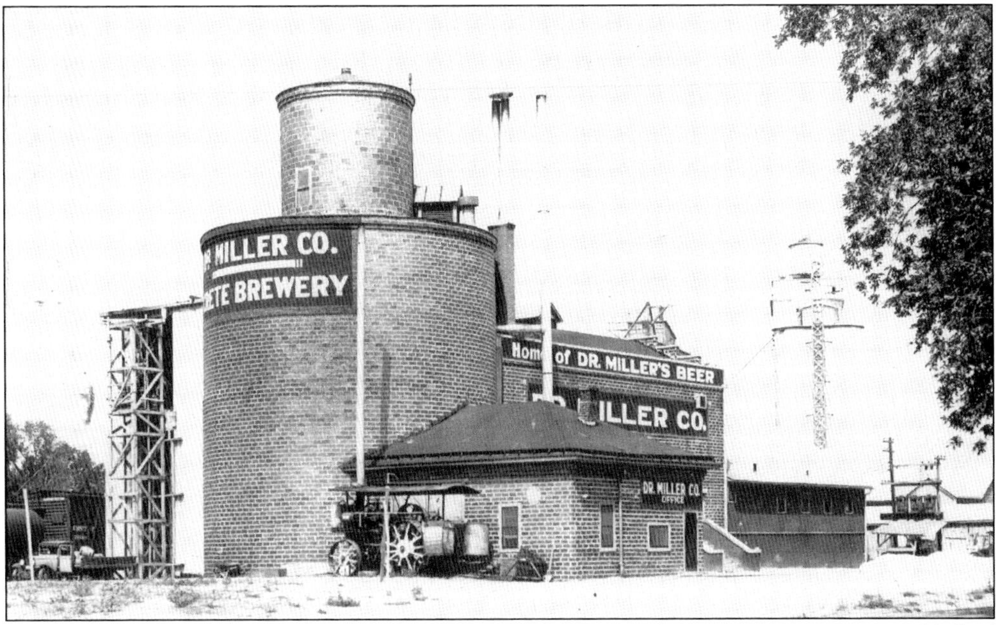

Crete's European population initiated local beer production. The Western Brewery, established in 1872 on the west side of the river near the cemetery, made Crete Beer. It was destroyed by fire in 1907. This brewery was built by a Dr. Miller in 1933 on West Thirteenth Street between Pine and Quince Avenues. Miller's Bohemian brewmaster produced the popular Golden Harvest and Kreet beers, but the plant closed in 1941 due to financial difficulties. (CHS.)

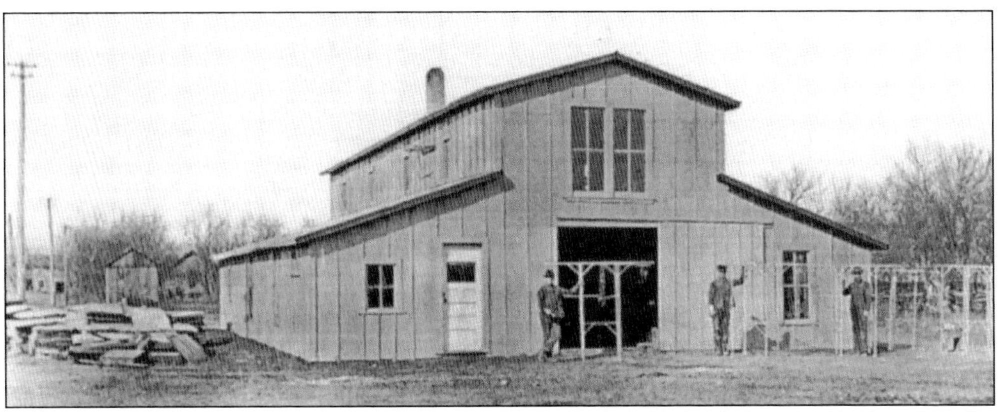

Douglas Manufacturing Company was founded in 1905 by Elizabeth Jane Robb Douglas, the designer of a collapsible voting booth. She patented the idea and launched a company, at Sixteenth Street and Pine Avenue, which expanded to serve customers worldwide. The company, which still produces voting booths, added ballot boxes, media storage containers, and more over the years. Elizabeth's great-grandson Roger Douglas is now president. The original plant building is seen here in 1912. (CHS.)

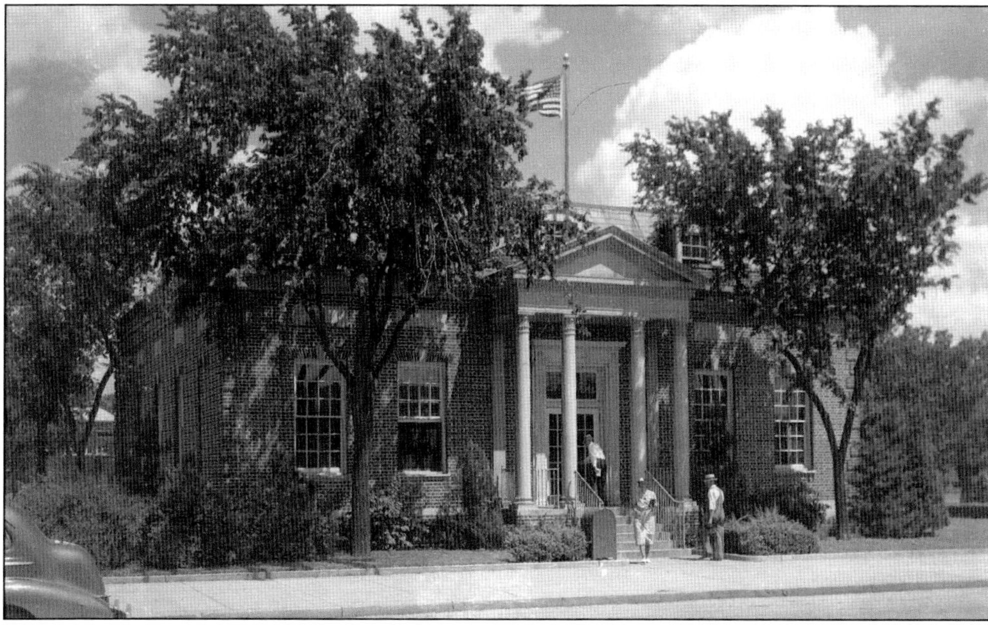

Crete's post office was dedicated on October 11, 1931, and more than 500 people toured the building that day. The first floor featured a postal workroom and service counter, and the second floor had offices for military recruiting and a lounge for employees, complete with a shower and bath. Constructed on the Central Park block, the $65,000 building is still in service. (Marti Ator Williams collection.)

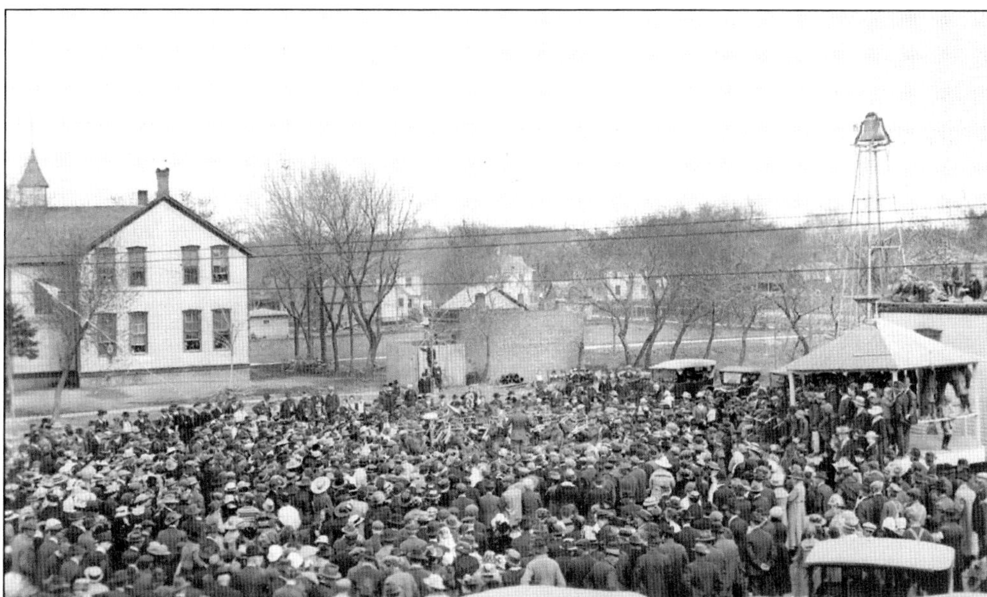

The occasion for this Central Park gathering is unknown, but the photograph contained the inscription "October 1918," which was the time of the Spanish influenza epidemic in Crete. These people apparently ignored the warnings to stay home. In the background are the old city hall, the jail, and the town bell. (SCHS.)

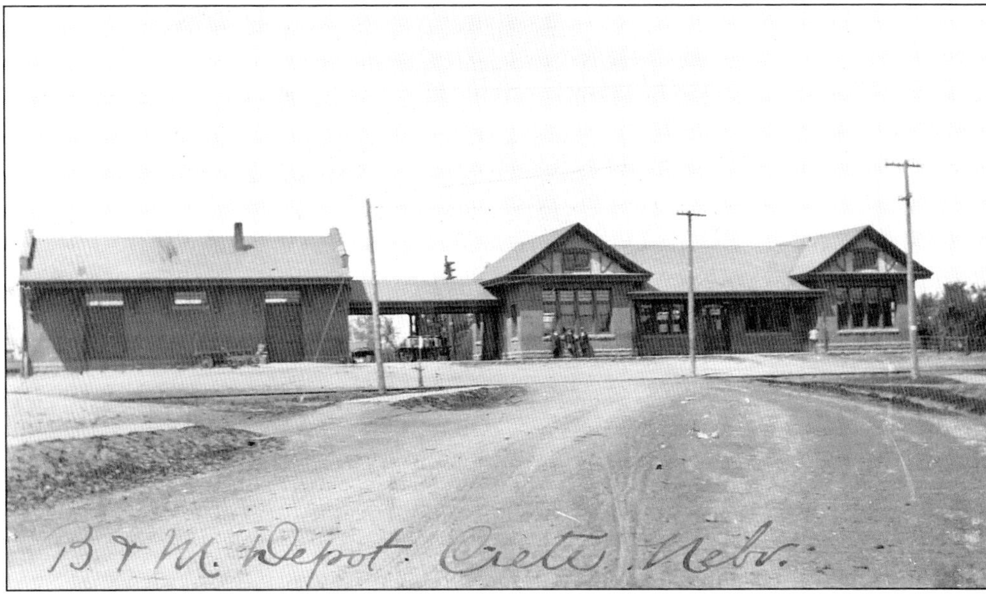

The original 1870s BMRR depot, built trackside on Oak Avenue, was replaced in 1905 by this brick depot about a block east. The new passenger depot was heated with steam, had electricity, and featured a modern "operating" room, a large waiting room, a smoking parlor, a mothers' lounge, and restrooms. A freight depot, connected by a covered walkway, was on the west. The building was razed in October 2011. (CHS.)

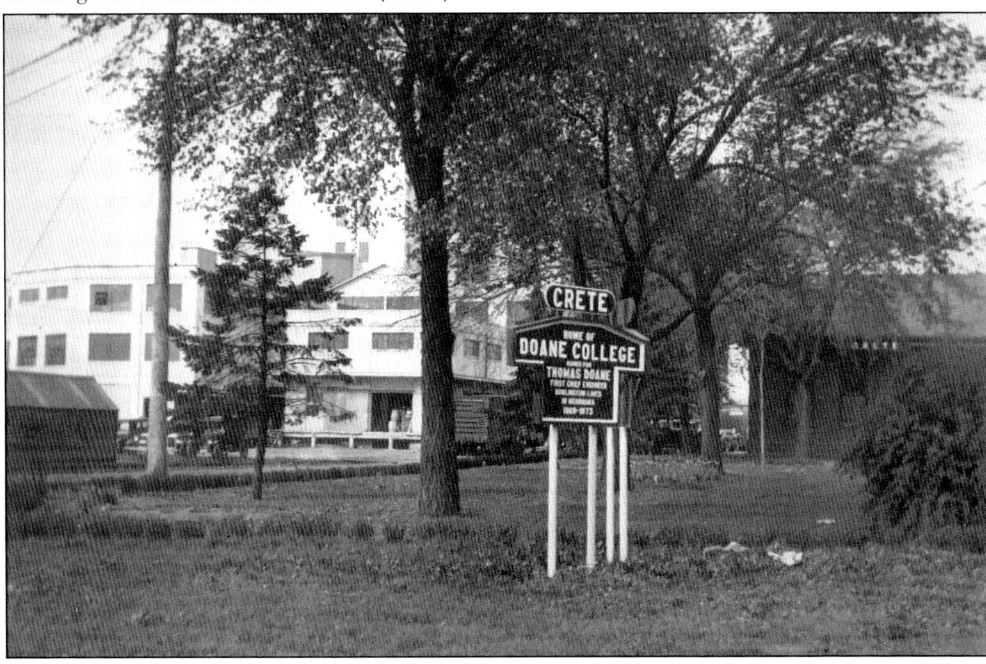

This two-sided sign stood trackside on the Burlington line, welcoming people to Crete. Doane alumni remember the familiar site as they returned to college. After the last passenger train came through Crete in 1971, the signs were abandoned but later rescued by local railroad historian Harold Jones. Now one sign is mounted in the local Edward Jones Investments office, and the other is displayed at Benne Memorial Museum. (Author's collection.)

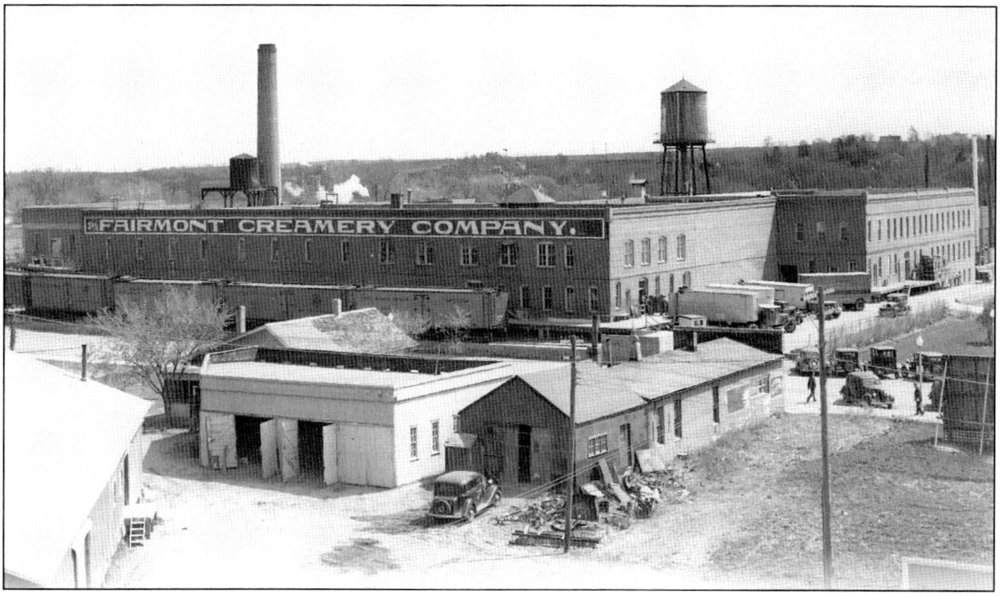

In 1889, Crete became the first expansion site for the Fairmont Creamery, founded in Fairmont, Nebraska, in 1884. In addition to processing cream and milk, the Crete operation made ice cream in many flavors, processed eggs and poultry, and made ice. The plant, at Maine Avenue and the Burlington tracks, was managed by M.D. Osterhout from 1903 to 1938, followed by Everett Darrington and Joe Magee, and closed in 1960. (CHS, Osterhout collection.)

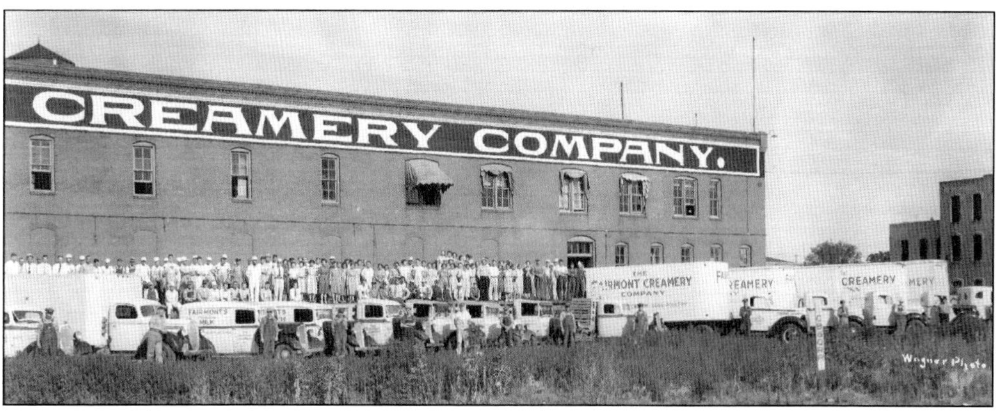

During World War II, the Fairmont Creamery employed 425 workers, compared to 175 workers in peacetime. The creamery produced 15,000 pounds of dried eggs daily during the war period. Annual picnics at Tuxedo Park and formal banquets at Sokol Hall were held for employees. This photograph from the 1940s shows the creamery staff and the company vehicle fleet. (CHS, Thelma Grasz collection.)

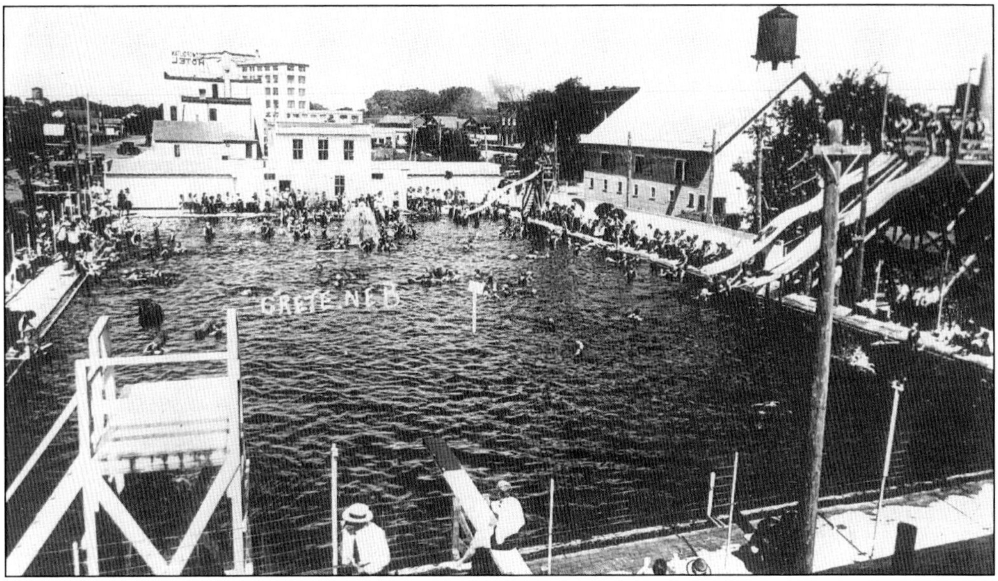

This swimming pool opened in 1921 and was fed from hot water condensers at the nearby Fairmont Creamery. Fairmont manager M.D. Osterhout chaired the building committee. A large pipe carried warm water from the creamery into the pool through a central fountain that ran constantly. The pool entrance, bandstand, ice cream parlor, spectator seating, and dressing rooms were on the west side. The pool closed in the 1940s, and the fire station now occupies this site. (SCHS.)

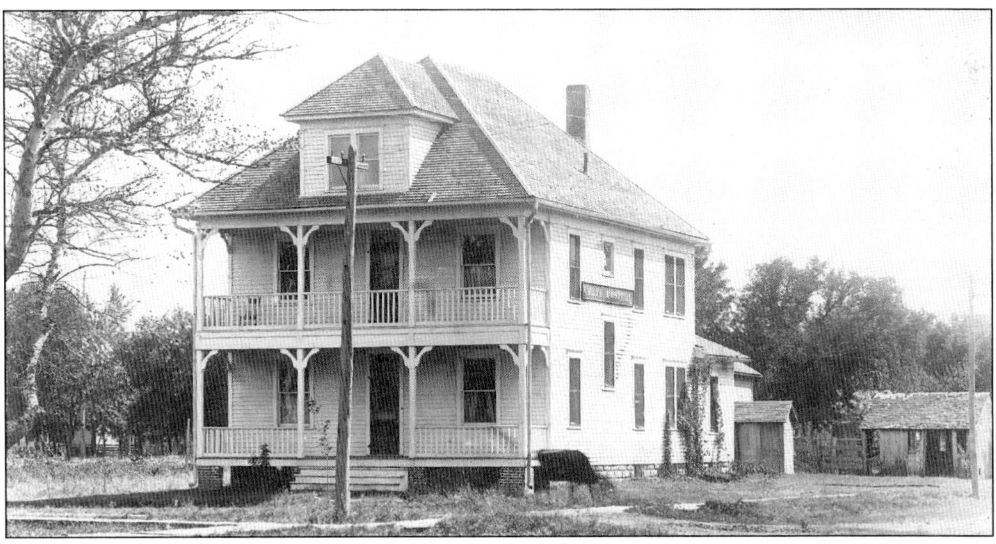

This building, on the southeast corner of Fourteenth Street and Juniper Avenue, was the first hospital in Crete. Built in 1902, the facility was run by Dr. C.H. Brewer, a surgeon, and was advertised as a well-equipped institution, capable of treating the most severe illnesses. The hospital was open to all qualified physicians, and visiting days were Wednesday and Sunday afternoons. The building is now an apartment house. (SCHS.)

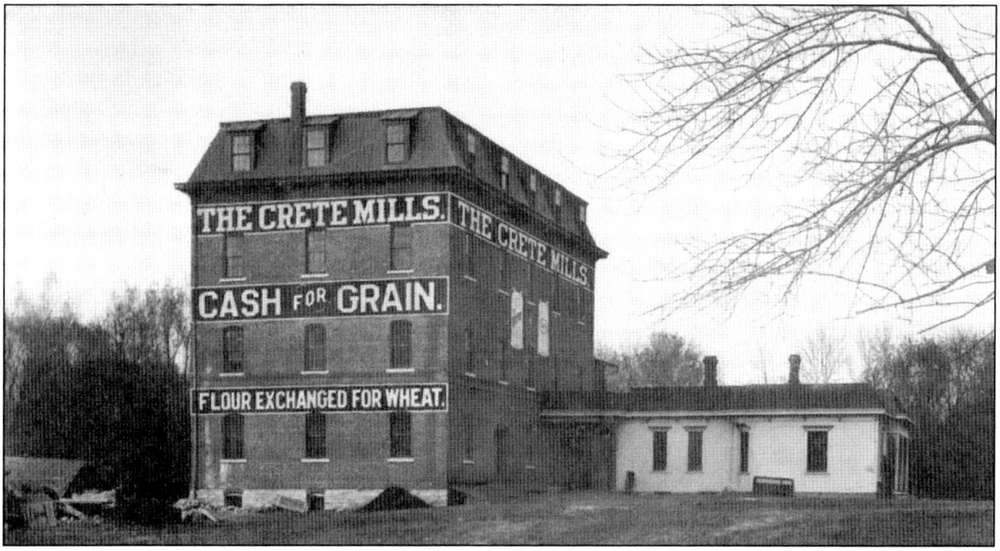

The Crete Mills began as a sawmill in 1869, run by George Bridges and Oliver Baltzley. A year later, they added a gristmill. Located on the river at about Third Street and Norman Avenue, this water-powered mill went through several names, finally becoming the Crete Mills in 1881. This view shows the south mill, later called Elevator A, which operated as a cereal mill into the 20th century. (Author's collection.)

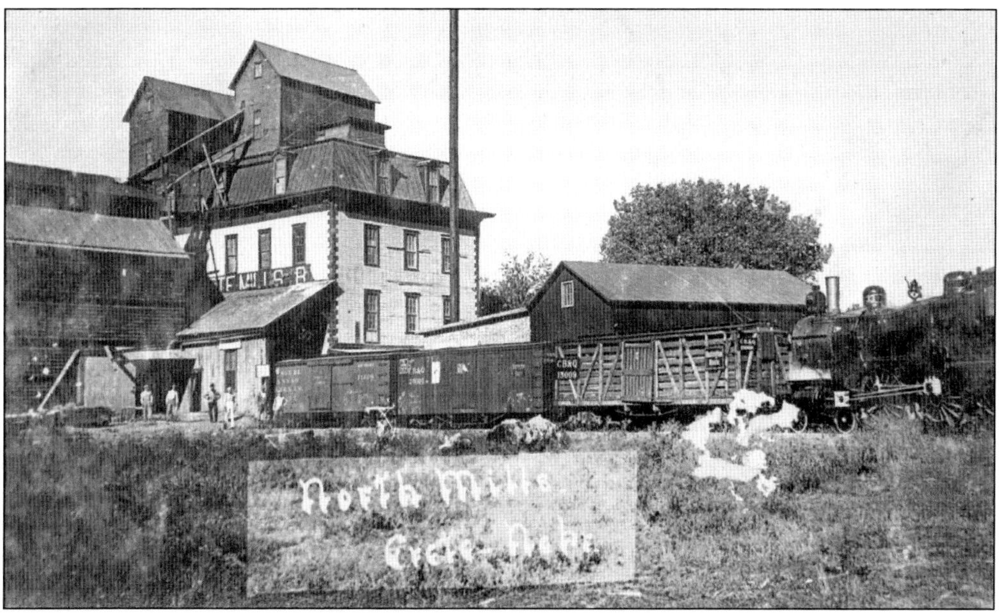

In 1881, Charles Seeley built a water-powered mill on the river north of the railroad tracks. By 1895, this mill had combined with the south mill, and the north mill was called Elevator B. The Crete Mills, operating from both sites, incorporated in 1901 with A.L. Johnson as president. This photograph shows the original north mill, or Elevator B, before it was destroyed by fire in 1912. (CHS, Krebs collection.)

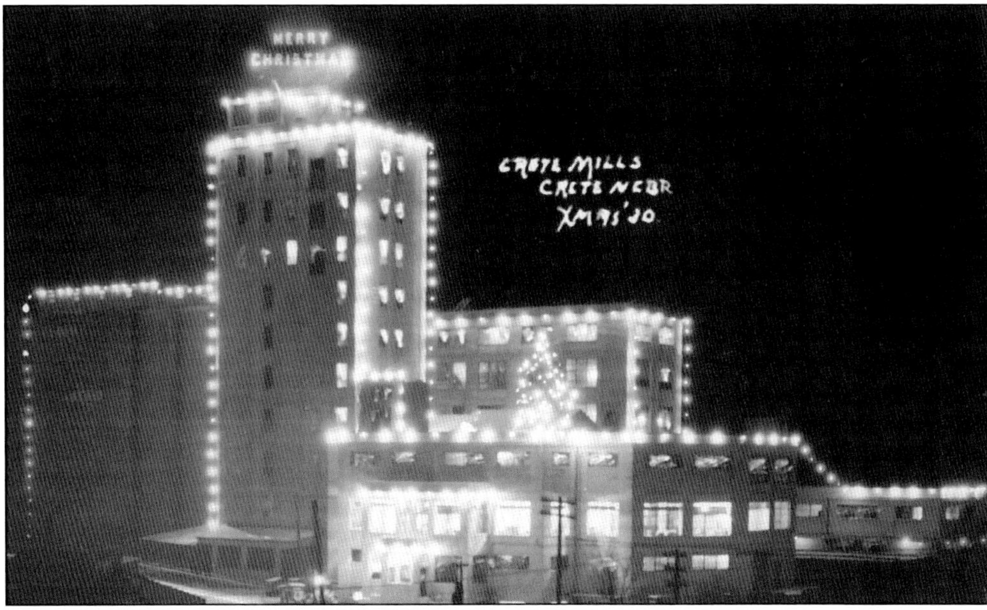

In 1913, after fire destroyed Elevator B, the Crete Mills moved to its present location, switched from water power to electricity, and expanded extensively. For years, the complex was decorated for the holidays, as captured in this 1930 photograph. Part of Bunge Milling, the Crete Mills currently grinds 50,000 bushels of corn per day into grits, meals, and flours for the cereal and snack food industries. (CHS, Butler collection.)

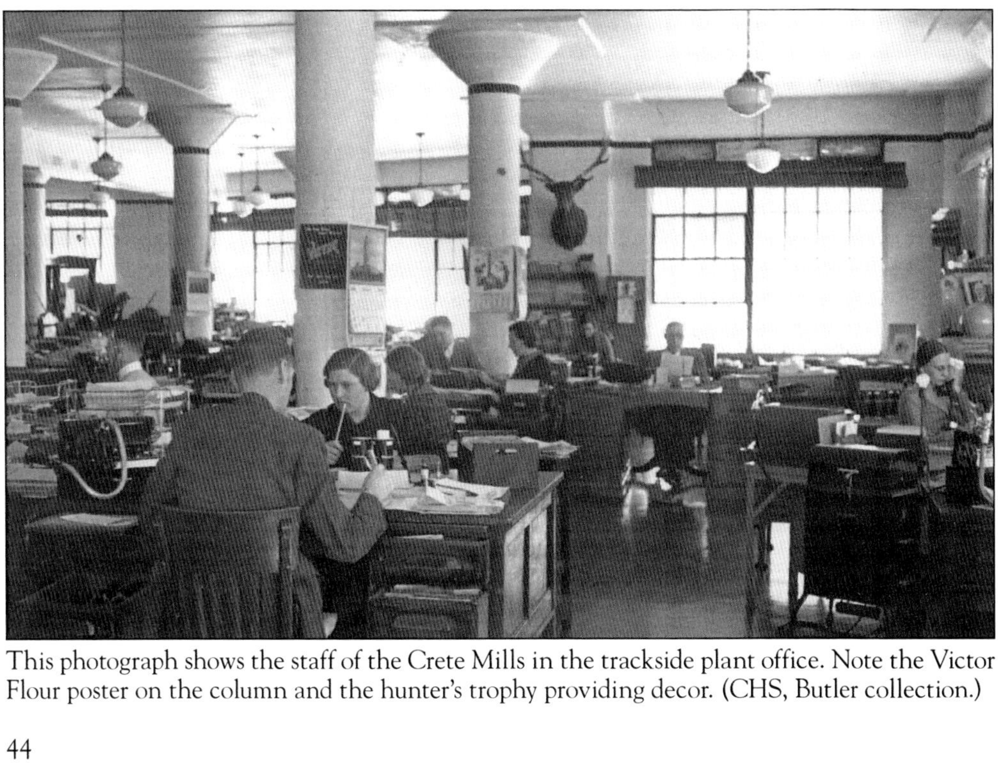

This photograph shows the staff of the Crete Mills in the trackside plant office. Note the Victor Flour poster on the column and the hunter's trophy providing decor. (CHS, Butler collection.)

This 1941 photograph looks northwest toward the Crete Mills in the foreground and the dam and former Elevator B mill site in the upper right corner. Douglas Manufacturing is in the trees on the right, and M.O. Smith's barn at The Maples is in the upper left. The Saline County Shop and the Burlington Northern depot are along the right side. The orderly plantings are the Crete Mills employee garden plots. (CHS, Krebs collection.)

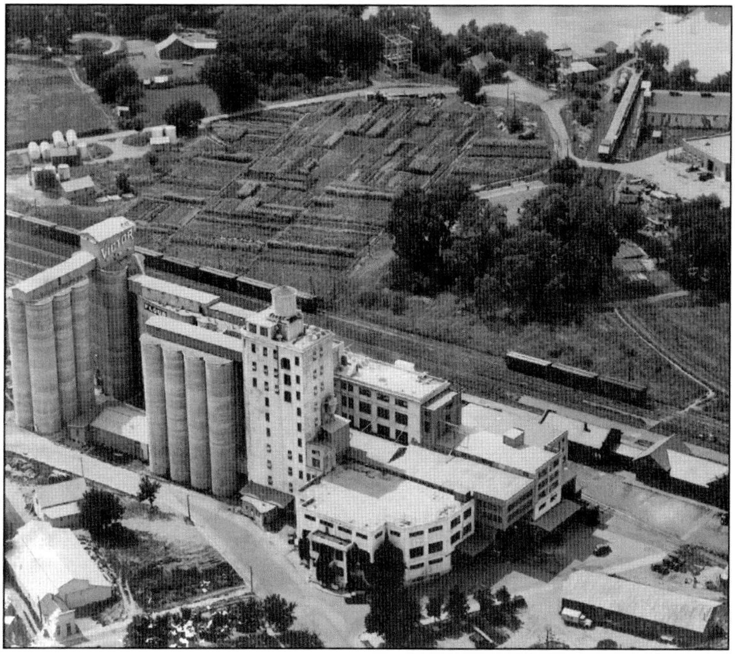

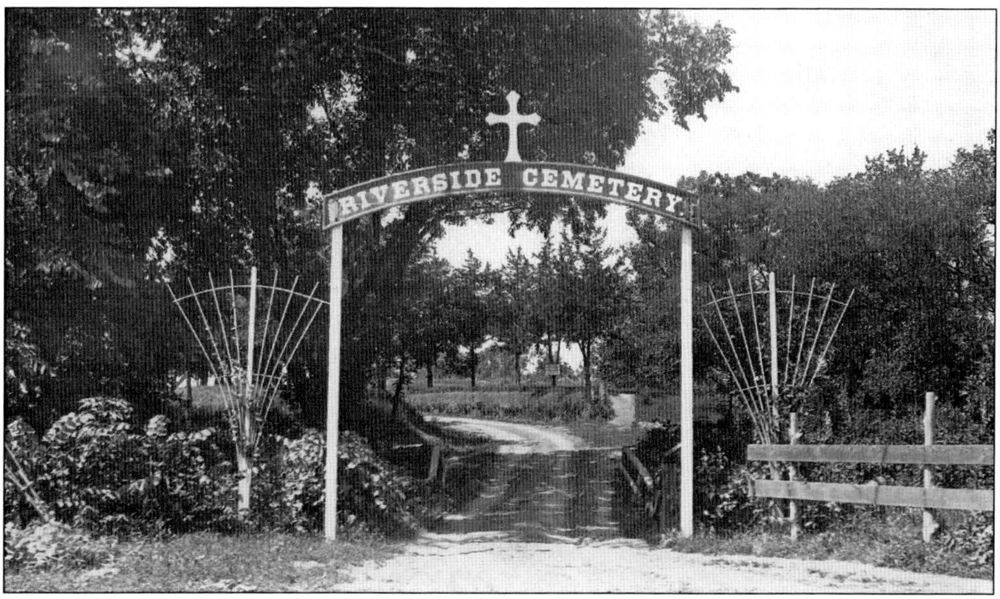

Doane professor Arthur Fairchild platted Riverside Cemetery in 1879. Graves were then moved from an unsightly graveyard south of town. Riverside was designed in parklike fashion, with tree-lined, curved roadways and limestone retaining walls. Patterned after Mount Auburn Cemetery in Cambridge, Massachusetts, the idea was brought to Crete by the easterners who founded Doane College. The Mount Auburn model urged a "garden of graves" rather than a "graveyard." (CHS, Krebs collection.)

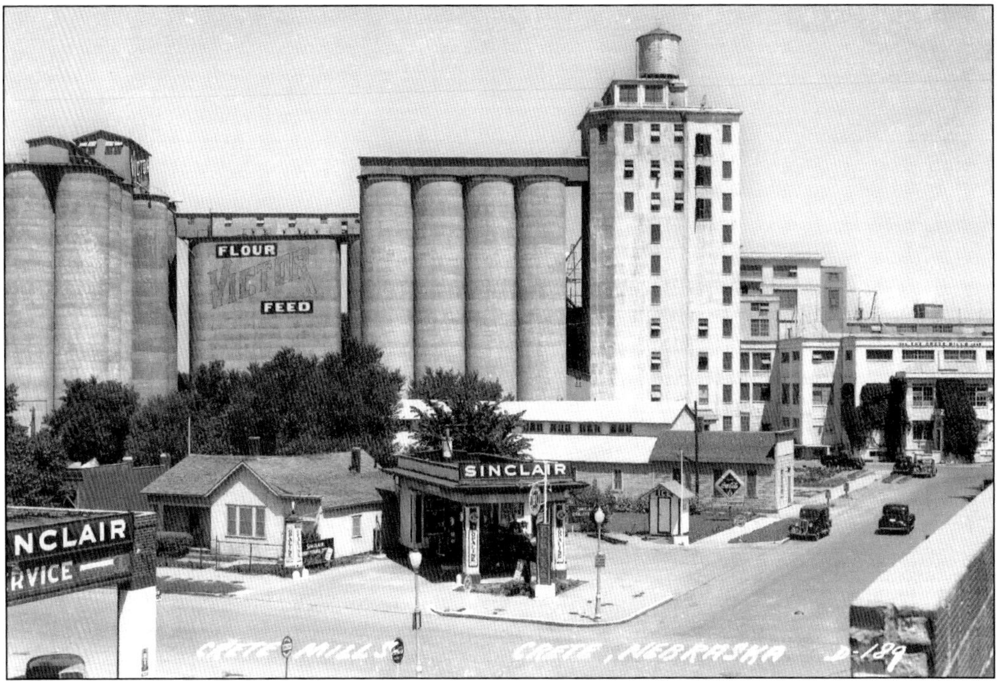

Crete's first gas station was on the northwest corner of Thirteenth Street and Norman Avenue, where a Crete Mills building now stands. The station was built by the Omaha Refining Company about 1916. John Menke, who later had his own filling station across from city hall, was the first manager of the facility. This station was purchased by Sinclair in the late 1920s. (Author's collection.)

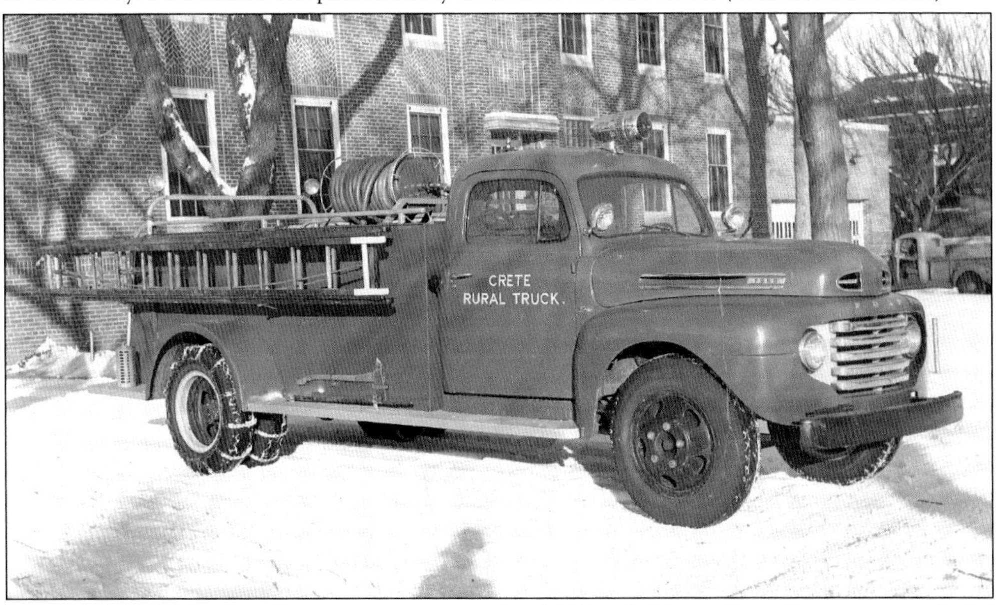

The Crete Volunteer Fire Department organized in 1888 with 18 members. Equipment included a hand-drawn cart, 750 feet of narrow hose, and one nozzle. The department became motorized in 1919. The department's 1948 rural pumper truck (above) was built by Bill Weidner and Alvin "Rosie" Rozdalovsky on a Ford chassis. The 50-member volunteer fire department and rescue squad now operate from a modern fire station with state-of-the-art equipment and vehicles. (CHS.)

Three

EDUCATION AND RELIGIOUS LIFE

As Crete became settled, educational programs and churches became important to the development of the town. In the winter of 1866–1867, thirteen pupils were taught in a dugout in the bank of the Big Blue River. Crete's school district was organized on February 13, 1868, and, in addition to dugouts, classrooms were located in store buildings and homes until proper schools could be erected.

Doane Academy was the classroom site for elementary students as well as college preparatory students during the 1871–1872 school year, and in 1873, three elementary schools, or wards, were built in Crete neighborhoods. Two of these buildings, the East and West Wards, were upgraded to two-story brick structures by the late 1880s, and a new North Ward was built in 1908.

The first school building on Block 158, on land purchased by the school district in 1881, was constructed in 1882. This frame structure, located on the southeast corner of Eleventh Street and Linden Avenue, was used as a school until about 1890, when it was moved to Central Park and became city hall. A new high school was constructed in 1888 just to the east of the 1882 building. By 1950, Block 158 and neighboring Block 157 housed four schools, all facing north to Eleventh Street—the 1882 frame school, "Old '88" high school, a second high school built in 1918, and Central Elementary School, completed in 1942. The Catholic parish built St. James School in 1887, serving grades one through eight.

A public library was organized in Crete in 1878. At first, books were housed in various downtown locations, including in a bookstore and in the rear of a law office. The library got a permanent home with the erection of the present Carnegie library in 1915.

Before 1872, three denominations—Methodists, Catholics, and Congregationalists—had organized. They were soon joined by the Episcopalian and Church of God congregations, and by 1880, eight different church organizations were active in Crete. Ethnic groups also had their own congregations, some short-lived. The Czechs had Catholic, Congregational, and Methodist churches, and the Germans had Congregational, Methodist, Catholic, and Lutheran congregations.

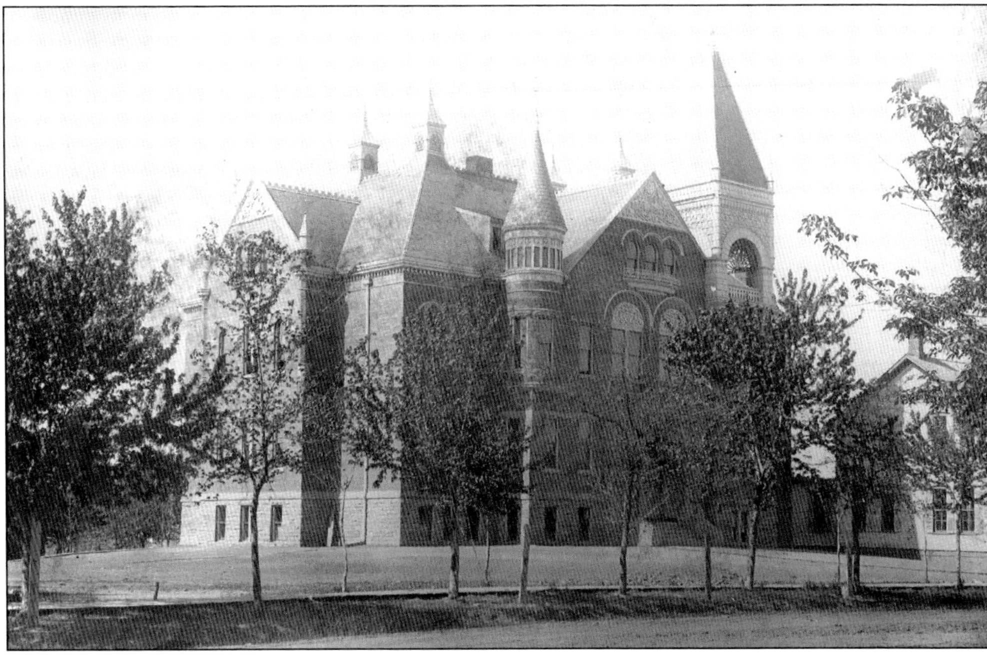

This high school was built in 1888 at a cost of $20,000 from plans by Omaha architects Fowler and Beindorf. Known as "Old '88," the three-level Queen Anne building served upperclassmen until a new high school was completed in 1918. It was then used into the 1950s as a grade school. The building faced north near the southeast corner of Eleventh Street and Linden Avenue. (CHS, Jennie Chapman Stevens collection.)

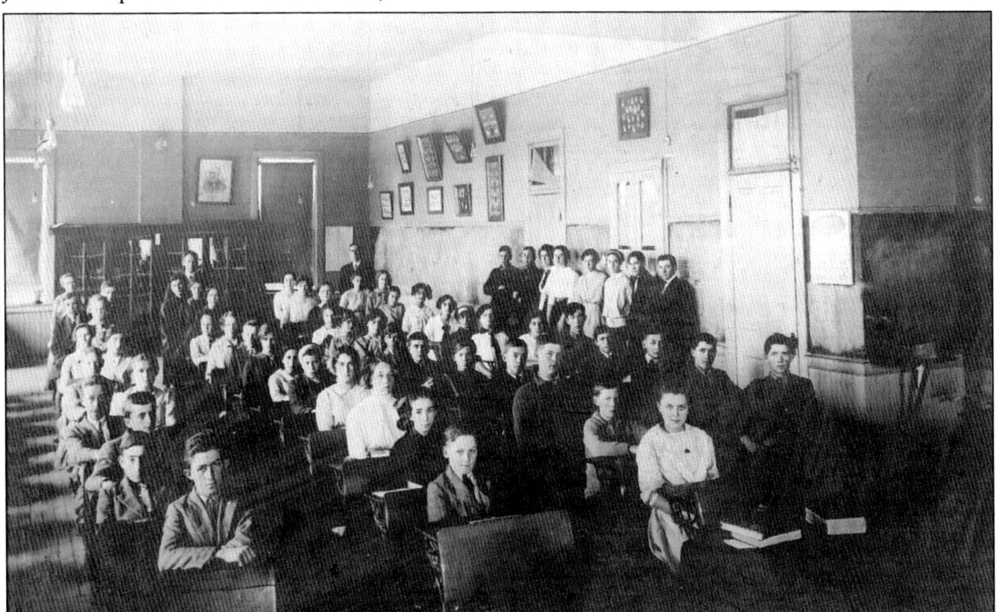

Eighth-grade students pose in the second-floor assembly room of "Old '88." The bell mounted in the school's tower is now exhibited at the Benne Memorial Museum in Crete. "Old '88" was razed in 1955 to make way for Crete's fourth high school building, which is still in use as an elementary school. (CHS.)

Supt. George A. Gregory created a manual training program in domestic science where Crete homemakers taught students how to cook. Gregory advocated hands-on training and felt that girls, like the boys who already had manual programs, should have the same opportunities. By having housewives teach, the budget was spared. The Crete Plan in Domestic Science was adopted by many school systems. (CHS.)

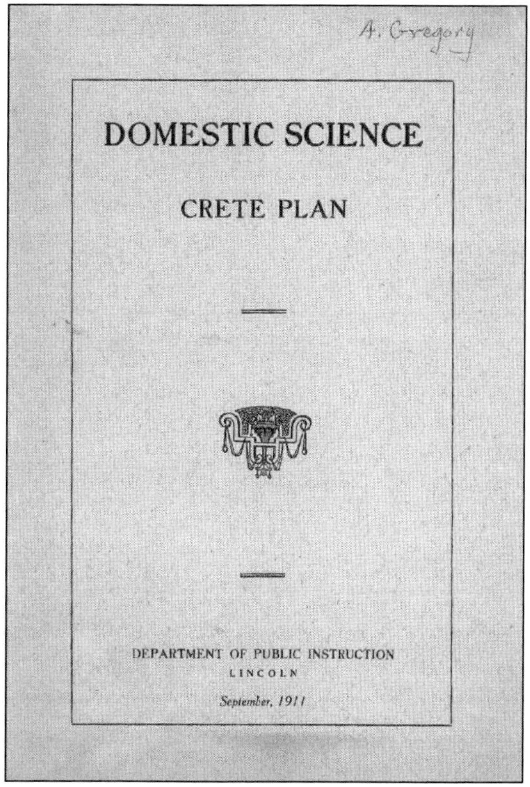

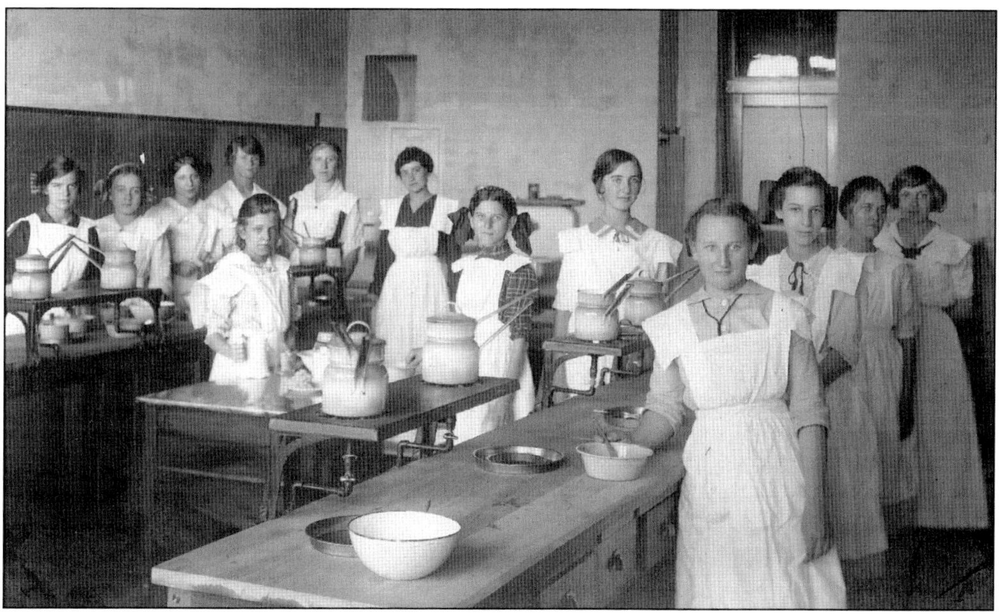

Students often met for cooking classes in the homes of their instructors but sometimes had class at school. Crete ladies focused on their areas of expertise; for example, one woman taught meats while another taught baking. Records show that when Superintendent Gregory suggested the idea of teaching to Crete homemakers, he had more volunteers than he needed and was forced to create a selection process. (CHS, Wallace collection.)

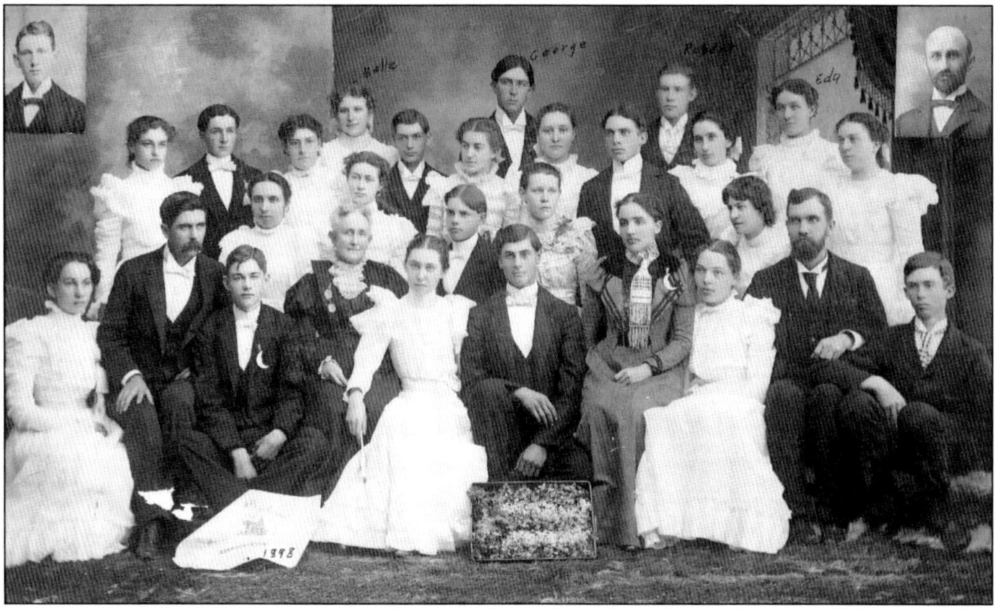

The Crete High School graduating class of 1898 posed for a formal group portrait with administrators and faculty. In the left foreground is a diploma featuring a line drawing of "Old '88," and in the center is a container of flowers. (CHS.)

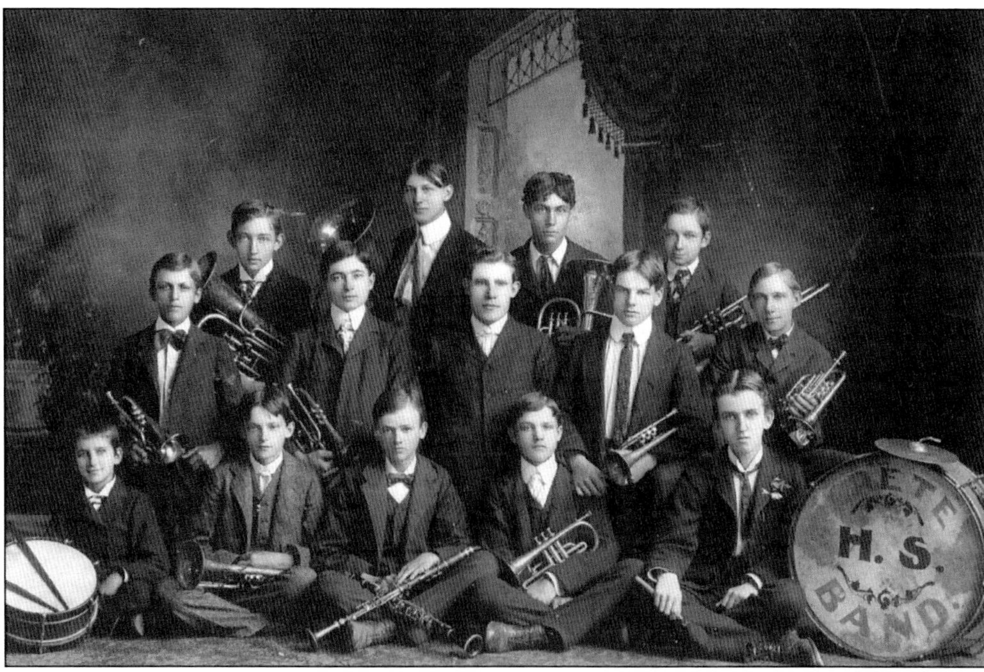

A Crete High School Band was the inspiration of Supt. George A. Gregory. Organized in 1901, the band gave concerts to help meet school expenses. The band included, from left to right, (first row) Stanley Maresh, Fred Kolouch, Adolph Gerner, Harry Hogue, and Herbert Dawes; (second row) Vance Jelinek, Frank Kolouch, Robert Rick, director Earl Johnson, and Otto Kopecky; (third row) Earl Talhem, Axel Smith, Ernest Chapelow, and John Johnson. (CHS, Gerner family collection.)

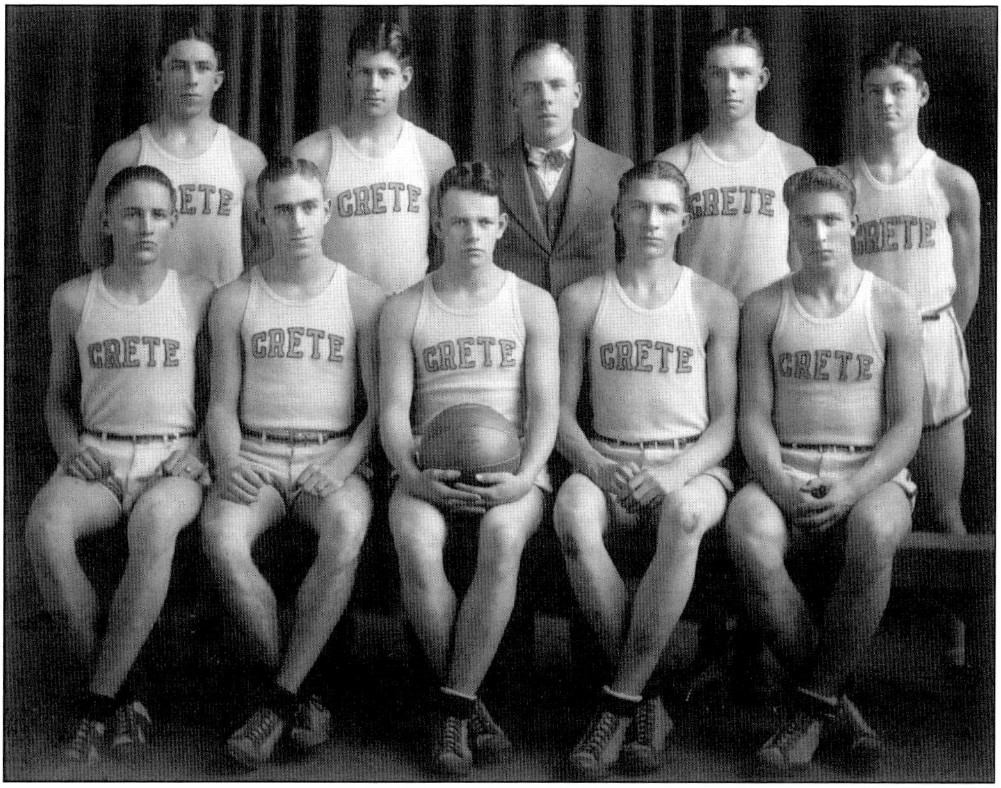

Members of Crete's 1927–1928 basketball team posed with coach L.F. "Pop" Klein after a successful season. They won the Cotner Tournament in March 1928 and immediately went on to Nebraska's state basketball tournament where they ended up 2-1. The team included, from left to right, (first row) Henry Krejci, Charles Aller, Paul Parker, Frank Belka, and Steve Hokuf; (second row) Theodore "Tater" Fahrnbruch, William Stone, Coach Klein, Red Whelan, and Ralph Adams. (*Crete News* collection.)

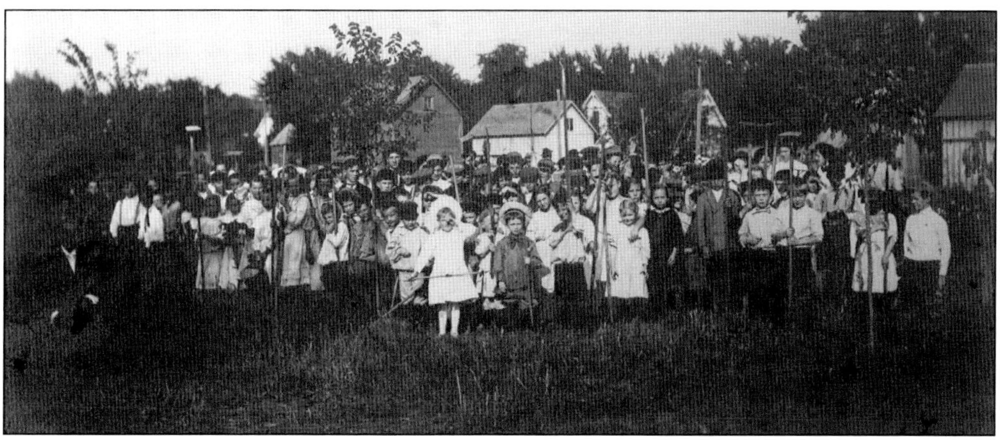

This photograph shows the Crete School Garden Club in 1909. Another of Superintendent Gregory's programs, the club promoted home and school gardening, even during the summer months. A vacant lot was loaned to the students who each tended their own small plot using free seeds distributed by their teachers. Students brought specimens for exhibition when school started in the fall. (CHS.)

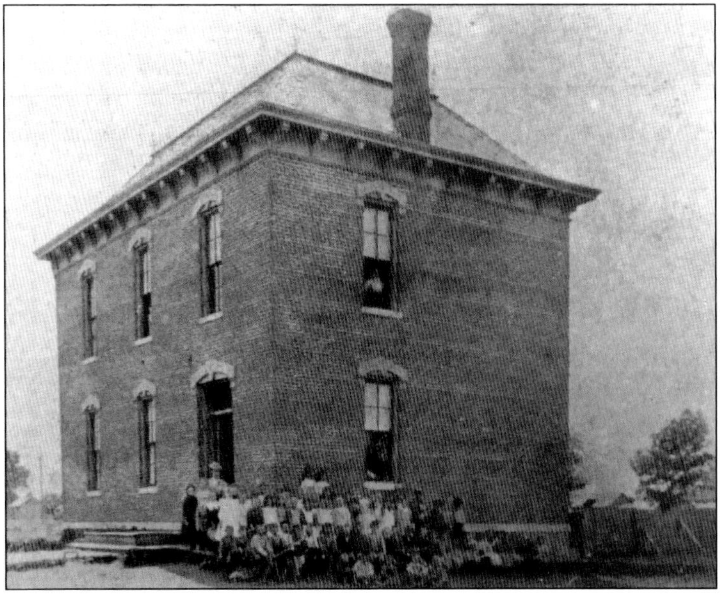

East Ward Elementary School was built in the late 1880s to replace an earlier frame structure. Due to high enrollment, a $3,645 extension was added in 1908. Located at Ninth Street and Hawthorne Avenue, the site is now part of the Bethlehem Lutheran Church property. The East and West Ward schools were used until Central Elementary was built in 1942, while North Ward continued to serve the district. (CHS.)

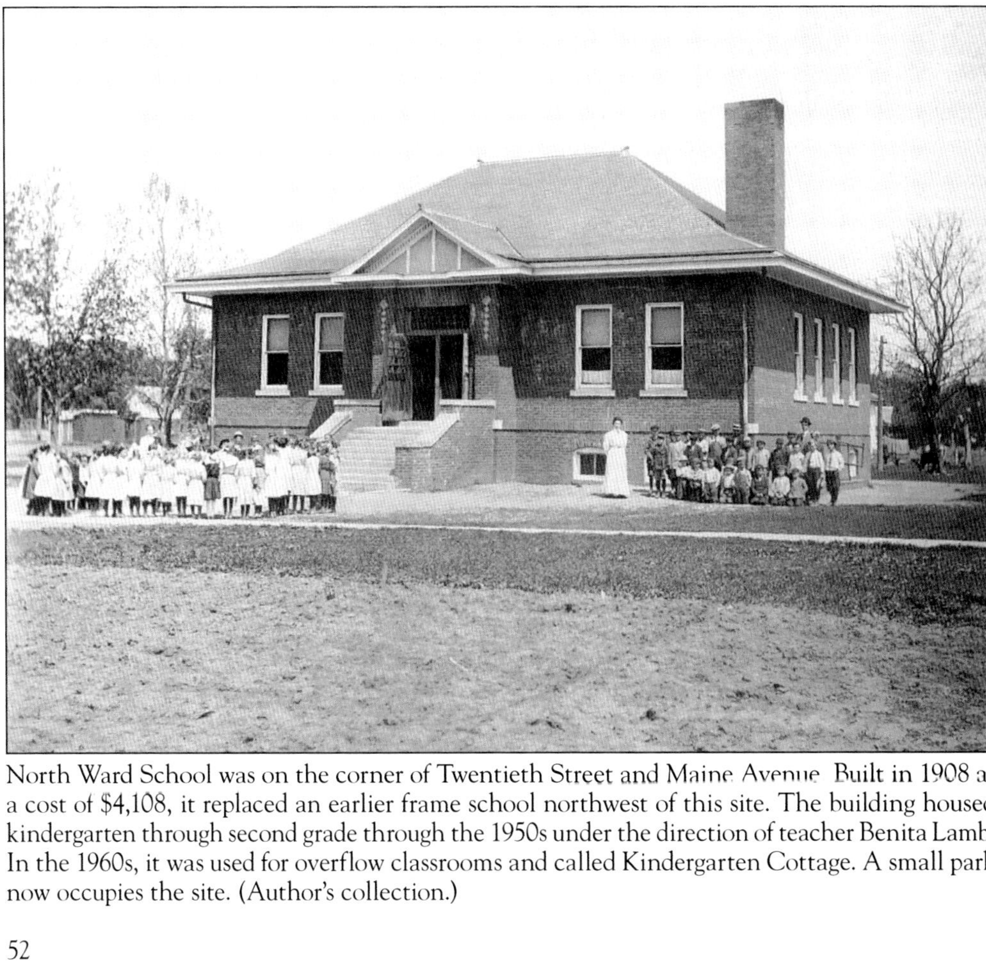

North Ward School was on the corner of Twentieth Street and Maine Avenue. Built in 1908 at a cost of $4,108, it replaced an earlier frame school northwest of this site. The building housed kindergarten through second grade through the 1950s under the direction of teacher Benita Lamb. In the 1960s, it was used for overflow classrooms and called Kindergarten Cottage. A small park now occupies the site. (Author's collection.)

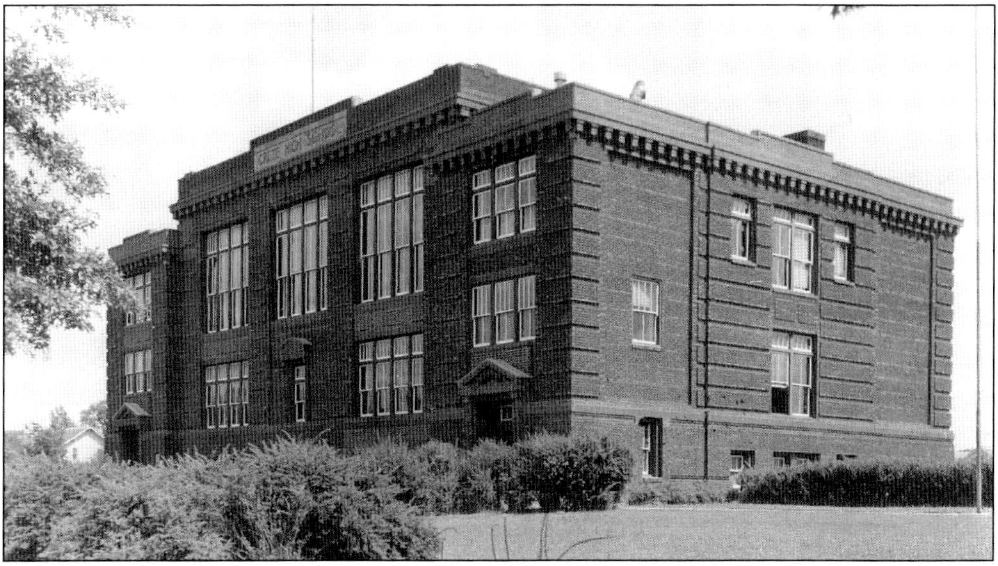

Crete's third high school was built in 1918 to the east of "Old '88." The older school then became home to grades four through eight, manual training, and band. Younger students were in the ward schools. This high school was replaced in 1956 by a fourth high school building, which is currently used for elementary students. Grades seven through nine were in the 1918 school until it was razed in 1976. (Marti Ator Williams collection.)

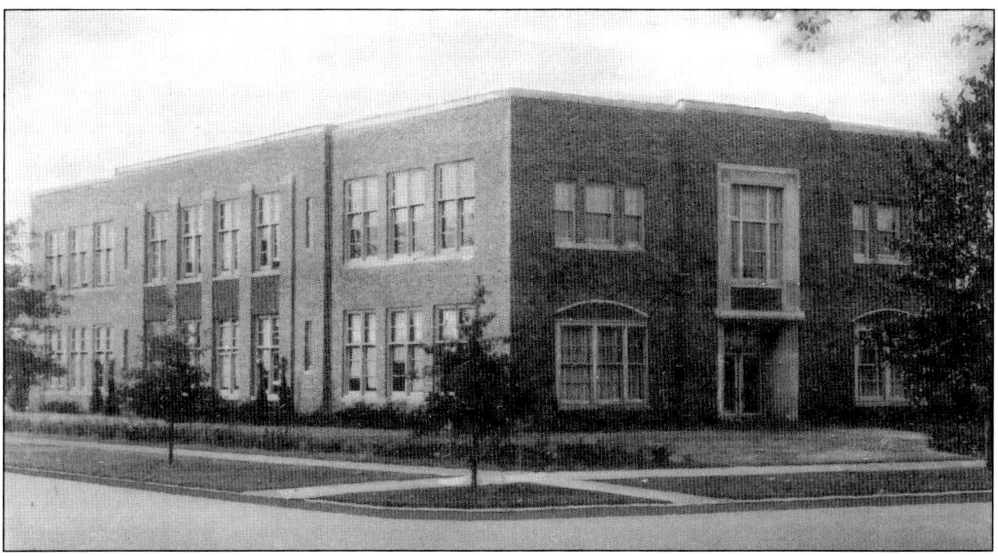

The Central Elementary School was completed in 1942. Contractors John Kerst and Anton Vasak won the bid and led a construction crew of Works Progress Administration (WPA) laborers assisted by local builder Otto Feeken. When completed, most of Crete's elementary age students were consolidated into the building, which is still in use as part of the elementary school complex. (Marti Ator Williams collection.)

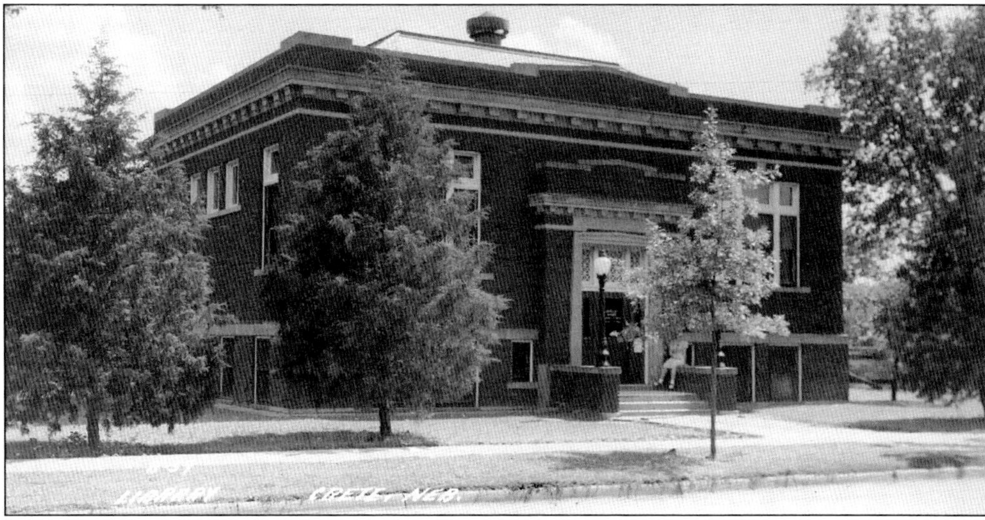

The Crete Public Library was built in 1915, aided by a $10,000 gift from the Andrew Carnegie Foundation. The library was designed by architect J.W. Salmon of Lincoln and was constructed by local contractor John W. Kerst. The nation's first living Christmas tree was planted north of the building in 1923 by Florence Hazen Miller and the Crete Chapter of the Children of the American Revolution. (Marti Ator Williams collection.)

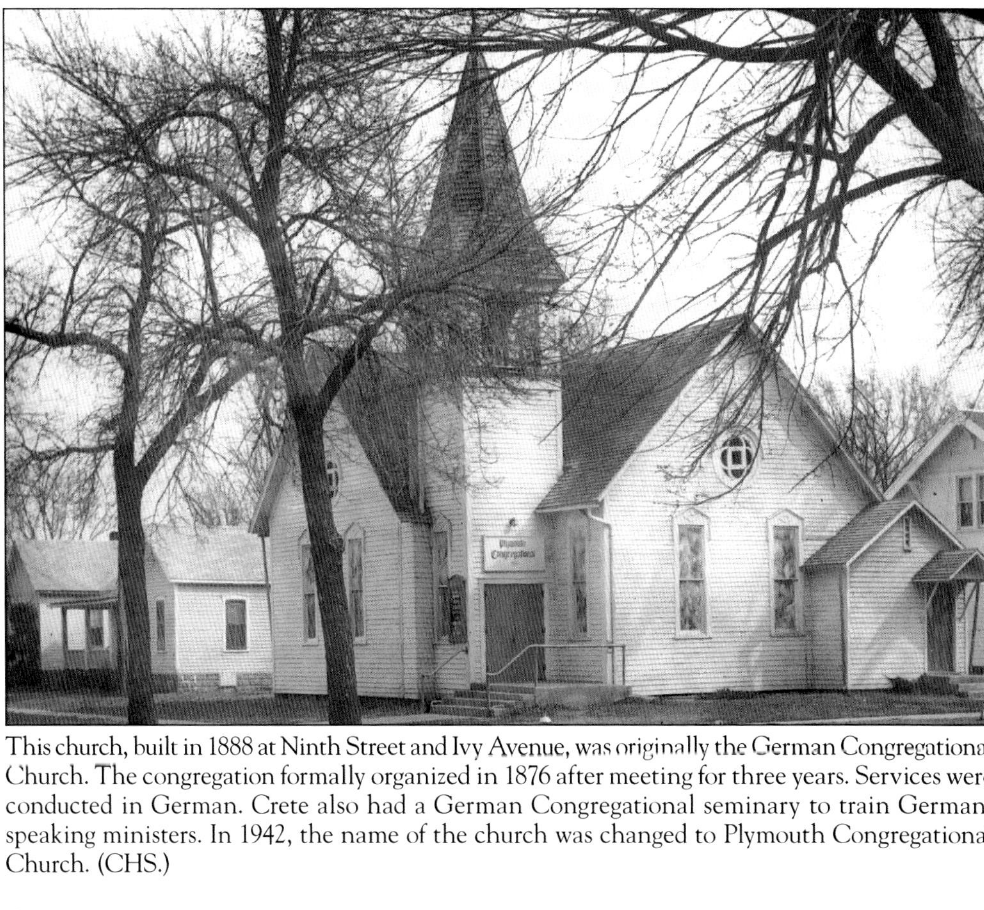

This church, built in 1888 at Ninth Street and Ivy Avenue, was originally the German Congregational Church. The congregation formally organized in 1876 after meeting for three years. Services were conducted in German. Crete also had a German Congregational seminary to train German-speaking ministers. In 1942, the name of the church was changed to Plymouth Congregational Church. (CHS.)

Crete Methodism began in 1869 in a cabin on Walnut Creek. The first church, named Grace Methodist Episcopal, after the deceased daughter of a member, was built in 1874 near the site of the current Crete power plant. This church, at Thirteenth Street and Juniper Avenue, was completed in 1887. This 1890s view shows the old high school/city hall in the background. (Liz Henning collection.)

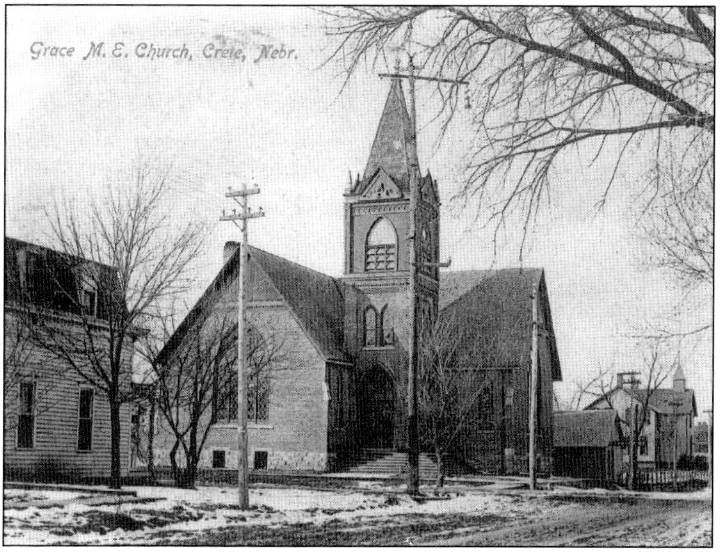

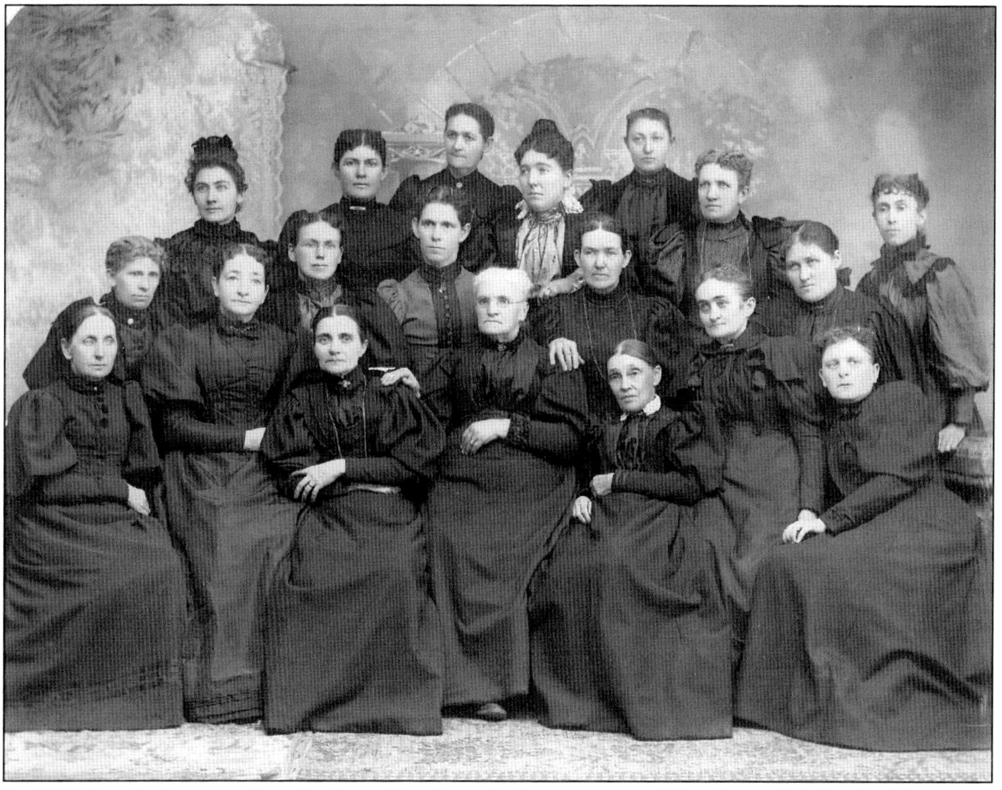

In 1895, local photographer Andrew Smith took this portrait of the Grace Methodist Episcopal Church Ladies Aid Society. Members included, from left to right, (first row) Miss Croston, Mesdames C.C. White, Ezra White, Fay, and French; (second row) Mesdames Guild, McCargar, Booth, Fiske, Ingles, Misner, and Frundell; (standing) Mrs. Fleming, Van Tyl, Martha Kimball, Mrs. Hollingshead, Mrs. Smith (the photographer's wife), Mrs. Norris, and Mary Shepherd. (CHS.)

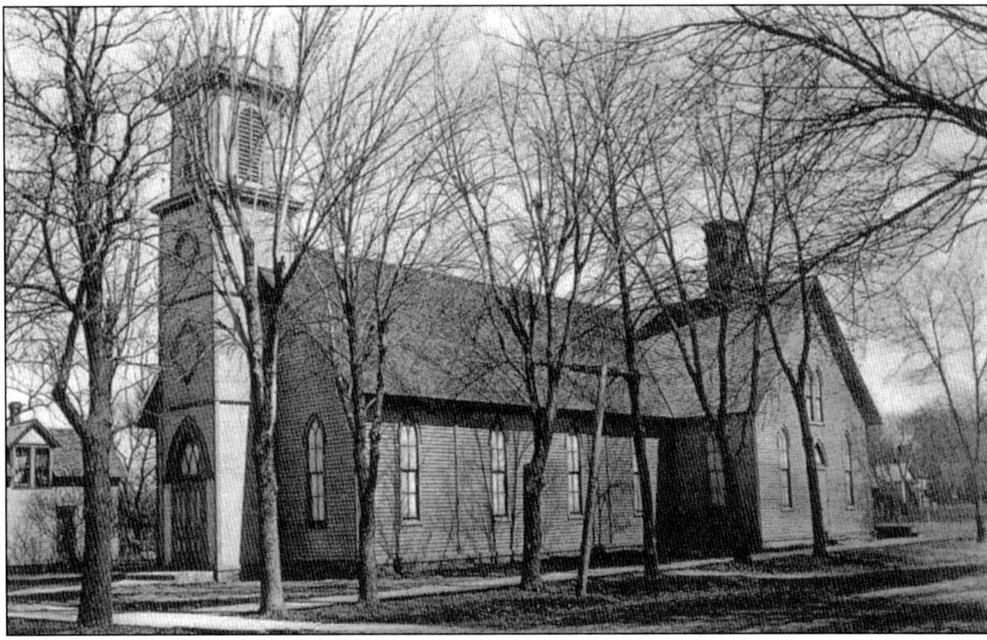

The original First Congregational Church building was dedicated in 1877. This frame building faced west at the northeast corner of Twelfth Street and Juniper Avenue. Later, a two-story parsonage occupied this site. The congregation was organized in 1870 in a downtown business building, at 1328 Maine Avenue, under the direction of Rev. Frederick Alley. (UCC collection.)

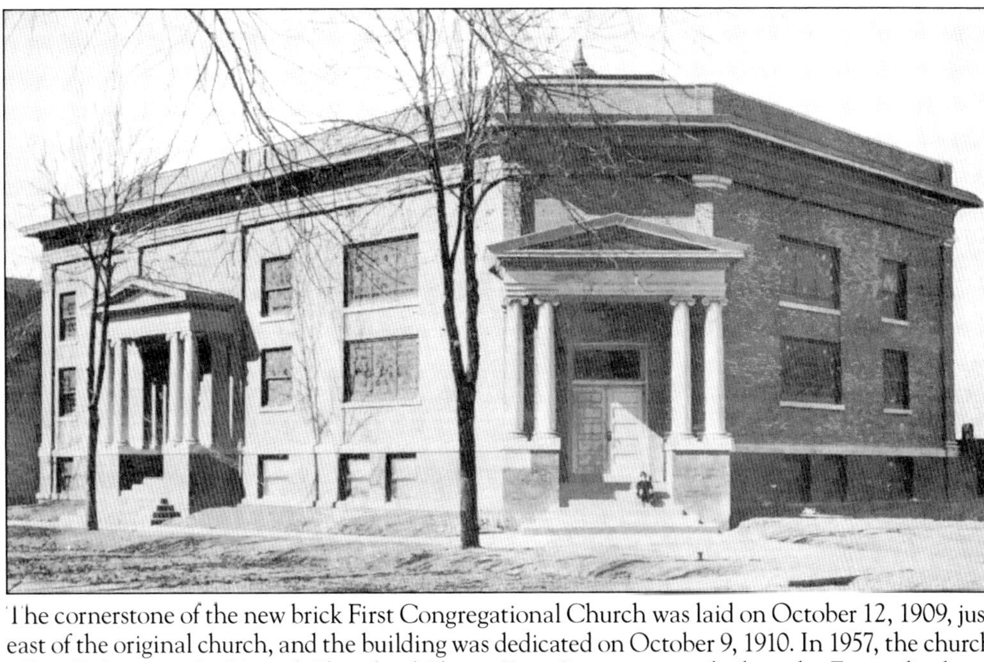

The cornerstone of the new brick First Congregational Church was laid on October 12, 1909, just east of the original church, and the building was dedicated on October 9, 1910. In 1957, the church officially became the United Church of Christ, First Congregational when the Evangelical and Reformed Church merged with the Congregational Church. (Marti Ator Williams collection.)

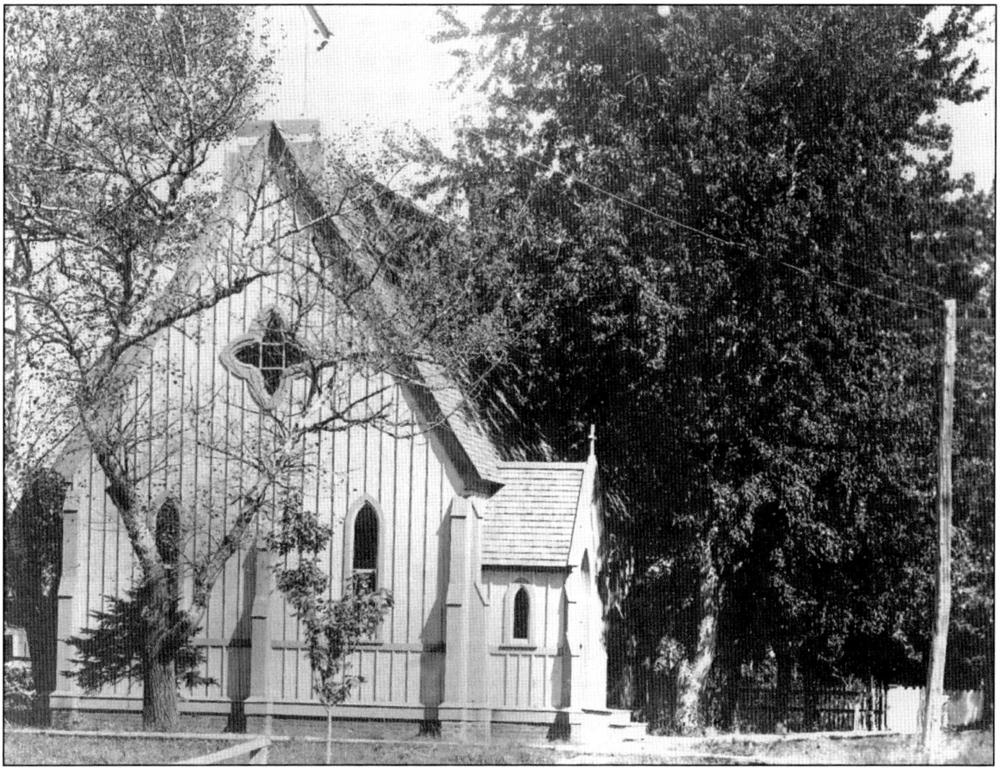

Trinity Memorial Episcopal Church was built in 1872 on the northeast corner of Fourteenth Street and Juniper Avenue. The congregation organized in 1871 and first met in a store attic. Trinity is one of four wood-frame, Gothic-inspired churches in Nebraska and is listed in the National Register of Historic Places. This view shows the original front entrance facing Fourteenth Street. (CHS.)

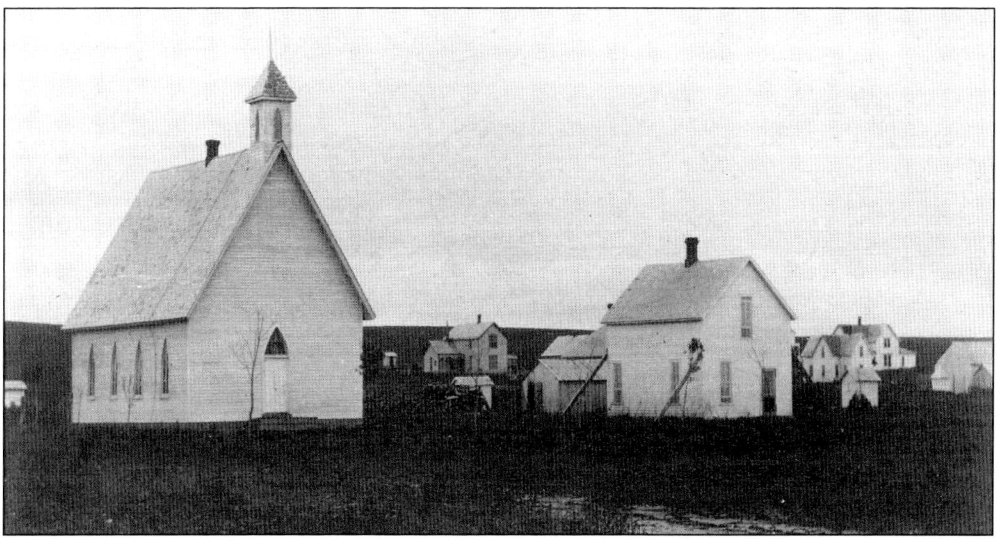

A Church of God organized in 1872 and built this church, the Bethel, at Eleventh Street and Ivy Avenue for $1,000. Pastor Elliott Aller's house is at right. The denomination left the Bethel in the 1880s, and the building was later used by the Lutheran congregation. In 1903, after the Lutherans outgrew the Bethel, they built a new church on the site. The parsonage still stands. (SCHS.)

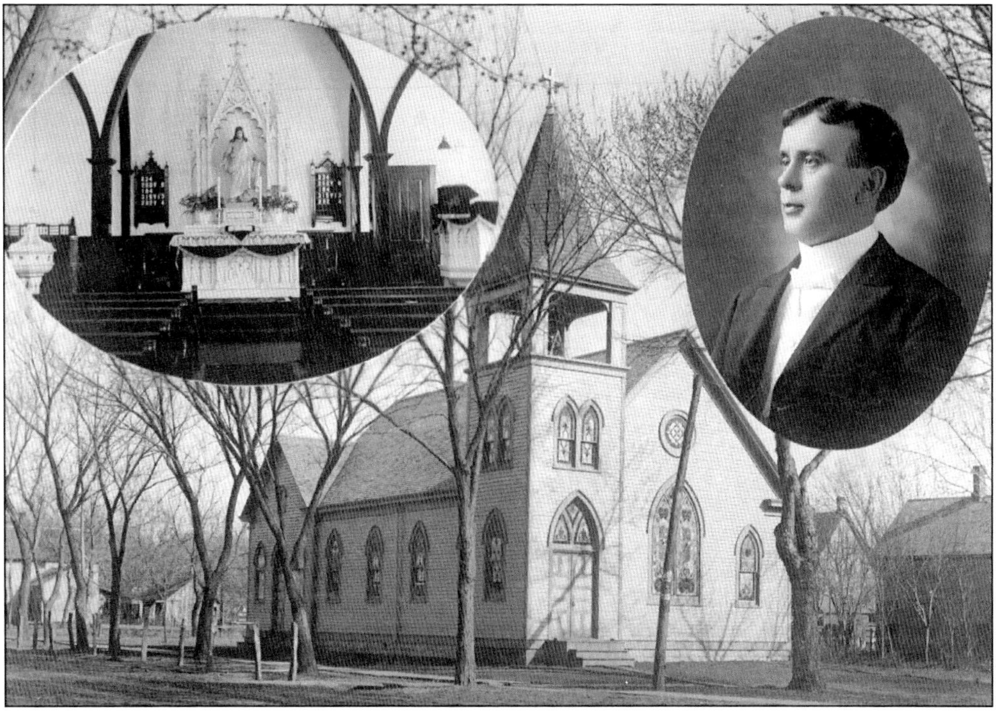

Crete Lutherans organized in the 1870s. They met at Doane Academy and then moved to the Church of God Bethel at Eleventh Street and Ivy Avenue in 1900. Soon, the first Bethlehem Lutheran Church building was erected on that site and the old Bethel was added to the east end of the new building for Sunday school classes. In the 1950s, the church became an IOOF hall, and it is now an apartment house. Pastor John Biehusen is shown here. (Bethlehem Lutheran Church collection.)

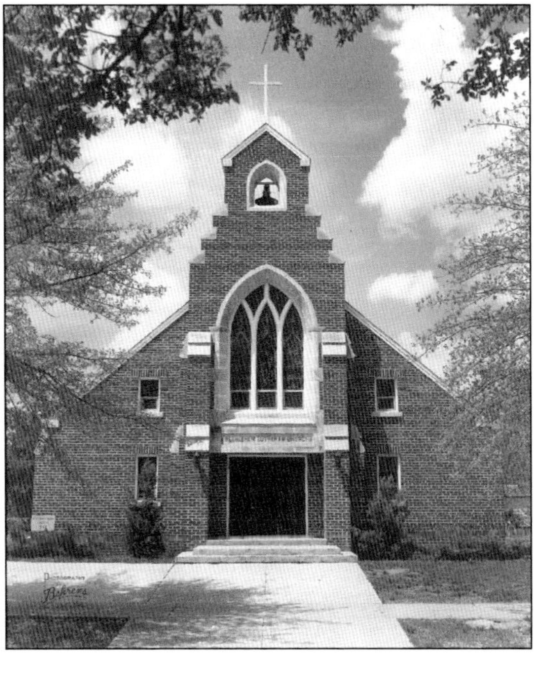

A new Bethlehem Lutheran Church was built in the early 1950s at Eighth Street and Hawthorne Avenue on the site of the old East Ward School. Over the years, the congregation made additions to the building, including an educational wing and a new church entrance. The Bethlehem Lutheran Lambs of Christ Preschool is now housed in the building north of the church. (*Crete News* collection.)

St. James Catholic Parish organized in 1870 and in 1873 built St. James Church on the northeast corner of Twelfth Street and Ivy Avenue. When the old church became too small, Sacred Heart Church of St. James Parish, seen here, was built one block north of the original church in 1892. William B. Hughes of Lincoln was awarded the contract for $9,685. (Marti Ator Williams collection.)

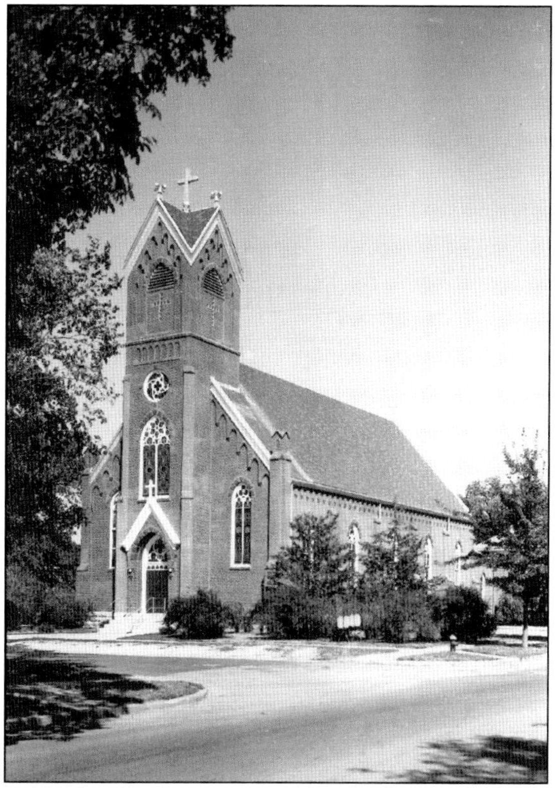

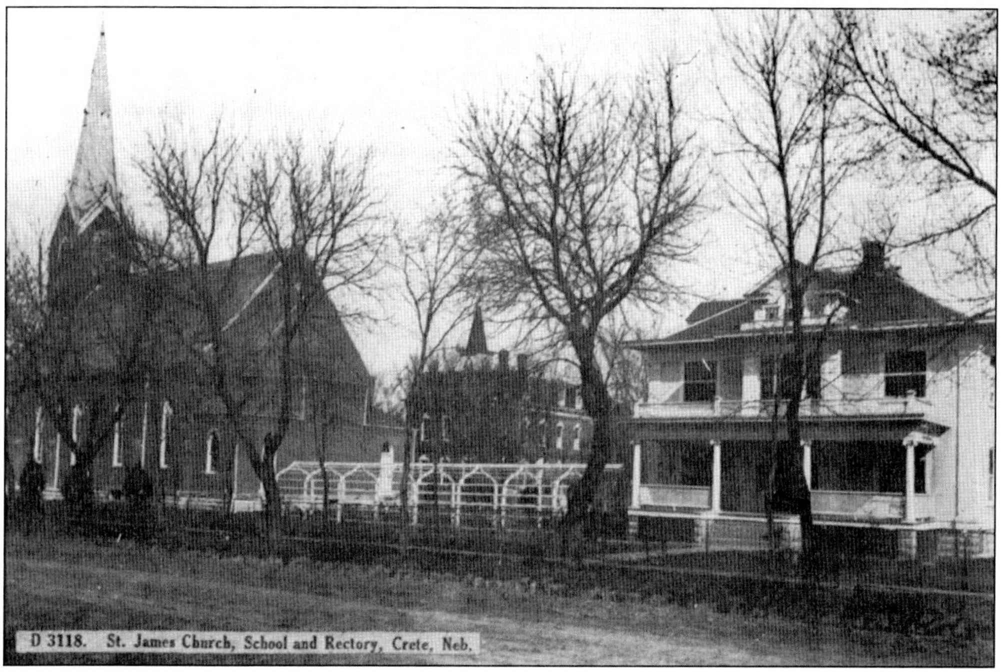

This view of the parish block looking northwest shows Sacred Heart Church on the left, the 1887 St. James School in the center, and the 1906 rectory on the right. The school was replaced in 1989, and the rectory was moved to 1330 East Fifteenth Street in 1995. (Author's collection.)

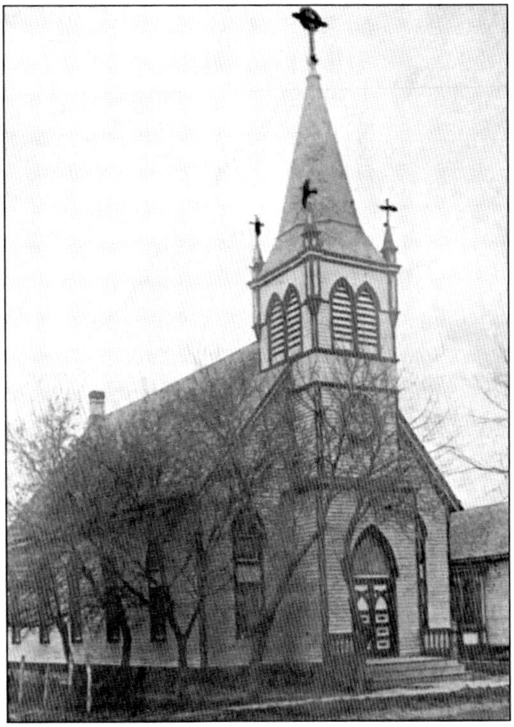

St. Ludmilla's Catholic Church served Crete's Czech population for more than 20 years. Built in 1890, this church was on the northwest corner of Tenth Street and Hawthorne Avenue. Czech-speaking priests served about 36 immigrant families there. By 1915, services stopped and the church was dismantled. The house at 1005 Hawthorne Avenue occupies the church site today. (CHS.)

This Czech Methodist Church was built in 1908 for $3,000 on the northwest corner of Tenth Street and Juniper Avenue, now part of the public school property. Church clergy published a Protestant monthly newsletter there in the Czech language. The church was moved to Ninth Street and Maine Avenue before 1920 and remodeled into a duplex that was razed in the 1970s when the Gibson/Pamida Company developed the property. (CHS.)

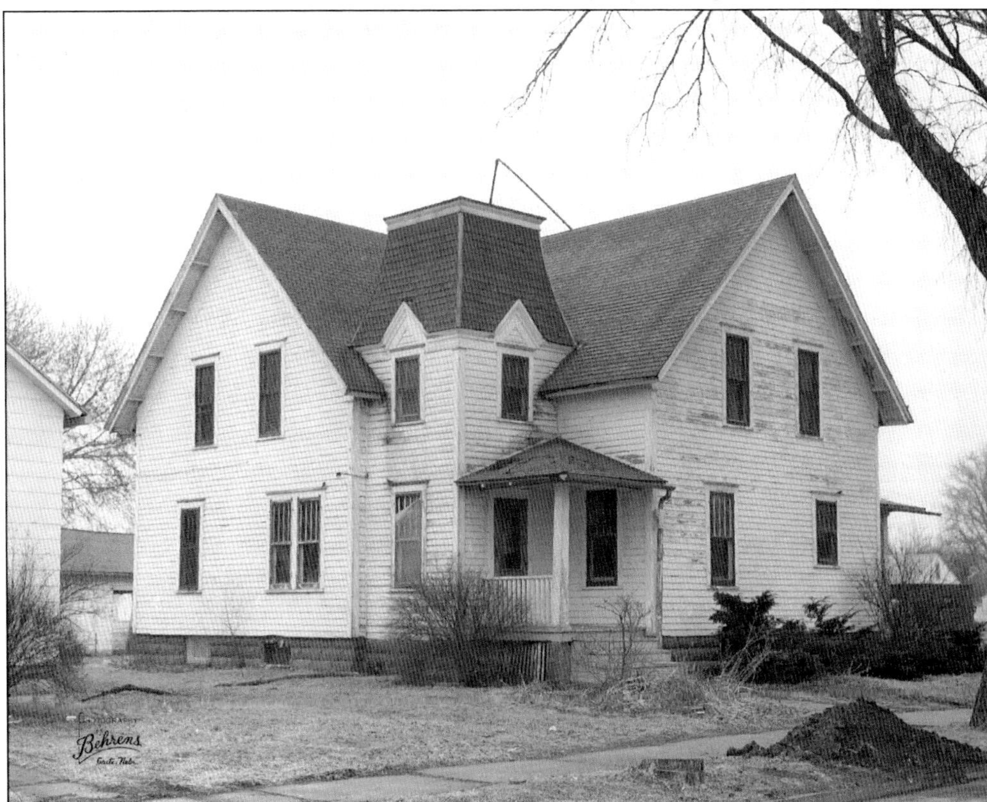

Four

THE COLLEGE ON A HILL

Doane College was created in the tradition of Harvard and Yale by New England Congregationalists who believed that pioneer children on the prairie should have the same educational advantages as children from more civilized areas. Among them was chief civil engineer Col. Thomas Doane of Massachusetts, builder of the Burlington Missouri River Railroad (BMRR) in Nebraska, and Rev. Frederick Alley, who was starting new Congregational Churches in the state.

The college, officially incorporated in 1872, began in an academy building completed in November 1871 between Fifth and Sixth Streets and Ivy and Hawthorne Avenues. The first substantial structure in Crete, the academy was funded personally by Thomas Doane and used for a variety of purposes. College, grammar, and high school classes; church services; and town hall meetings were held there.

In the mid-1870s, campus planning began on a 600-acre hilltop tract donated by the BMRR. The land was platted and landscaped by Thomas Doane, school president David Brainerd Perry, Prof. Arthur B. Fairchild, and nurseryman E.F. Stephens, who planted hundreds of trees.

In 1879, ground was broken for Merrill Hall, a three-story administration and classroom building. This landmark structure stood until 1969, when it was destroyed by fire. The erection of Boswell Observatory, Gaylord Hall, and Whitin Library transformed the barren land into a respectable campus by 1900.

College administrators embraced the area's ethnic population and integrated into the community. President Perry learned Bohemian to communicate with immigrant students and their families. Thomas Doane became involved with a local bank and built a home, The Grange, south of the campus, where he lived several months each year. Doane College provided citizens with cultural events, such as plays, concerts, recitals, and sky-viewing.

Doane College caught the attention of *Life* magazine officials, who included a piece on "Little Doane a Fresh Water College" in its June 7, 1937, special college edition.

The Doane College campus still comprises about half of the original BMRR tract. The physical plant consists of nearly 30 buildings, including three that are listed in the National Register of Historic Places. Today, student population on the Crete campus is more than 1,000, and satellite campuses in Lincoln and Grand Island serve nearly 1,100 undergraduate and graduate students.

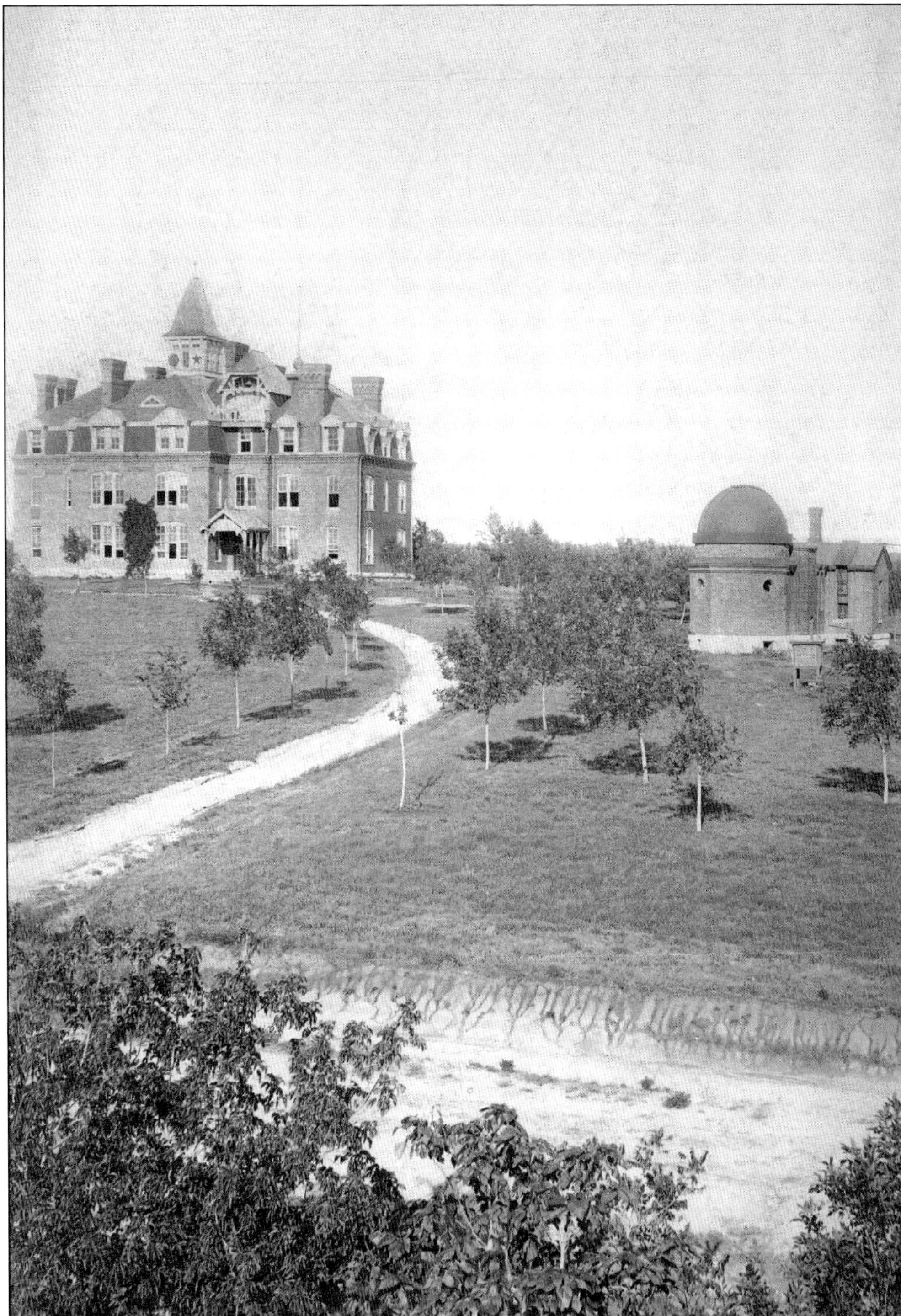

This 1887 view of Doane College, taken by photographer Andrew Smith, looks east toward Merrill Hall and Boswell Observatory. New trees line the drive circling in front of Merrill Hall. Note the unimproved Boswell Avenue in the foreground. (DCA, Helen Perry Curtis collection.)

In 1869, civil engineer Col. Thomas Doane arrived in Nebraska to build 240 miles of railroad west from the Missouri River. He and others founded the college bearing his name. Doane, who lived in Boston part of the year, was a hands-on administrator at the institution and designed the official college seal. He sat on the board of trustees from 1872 until his death in 1897 and seldom missed a commencement. (DCA.)

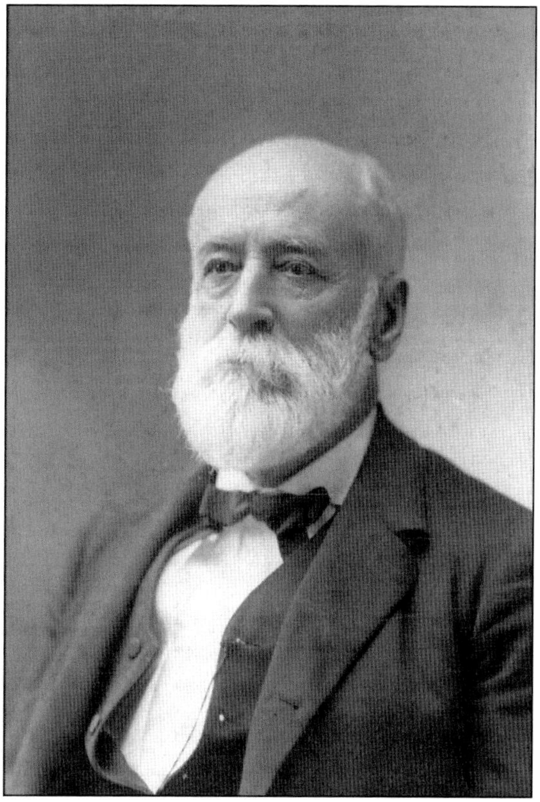

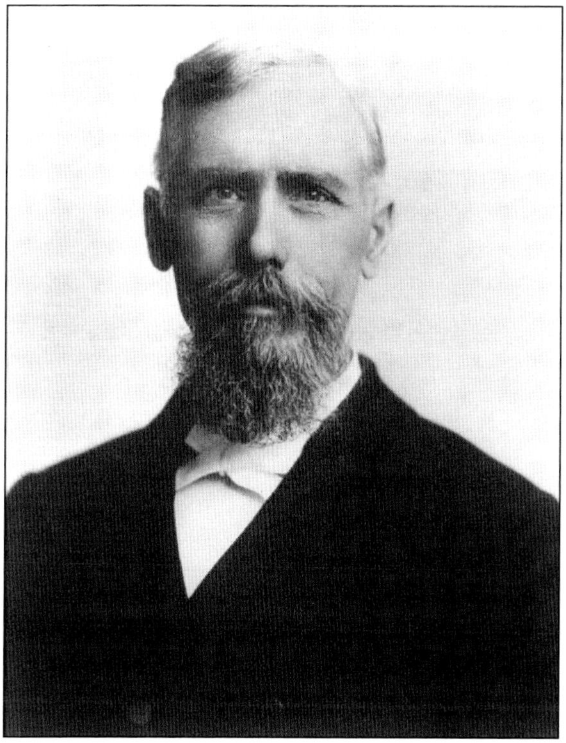

Rev. Frederick Alley was a driving force in establishing Doane College. Reverend Alley emigrated from Ireland in 1856 and founded several Congregational Churches in Nebraska during early statehood. He came to Crete in 1870 to establish a Congregational Church and an academy. Alley became the first principal, professor, and business agent of the academy and suggested the school be named Doane to honor its staunch supporter. (DCA.)

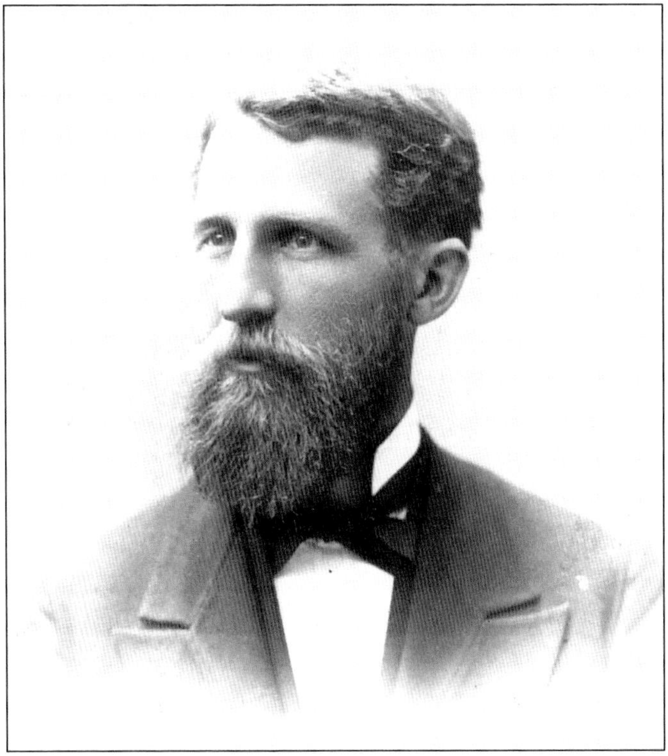

The first Doane president, Rev. David Brainerd Perry, came to Nebraska as a circuit-riding preacher in 1872. Soon, he was the chief administrator of Doane Academy and the college, had married Thomas Doane's daughter Helen, and was settled into The Grange, Thomas Doane's country house near campus, with his young family. Reverend Perry served Doane for 40 years until his death in 1912. (DCA.)

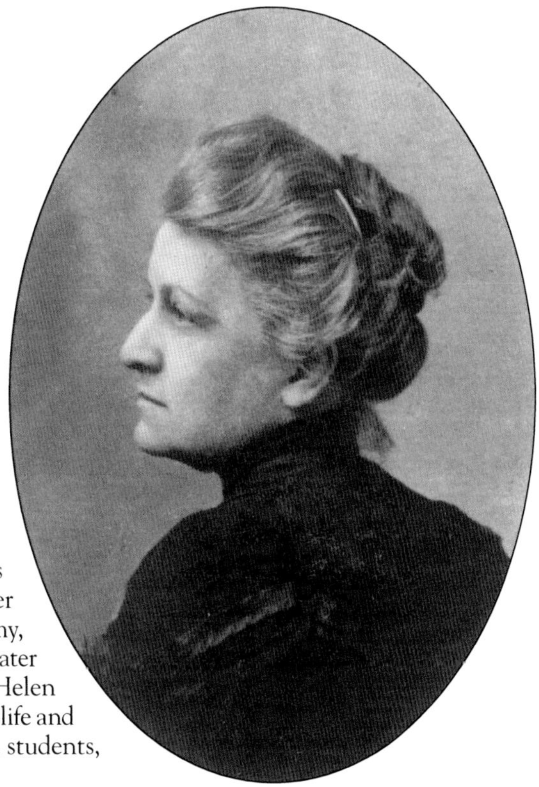

In 1870, young Helen Doane moved to Nebraska from Boston with her father, Thomas Doane; her new stepmother, Louisa; and her three siblings. Helen attended Doane Academy, where she was taught by Reverend Perry. She later married Perry, who was 15 years her senior. Helen brought refinement to college and community life and made The Grange a social center for faculty, students, friends, and visiting dignitaries. (DCA.)

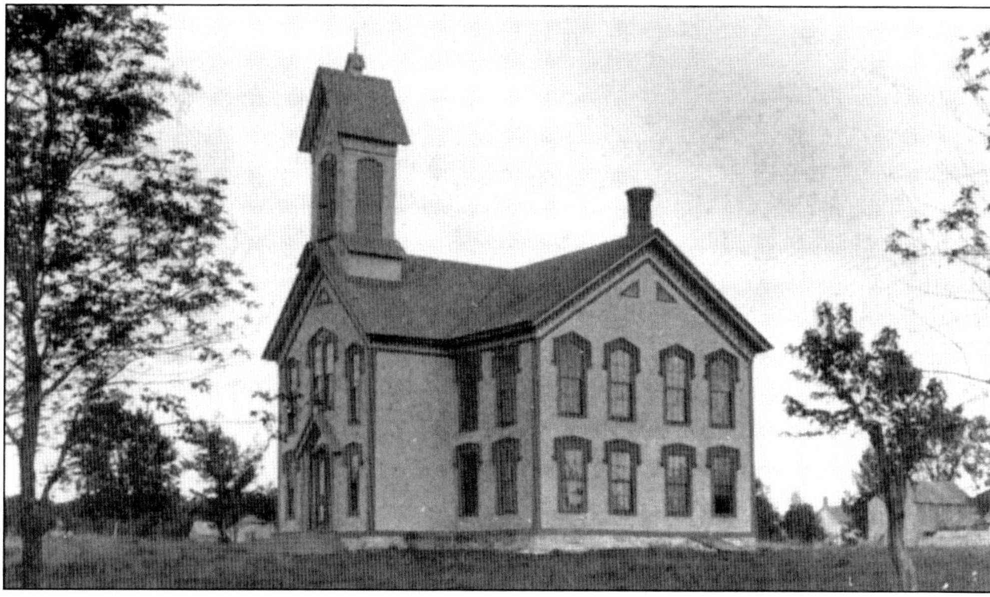

The Doane Academy was completed in the fall of 1871 in south Crete. Students prepared there for entrance to Doane College. The school, one of five Congregational academies in Nebraska, also offered college-level classes to those who qualified. The building was vacated in the late 1880s and was razed about 1900. (DCA.)

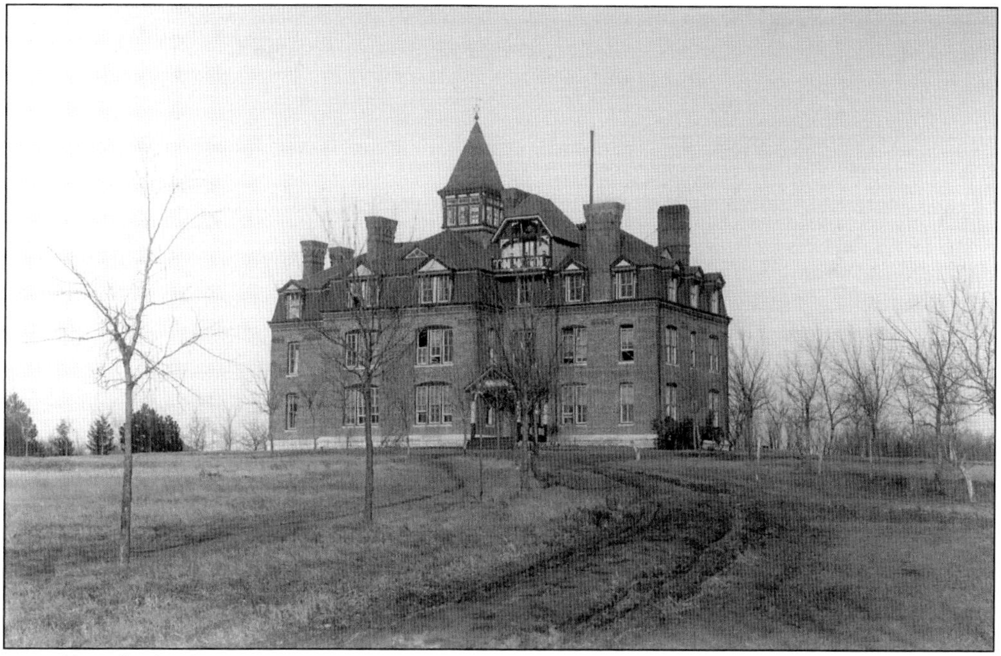

Merrill Hall, the first structure on Doane's hilltop campus, was built in 1879. Designed by the prominent Boston architectural firm Cabot and Chandler, the building was named for Rev. O.W. Merrill, a member of the General Association of Congregational Churches. Merrill Hall was the hub of campus activity for 90 years. Administrative and faculty offices, classrooms, male student housing, the campus print shop, and the mail room were housed in this building. (CHS, Jennie Chapman Stevens collection.)

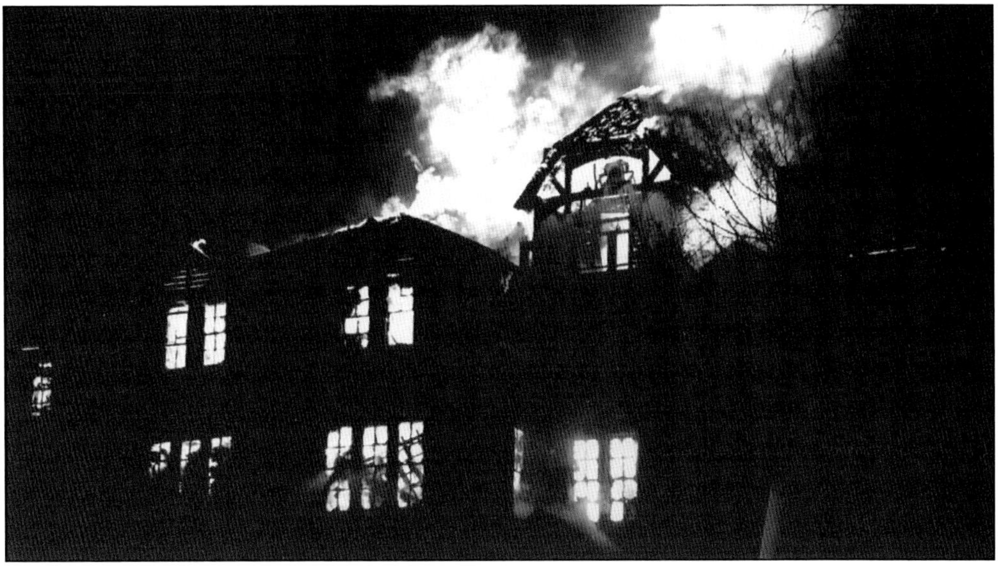

On February 28, 1969, Merrill Hall was destroyed by fire. At 3:07 a.m., alarms alerted campus and community residents to the blaze, and 90 minutes later, Doane's oldest campus building was reduced to rubble. The building is memorialized by the Merrill Bell Tower, erected in 1971 on the site of the original structure. The charred remains of the original bell are mounted at the tower's base. (DCA.)

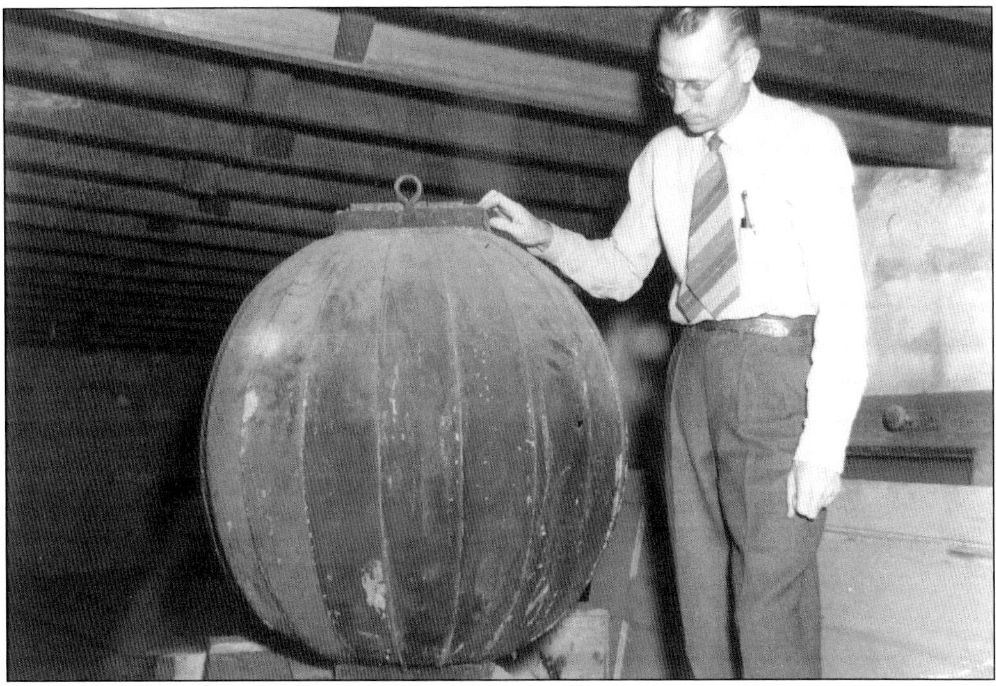

Longtime college registrar and professor of mathematics and astronomy Loyd Oleson examines the time ball in the Carnegie Science Hall attic. Originally mounted atop Merrill Hall and signaled by a clock in Boswell Observatory, the ball dropped every day at noon so that community time pieces could be synchronized. The time ball was removed from Merrill's roof about 1920 and is now on display in Boswell Observatory. (DCA.)

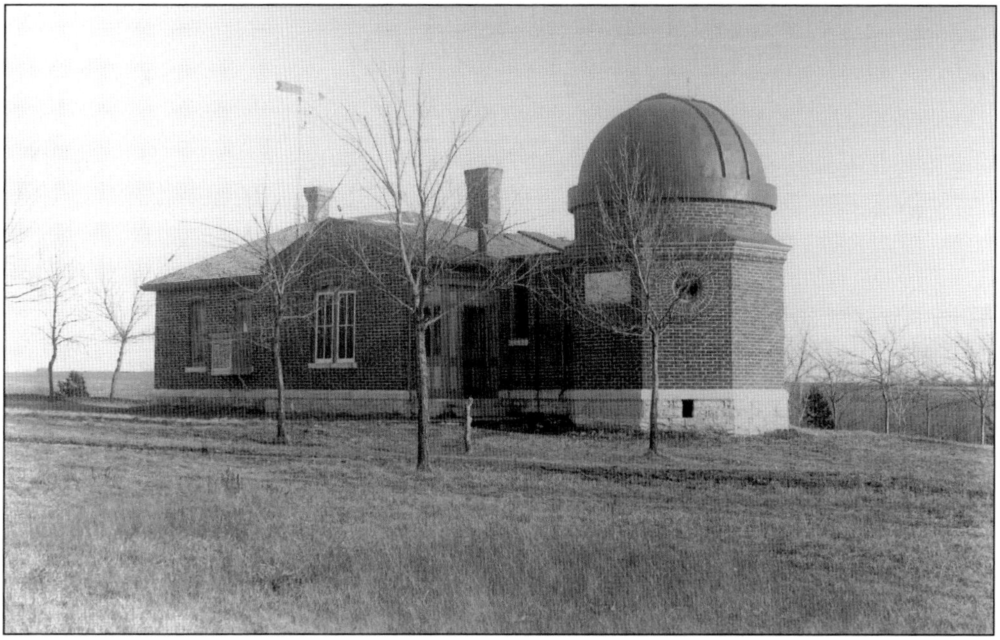

Boswell Observatory, built in 1883, was named for Connecticut benefactor Charles Boswell. It is the oldest extant operating observatory west of the Missouri River. The original 1884 telescope is mounted in the dome and sky-viewing still takes place. Time-keeping, weather-recording, and astronomical equipment is housed in the building, now also a museum. The observatory was the first home of the Nebraska Signal Service Office of the National Weather Service. (CHS, Jennie Chapman Stevens collection.)

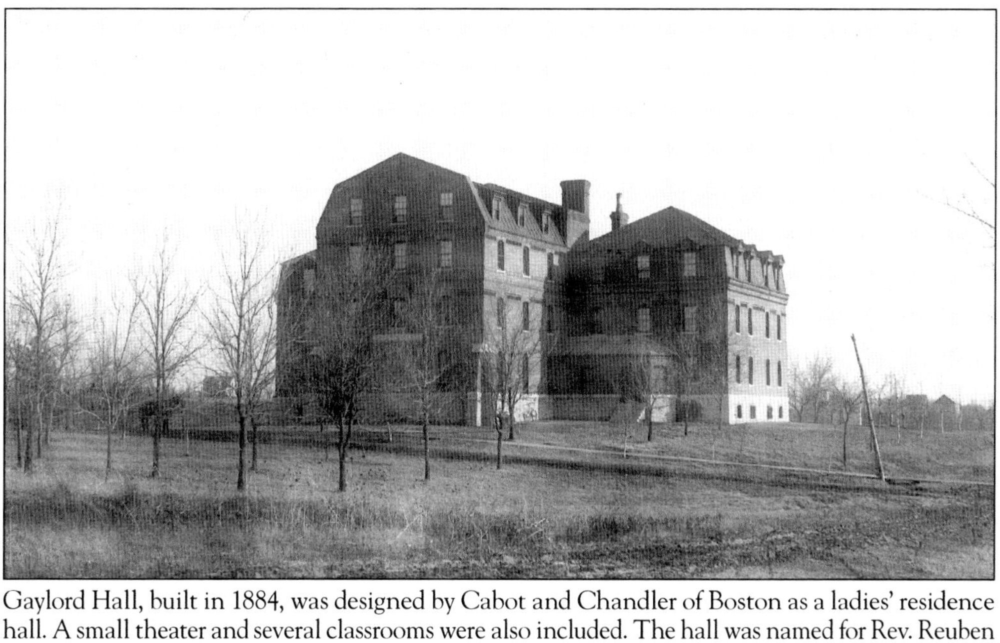

Gaylord Hall, built in 1884, was designed by Cabot and Chandler of Boston as a ladies' residence hall. A small theater and several classrooms were also included. The hall was named for Rev. Reuben Gaylord, a pioneer home missionary for the Congregational Church. Gaylord was constructed as three separate elements tied together in a Y-shaped plan, reflecting the vernacular Victorian collegiate buildings of the time period. (DCA.)

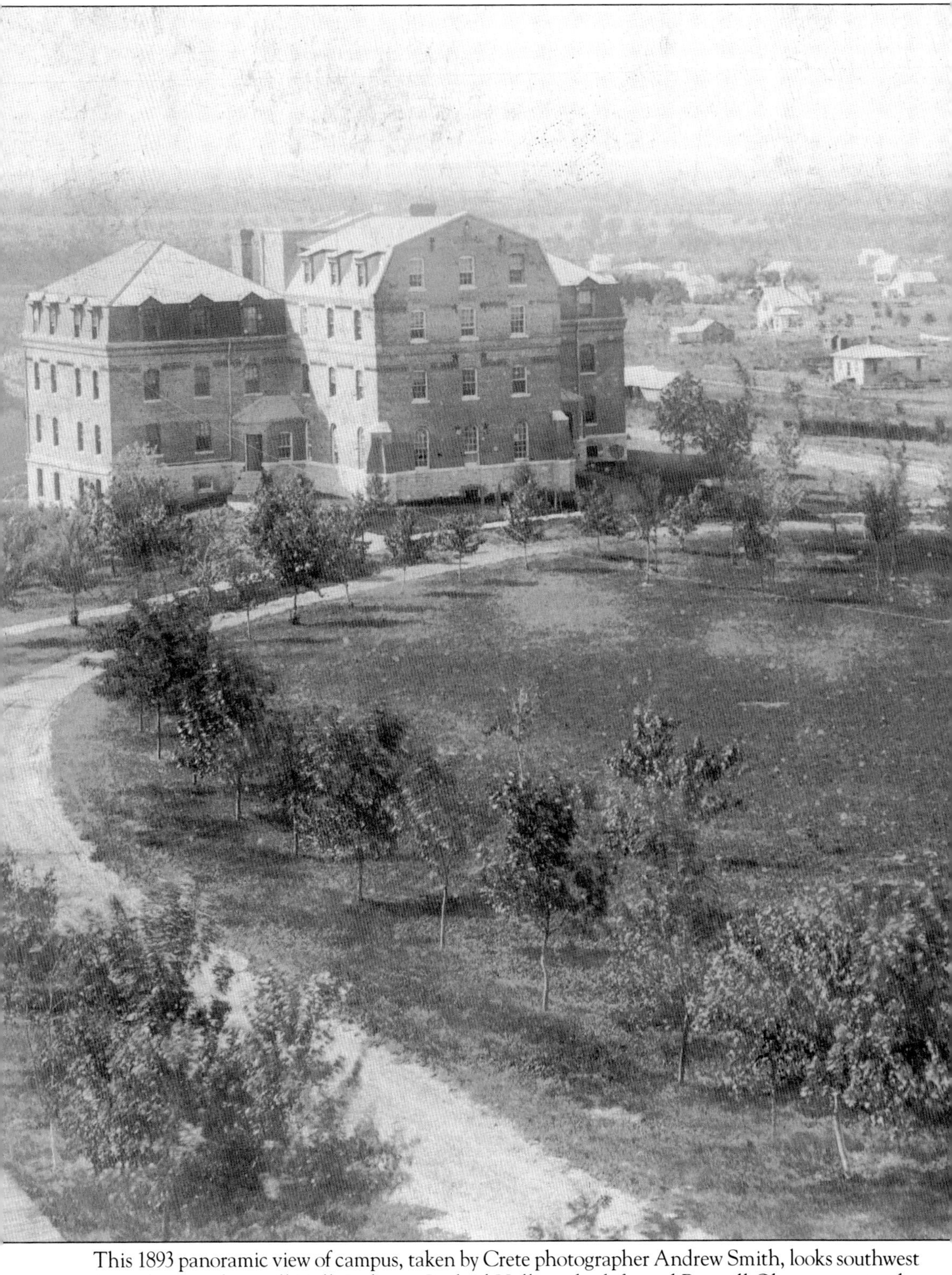

This 1893 panoramic view of campus, taken by Crete photographer Andrew Smith, looks southwest from the top of Merrill Hall. It shows Gaylord Hall on the left, and Boswell Observatory in the

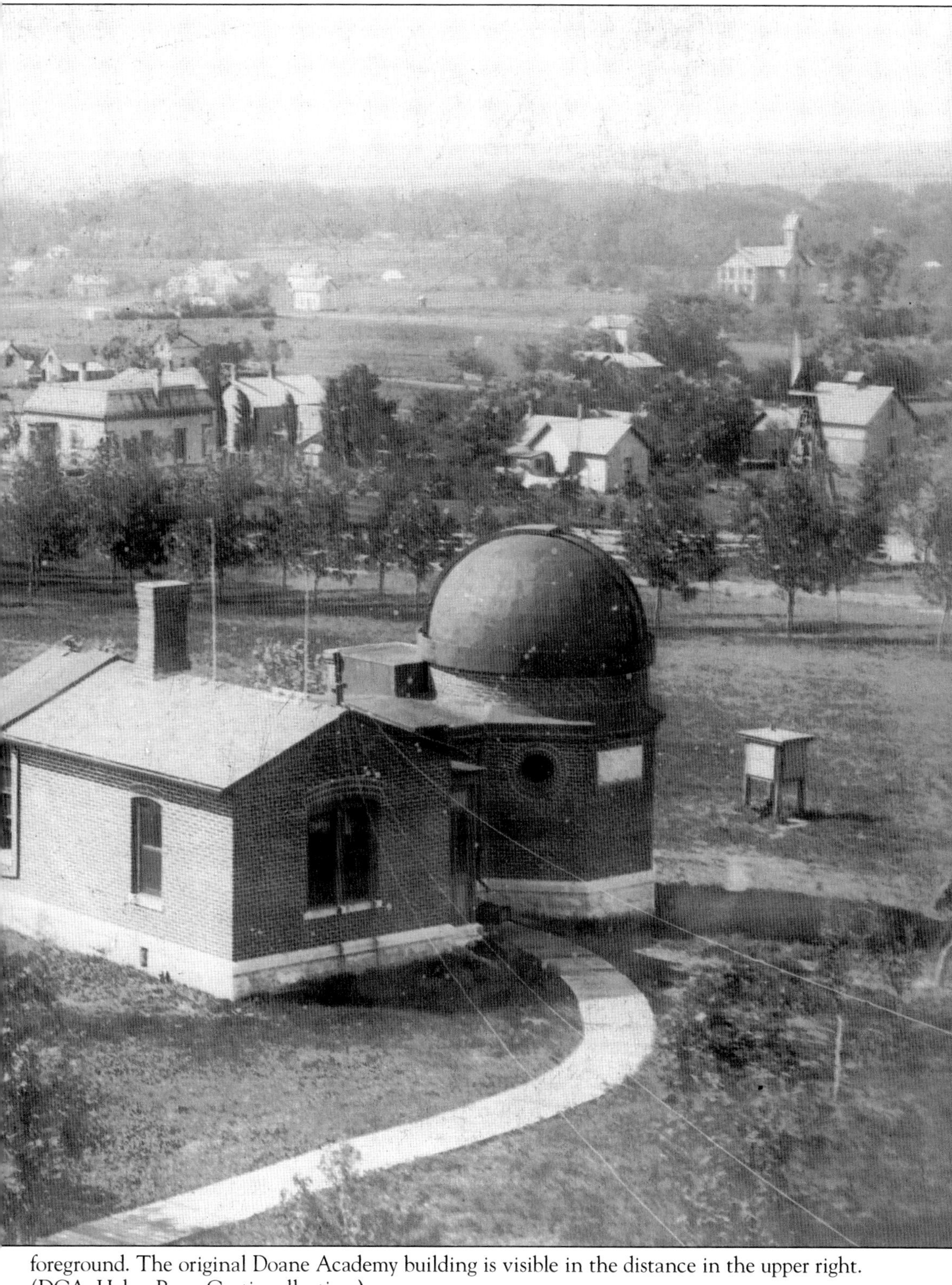

foreground. The original Doane Academy building is visible in the distance in the upper right. (DCA, Helen Perry Curtis collection.)

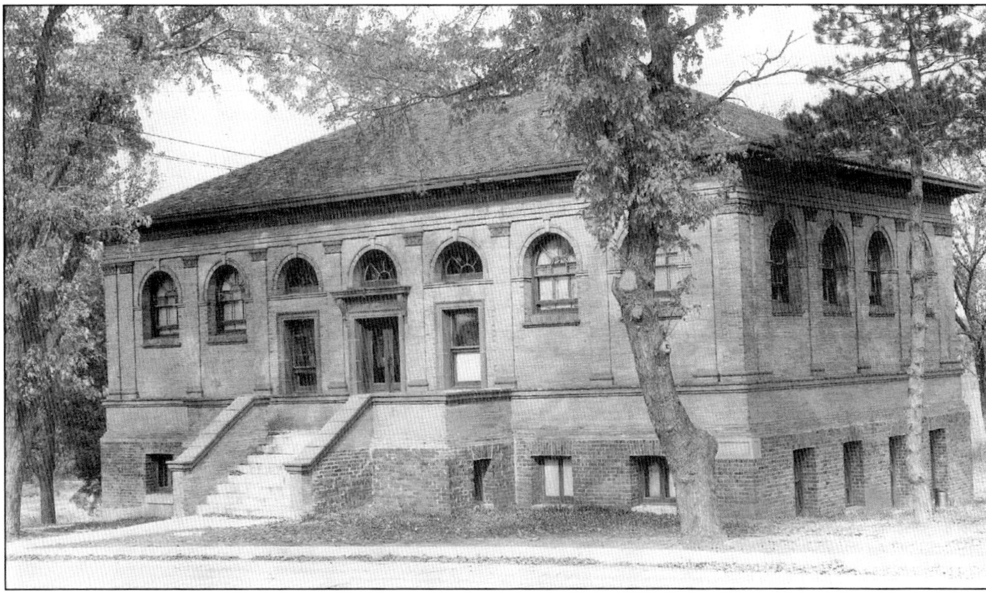

Whitin Library was built in 1894 in Renaissance Revival style from plans by architects and Doane alumni George and Arthur Dean of Chicago. In 1971, the library moved to a new facility, and Whitin was renovated into the art department. The structure was recently razed, but architectural elements from the front facade were incorporated into a new art and education building. (DCA.)

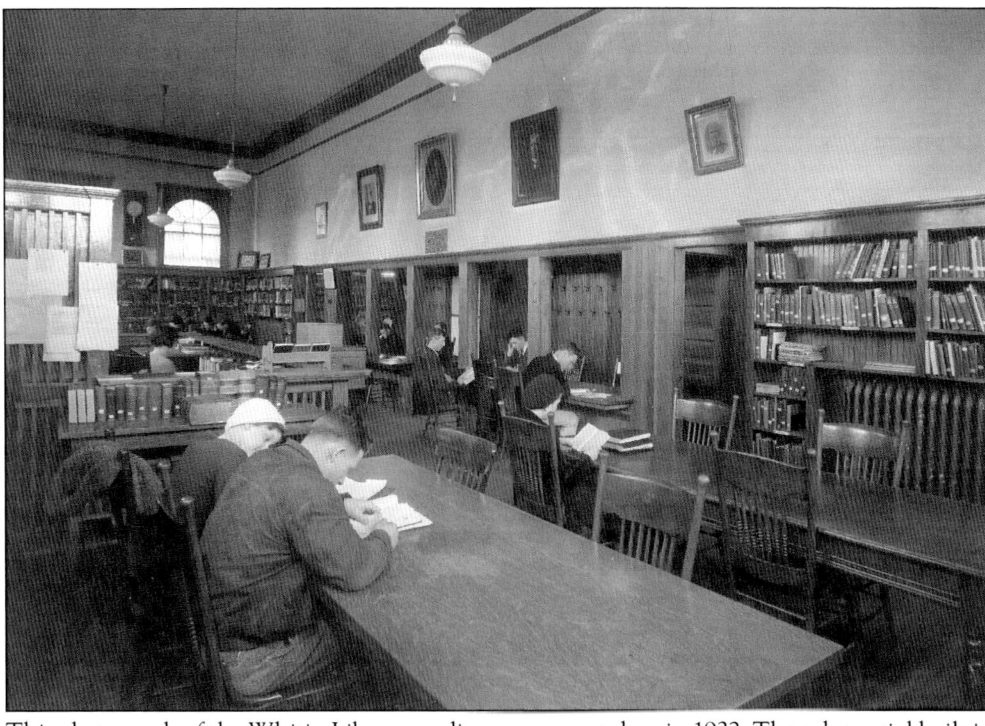

This photograph of the Whitin Library reading room was taken in 1932. The substantial built-in circulation desk is on the left. Furnishings include quality hardwood tables and chairs, many of which have been restored and are still in use on campus. Portraits of college founders hang on the wall. (DCA.)

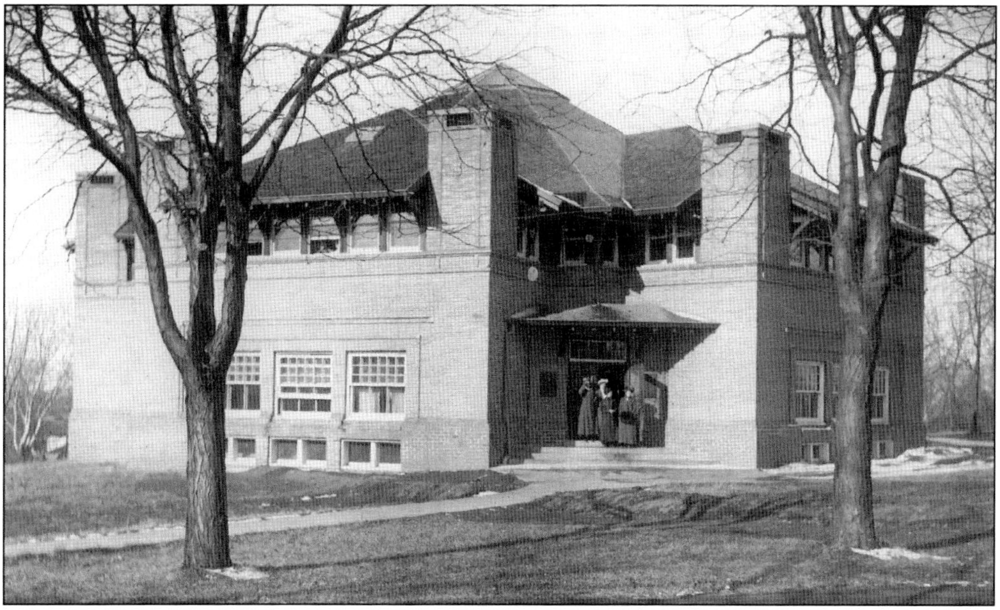

Whitcomb Conservatory/Lee Memorial Chapel is a five-sided, Prairie School building designed by the Dean and Dean architectural firm. George and Arthur Dean were Doane alumni and their brother Edwin was college president from 1925 to 1936. Affectionately called The Con, the building was named for Henry Whitcomb and George F. Lee. Built in 1906–1907, it was completely renovated in 2005 and is listed in the National Register of Historic Places along with Boswell Observatory and Gaylord Hall. (DCA.)

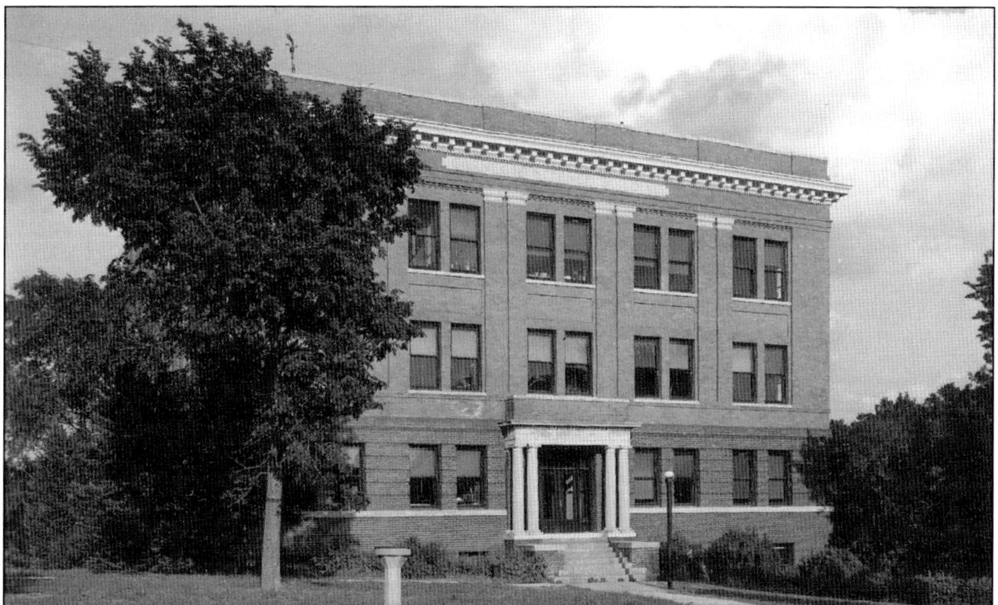

Carnegie Science Hall was built in 1909 with $25,000 from philanthropist Andrew Carnegie. The three-story building, which sat east of Boswell Observatory, was designed by Fiske and Dieman of Lincoln. It provided one entire floor each for biology, physics, and chemistry and was well-equipped with laboratories and lecture rooms. The building was razed in 1977. (DCA.)

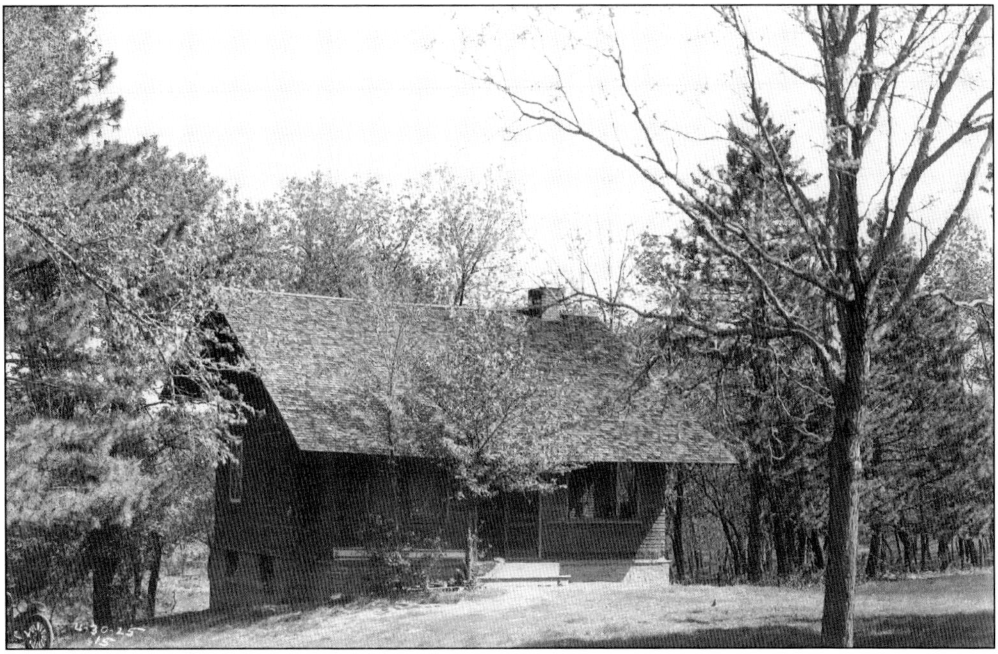

Fiske Lodge was built in 1909 with funds from Charlotte Fiske of Boston. The four-room Craftsman cottage was designed by Dean and Dean architects as the campus infirmary. When a new infirmary was incorporated into Men's Hall in 1929, Fiske Lodge served several other purposes that included time as the Tiger Inn snack shop and an art department annex. It is now a concession stand near Simon Field. (DCA.)

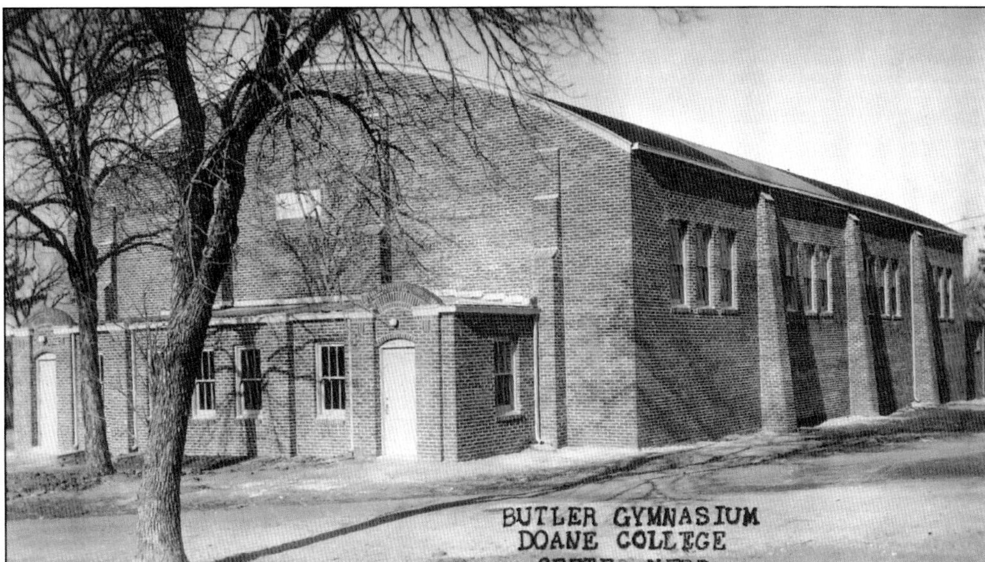

Butler Gymnasium honors Doane alumnus and US senator Hugh Butler. The gym was built in 1936 over a 1915 wooden gymnasium constructed by students. The old building was covered with brick and enhanced with engaged buttresses. In the 1940s, a swimming pool was added to accommodate the World War II Navy V-12/V-5 officer training program, and in the 1950s, the Byrnes Addition created classroom space. (DCA.)

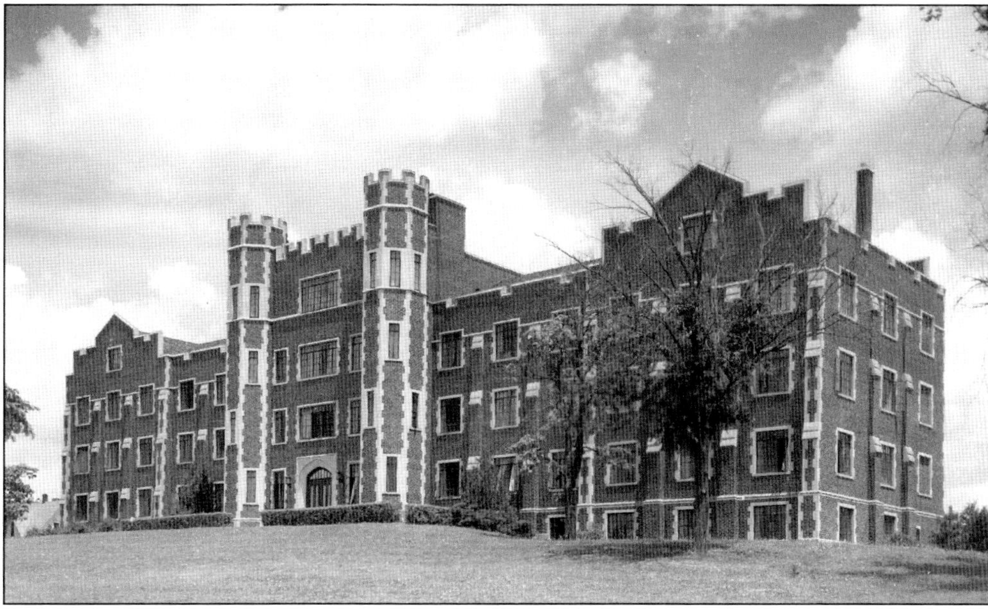

Smith Hall, originally named Men's Hall, was built in 1929 from plans by Dean and Dean architects. This Collegiate Gothic dormitory housed male students and also had a small infirmary. The building was renamed Smith Hall in 1977 to honor Charles C. Smith, a Doane alumnus, Nebraska businessman, and longtime trustee who made an anonymous donation in 1929 to ensure the structure's completion. The hall was completely renovated in 2011. (DCA.)

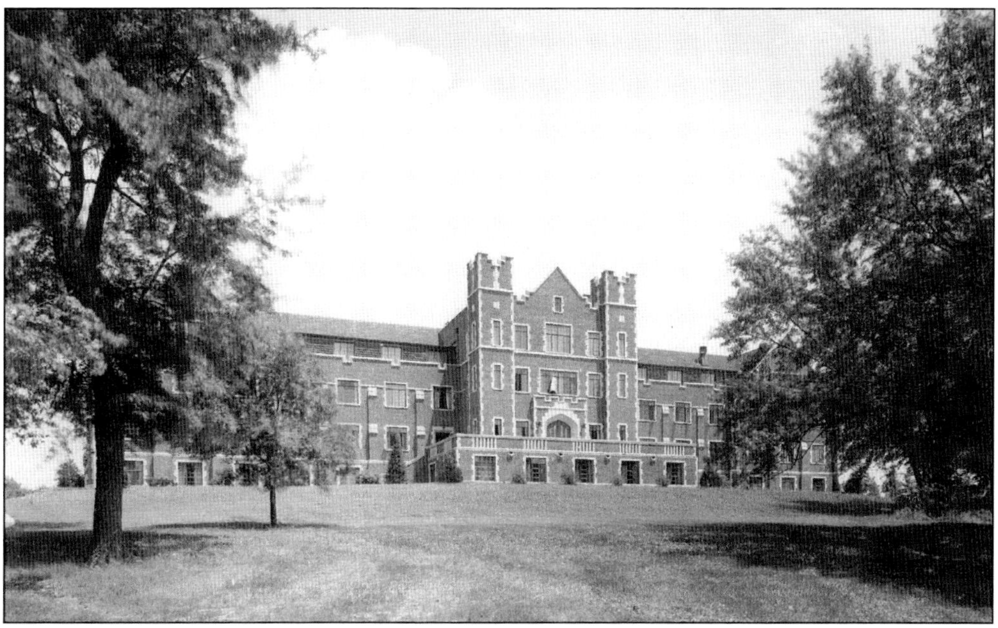

Frees Hall, a women's residence hall on the opposite side of campus from Men's Hall, was completed in 1931. The building, also designed by Dean and Dean architects, originally accommodated 185 residential students and had a 450-seat dining room in the basement. The Collegiate Gothic building was named for Mr. and Mrs. Benjamin Frees and was completely renovated in 2010. (Author's collection.)

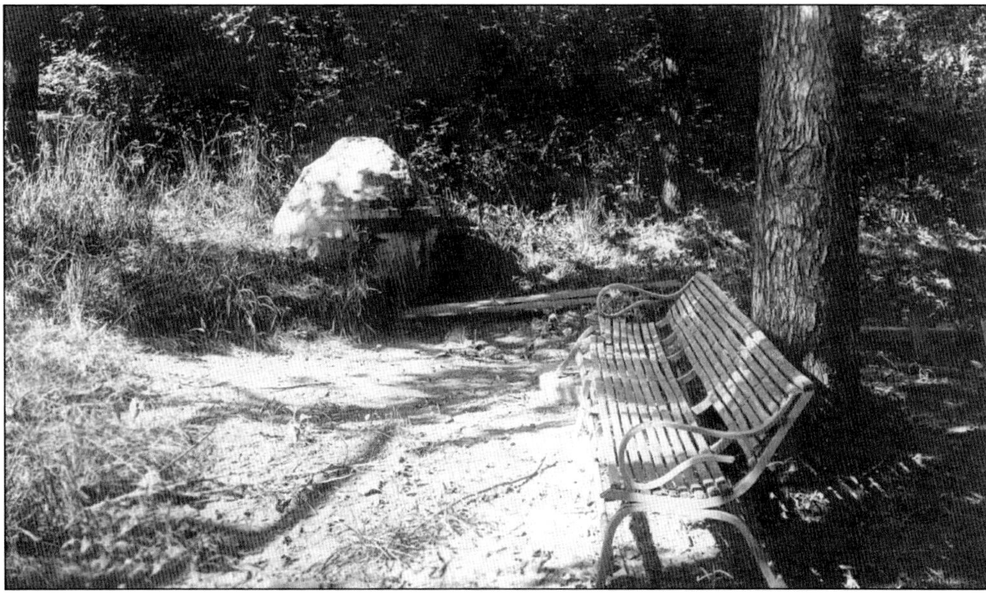

In the 19th century, the main campus water supply was a spring east of Gaylord Hall. Ladies residing in Gaylord and the staff came here for water. For decades, Spring Hollow (above) was a rustic setting, but in 1930, Carrie Dean, a member of the class of 1880, built a classical pergola over the water source in honor of her missionary parents, Samuel and Augusta Dean. Carrie was the sister of the architects George and Arthur Dean and college president Edwin Dean. The photograph below was taken at the dedication of Dean Memorial Pergola. The spring is still active today. (Above, CHS, Krebs collection; below, DCA.)

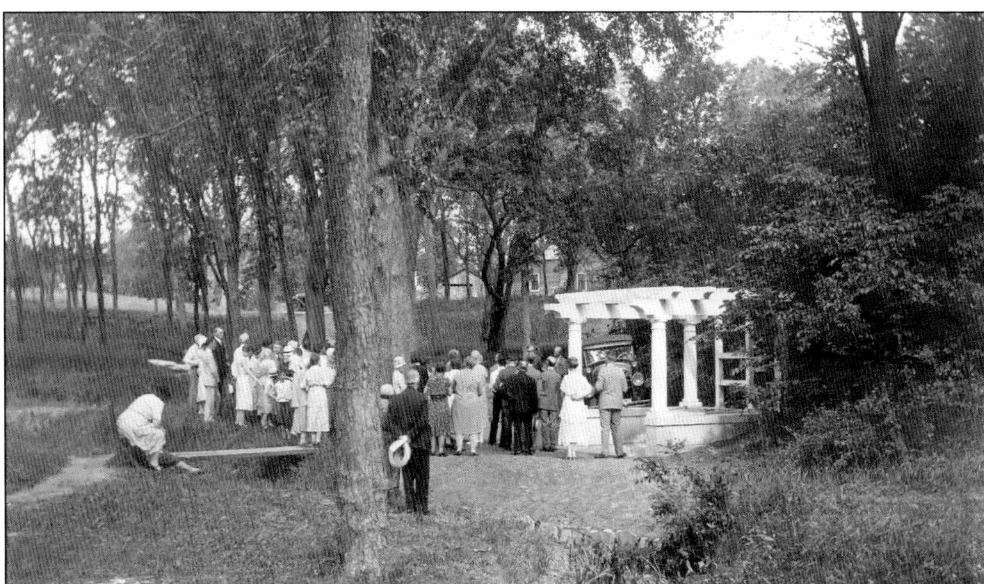

Five

Home Sweet Home

Crete boasts a variety of late-19th-century and early-20th-century residential architectural styles. Several houses are listed individually in the National Register of Historic Places, and others are part of the College Hill Historic District. Crete's assortment of house types provides a lesson in Nebraska's architectural history.

A few Crete leaders built substantial homes as early as the 1870s, but most upgraded from original simple cottages after 1880. Most of these new houses were built east of the downtown area on College Hill, between the Big Blue River valley, where the business district is located, and Doane College, situated on top of the hill. Styles ranged from Thomas Doane's 1871 vernacular Gothic Revival country house, The Grange, to the architect-designed Queen Anne and Shingle-style homes of prominent 19th-century businessmen.

Crete neighborhoods also feature many vernacular Victorian homes and a large assortment of 20th century bungalows and Prairie Box dwellings. Spanish Revival, Pueblo Revival, Dutch Colonial, and Tudor Revival homes appeared between 1920 and 1940. Crete is even home to a rare mid-century Lustron home, the metal prefabricated house type with a short-lived existence.

Crete's proximity to Lincoln and Omaha made it easy for affluent residents to network with architects to create stylish, quality dwellings. Crete was also home to several talented carpenters and contractors, who, although they had no formal architectural training, were adept at custom design and worked alongside city architects, or independently, to develop Crete's built environment.

One of these construction masters was John W. Kerst, who produced numerous residential, farm, church, college, school, and business buildings in the late 19th and early 20th centuries. It is often said that John Kerst and his crew built Crete. Two other notable builders were contractor Otto Feeken, who erected several fine early-20th-century homes in addition to the Isis Theatre, elementary school, and other buildings, and carpenter and bricklayer James Sinkule, who made his mark with several service stations and 1930s and 1940s Tudor Revival homes.

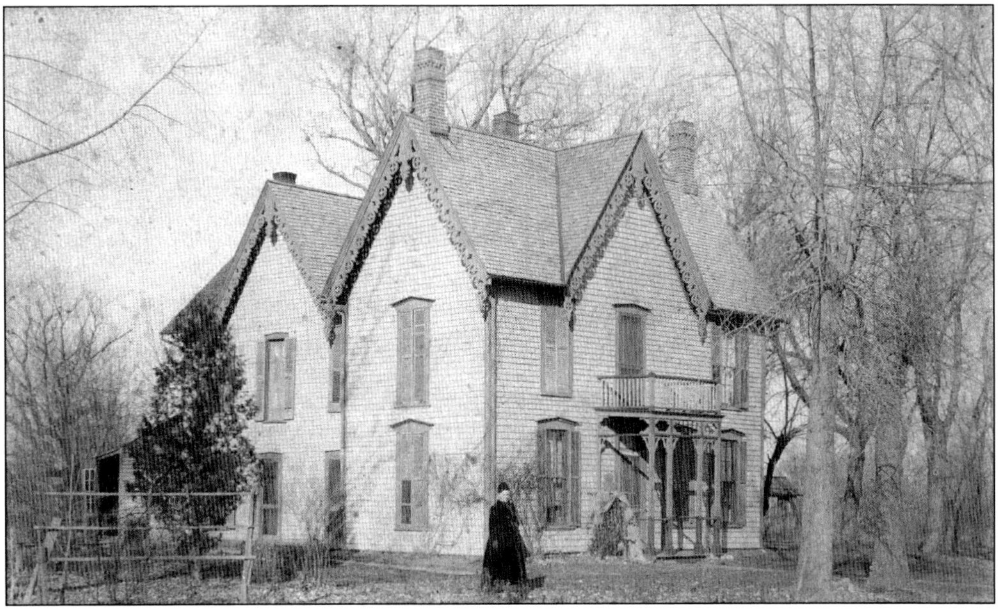

Jesse C. and Elizabeth Bickle homesteaded in 1863 on what became part of the Crete townsite. This Carpenter Gothic house began as a one-story log cabin, which was their residence and also the Crete Post Office. Later additions covered the cabin, and by 1880, it became an attractive home. The house still stands on the 18-acre Crete Heritage Society grounds. Elizabeth Bickle stands in front of her house in this photograph. (CHS.)

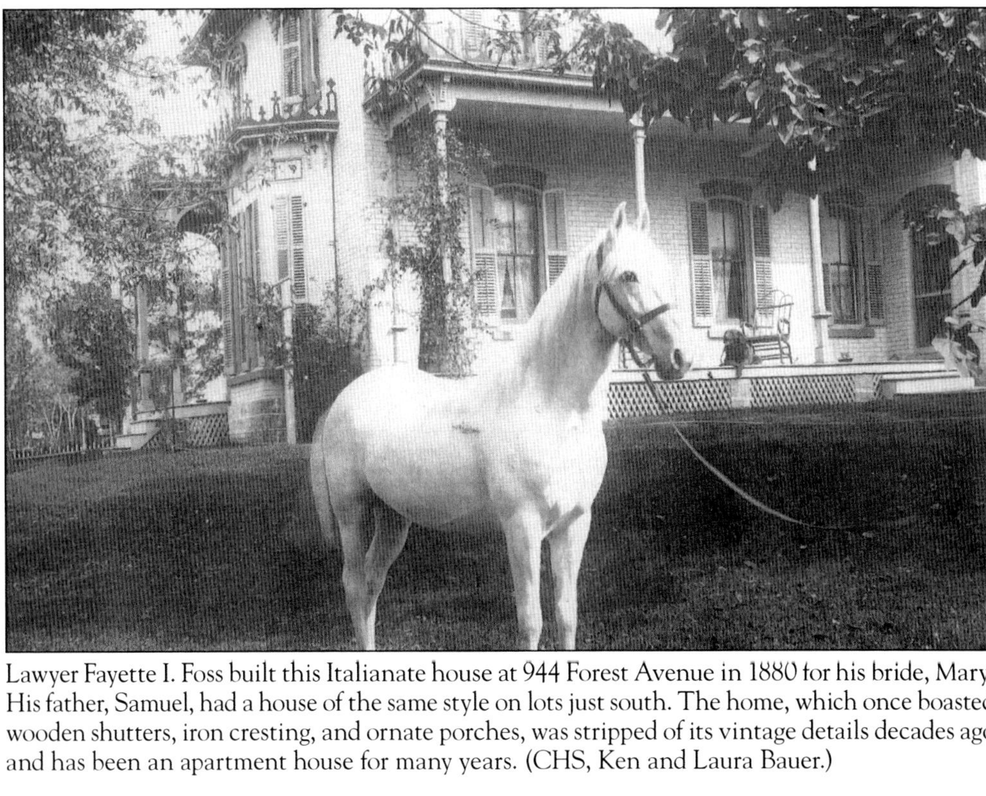

Lawyer Fayette I. Foss built this Italianate house at 944 Forest Avenue in 1880 for his bride, Mary. His father, Samuel, had a house of the same style on lots just south. The home, which once boasted wooden shutters, iron cresting, and ornate porches, was stripped of its vintage details decades ago and has been an apartment house for many years. (CHS, Ken and Laura Bauer.)

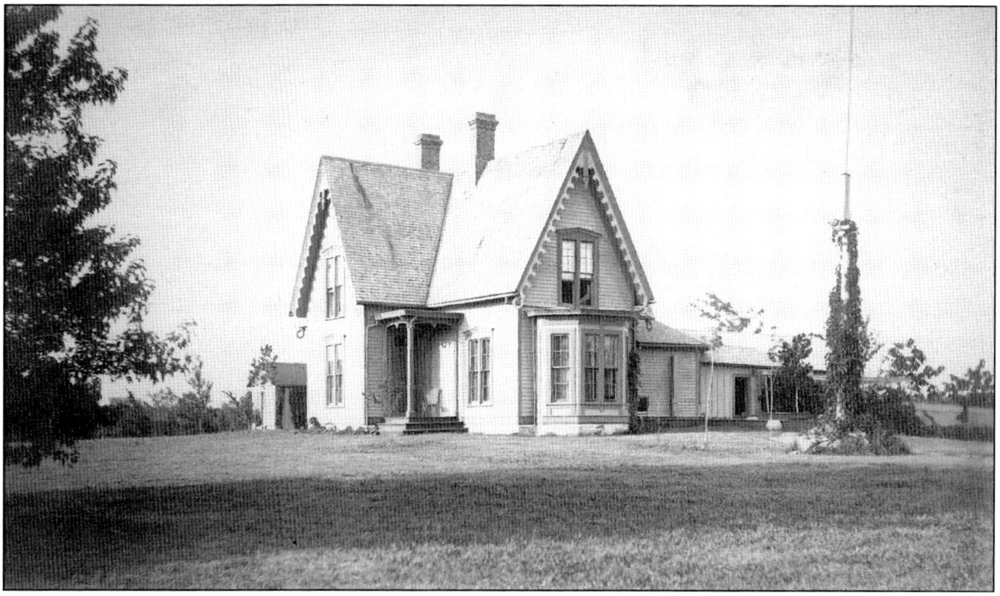

In 1871, college founder Thomas Doane built this country house, The Grange, on a 40-acre tract south of campus. Doane spent part of each year there. When his daughter Helen married college president David Brainerd Perry, they too lived at The Grange with their family. The site of many college activities during the Doane/Perry years, the house was destroyed by fire in 1942. (DCA, Helen Perry Curtis collection.)

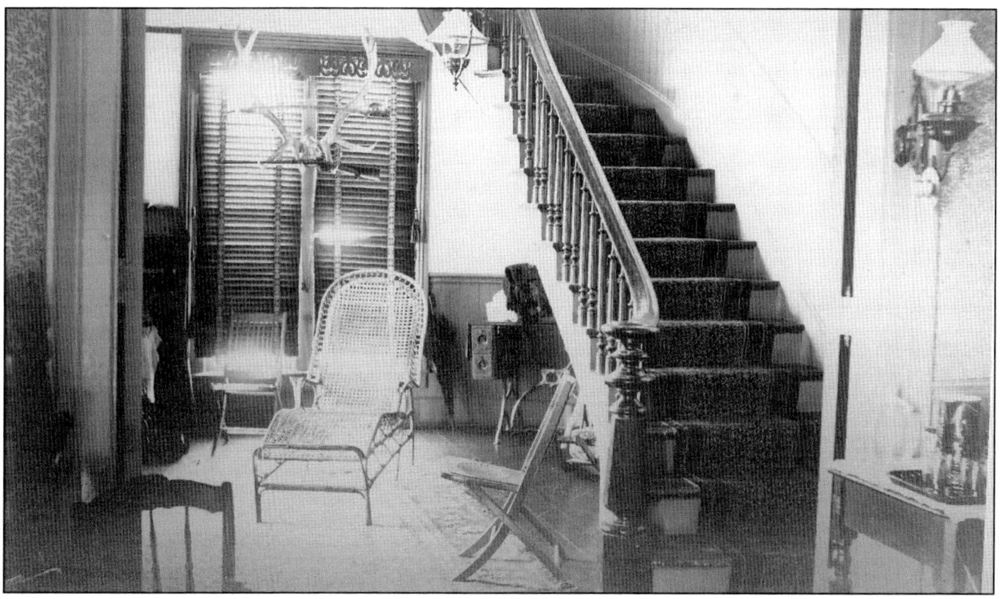

The interior of The Grange, seen here about 1890, shows refinement and rusticated decor. The open staircase is formal, as are the light fixtures, window treatments, and wallpaper. The caned, grasshopper chair and the gun rack made of elk antlers represent the rural Nebraska frontier, which was not yet totally tamed. (DCA, Helen Perry Curtis collection.)

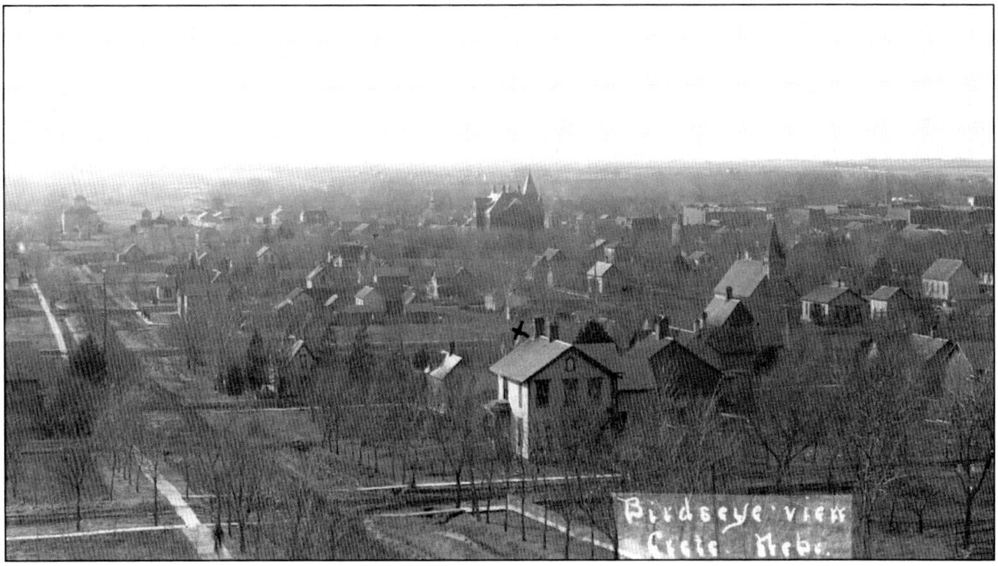

This view of the expanding College Hill residential neighborhood looks west-northwest from the top of Gaylord Hall at Ninth Street and Boswell Avenue. Reverend Eyster's house is visible in the foreground, and Crete High School, with its tall bell tower, is in the distance. St. Ludmilla's Catholic Church is located to the northwest of the Eyster house. (CHS.)

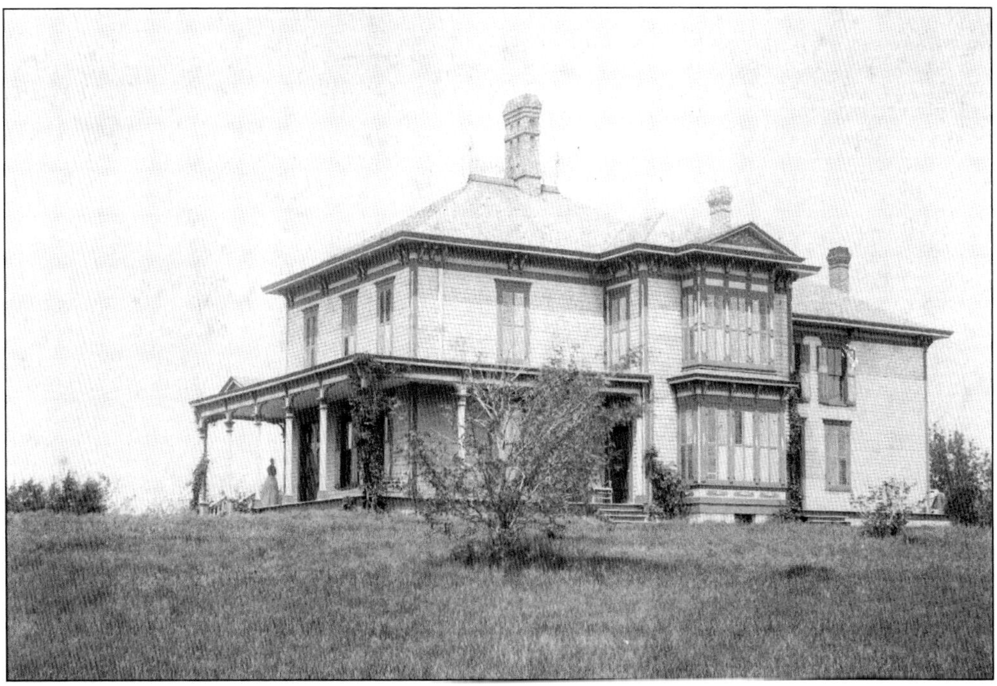
This house at 1310 East Thirteenth Street was built by grain buyer and insurance man Samuel L. Andrews in 1879. Situated just north of the college campus, the acreage allowed the Andrews family space to raise farm animals and grow orchard and garden produce. For many years, it was home to the Osterhout family. (Osterhout family collection.)

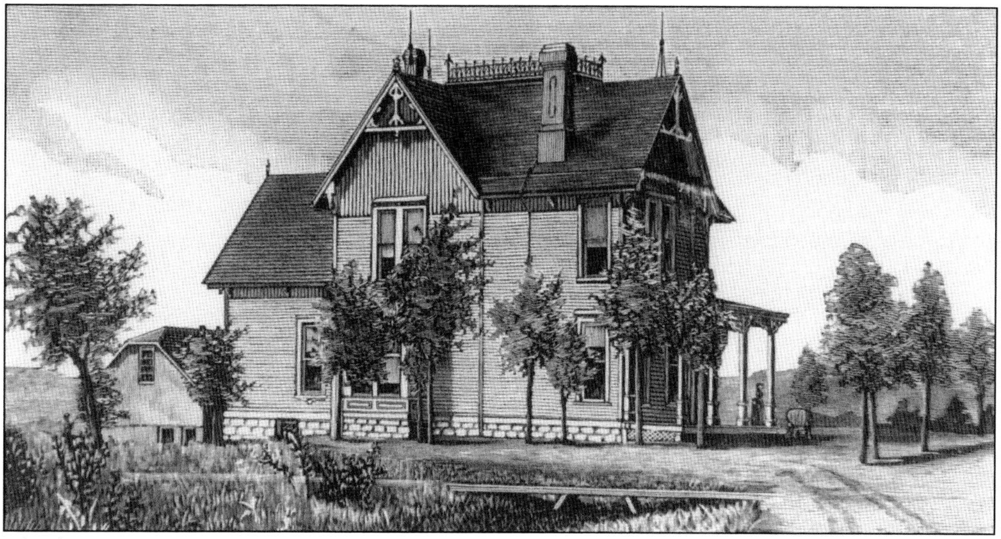

This house at 1205 Forest Avenue was built by lumber dealer Zephaniah Waterman about 1885. The Waterman Lumber and Coal Company was in business from 1883 until 1910. This house featured many decorative details, but in 1910, a two–story sleeping porch was added, substantially changing the appearance. Over time, all ornamentation was removed and the house was remodeled into apartments. (Drawing from J.A. Finch's *Map of Crete,* 1887.)

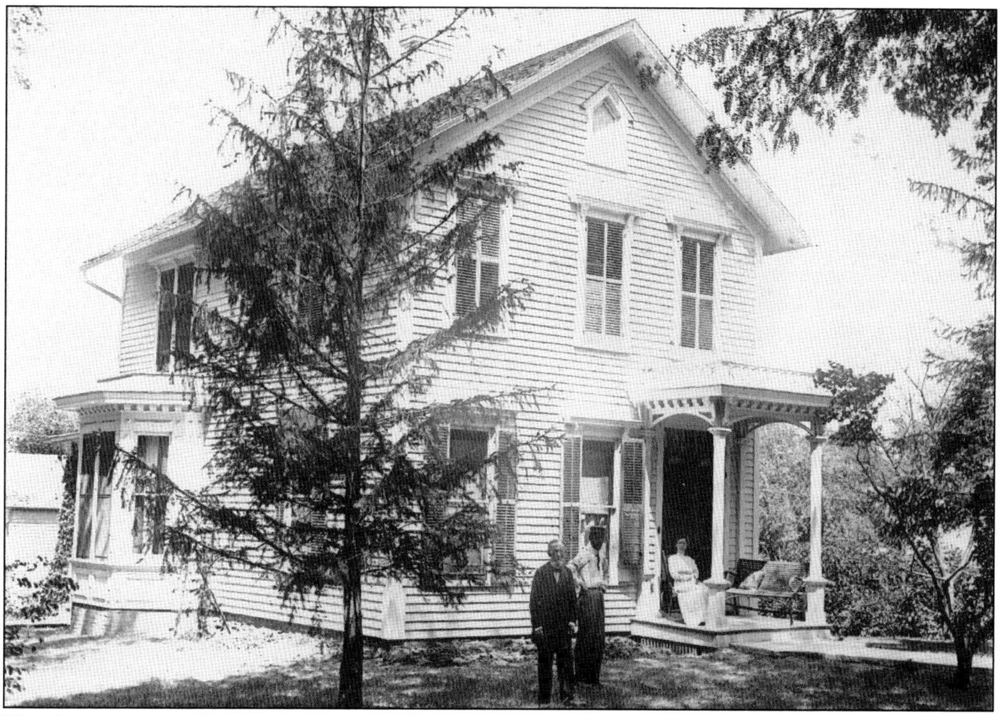

The house at 909 Forest Avenue was built about 1883 as a retirement home for Rev. William and Lucretia Eyster of Pennsylvania. The simple style is enhanced by a decorative front porch and bay window. Reverend Eyster, who often told of how he heard Abraham Lincoln give the Gettysburg Address, is at far left, and his daughter Alice is on the porch. (James and Sharon Crouse collection.)

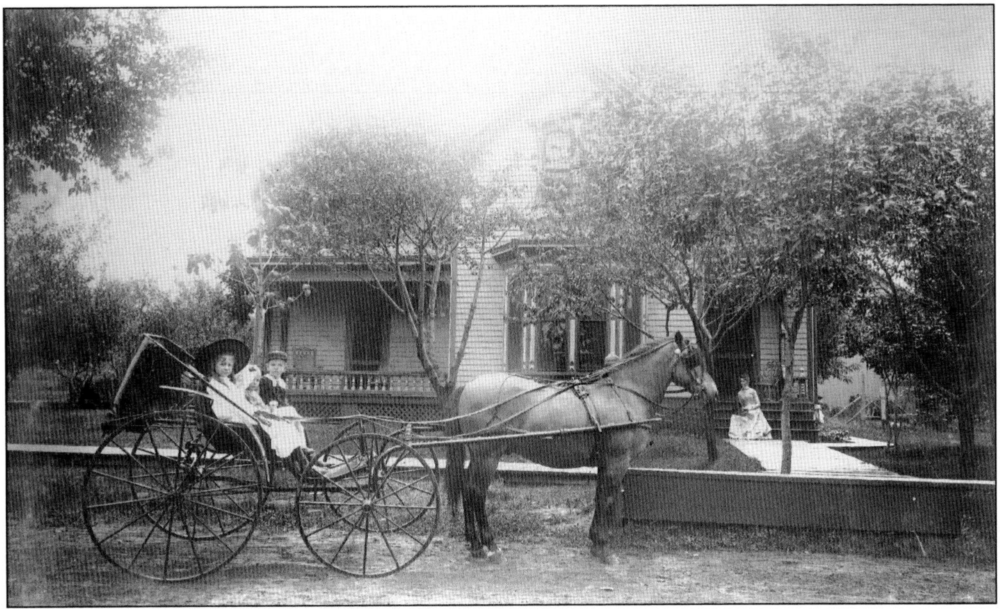

Banker George Stevens and his wife, Jennie, built this house at 924 Grove Avenue in 1885. It is a simple cross shape, but the decorative features surrounding the doors and windows, the bay window, and the porch balustrades give the house its distinctive Victorian appearance. The house has always been painted in contrasting colors to showcase its gingerbread ornamentation. (CHS, Jennie Chapman Stevens collection.)

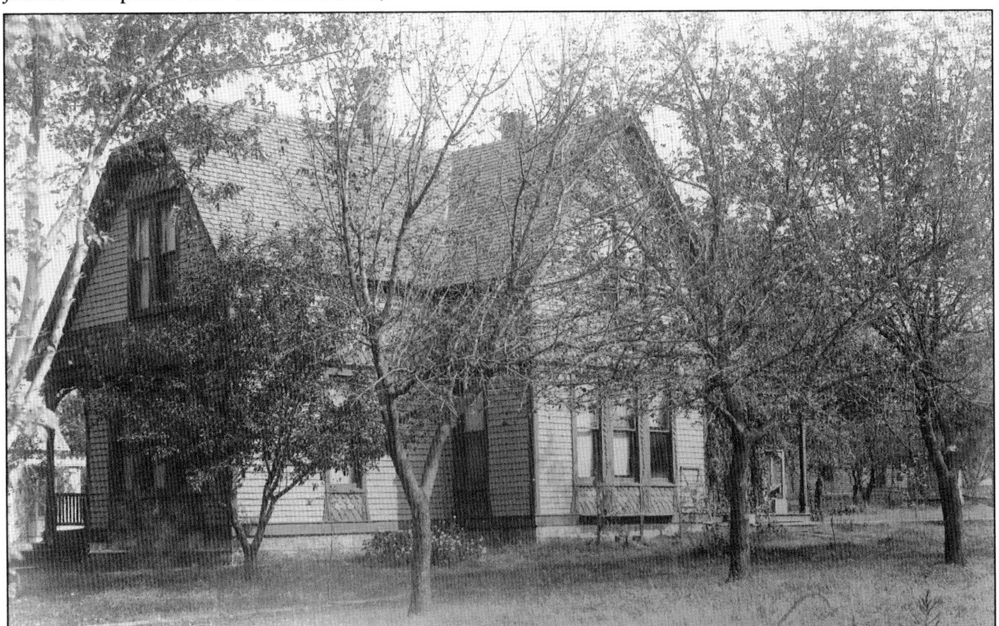

This late-1880s house at 1126 Hawthorne Avenue was built by George W. and Vietta Church. Church was an early Crete grocer and dealer in grain and seed. After 1900, it became home to two generations of the Conrad family. It was renovated extensively for Dr. Alexander Conrad in the 1930s by Lincoln architect Benjamin F. Hemphill and now has a period revival look. (CHS, Jennie Chapman Stevens collection.)

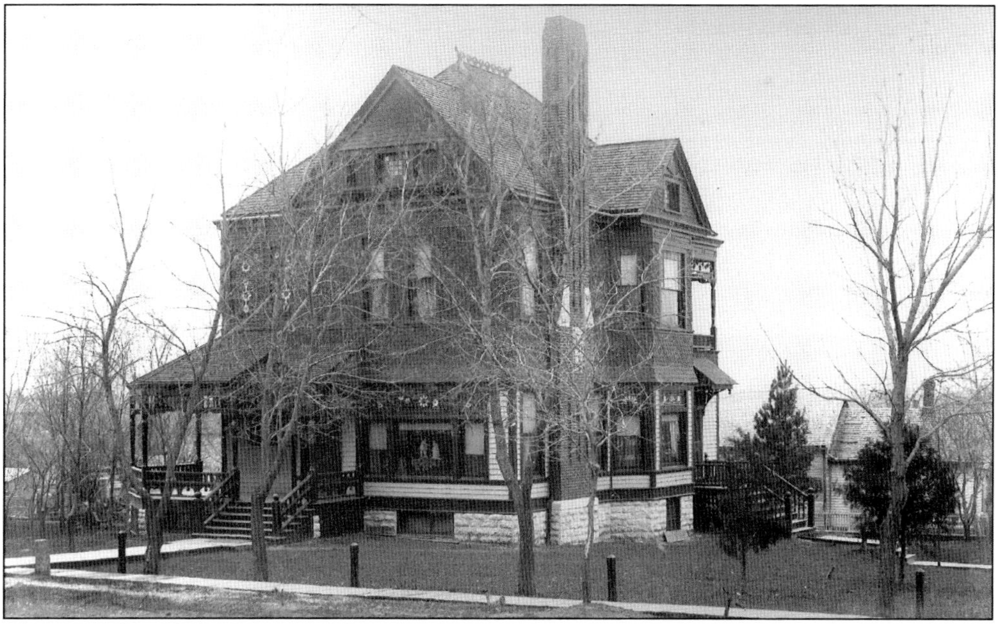

This Shingle-style/Queen Anne house at 1039 Forest Avenue was built in 1888 for the family of Judge William H. Morris. Designed by prominent Omaha architect J.H.W. Hawkins, the Morris house cost about $7,000 and boasted electrical appliances and running water. The frame exterior features patterned shingles and a massive Eastlake porch. Many well-publicized social activities took place here in the 19th century. (CHS, Jennie Chapman Stevens collection.)

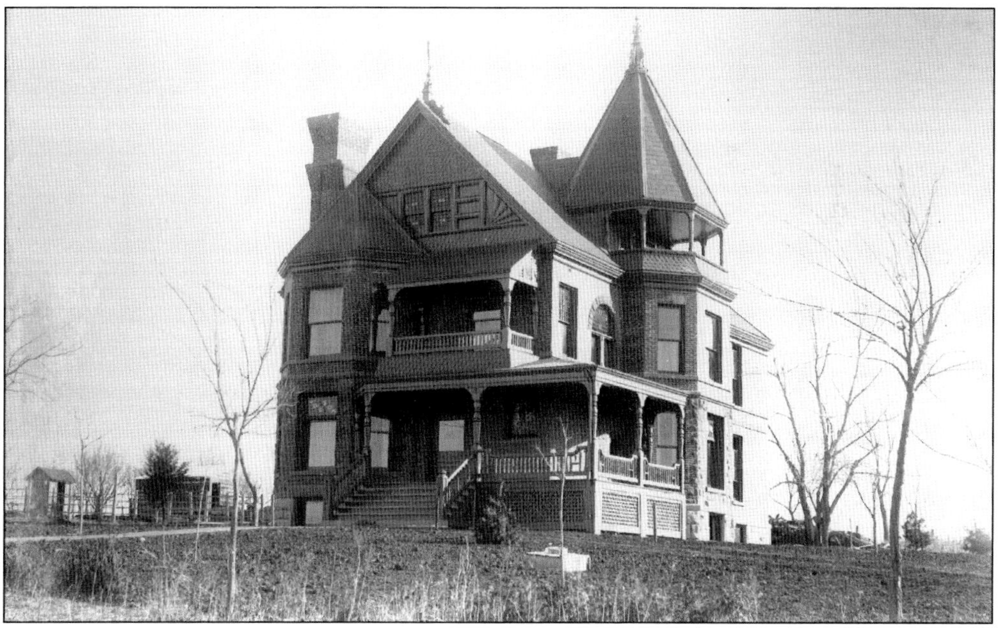

The house at 1422 Boswell Avenue was built between 1887 and 1889 for local entrepreneur and banker John R. Johnston and his wife, Ida. Designed by Lincoln architect James Tyler Sr., the Queen Anne house was originally part of a 15-acre estate. The house, which cost $15,000 and had electricity and running water, features multiple materials, including sandstone, brick, and wood, as well as a side tower and much ornamentation. (CHS, Jennie Chapman Stevens collection.)

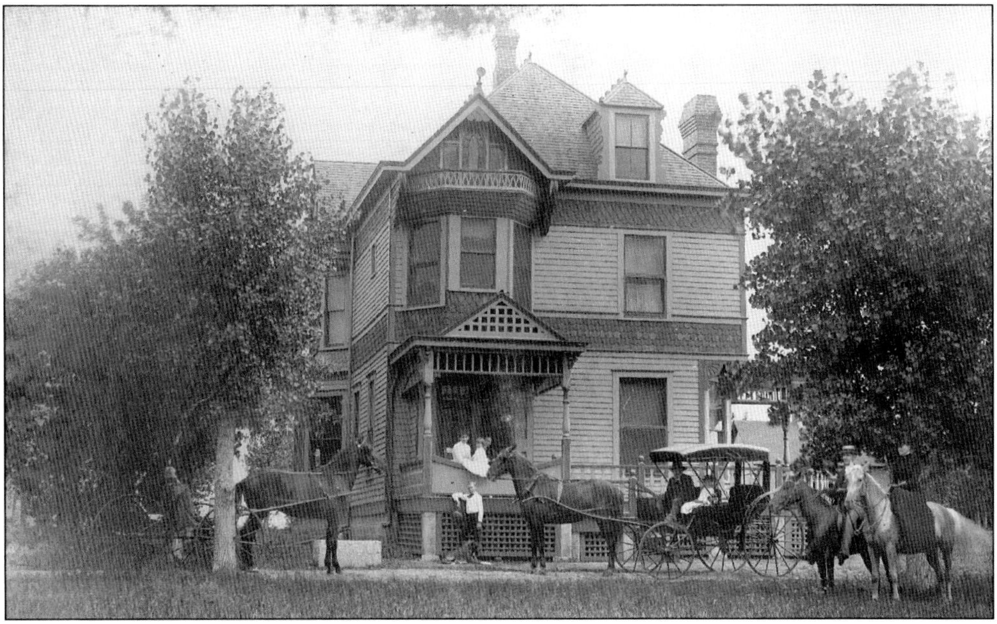

Hotel proprietor Henry Code built this house at 1120 East Thirteenth Street about 1886 as a retirement home. Code came to Crete in 1871 and built the Cosmopolitan Hotel in downtown Crete in 1879. Code's house, built for $10,000, originally had Queen Anne features but was remodeled with a new front porch and sleeping porch additions in the early 20th century. (CHS, Jennie Chapman Stevens collection.)

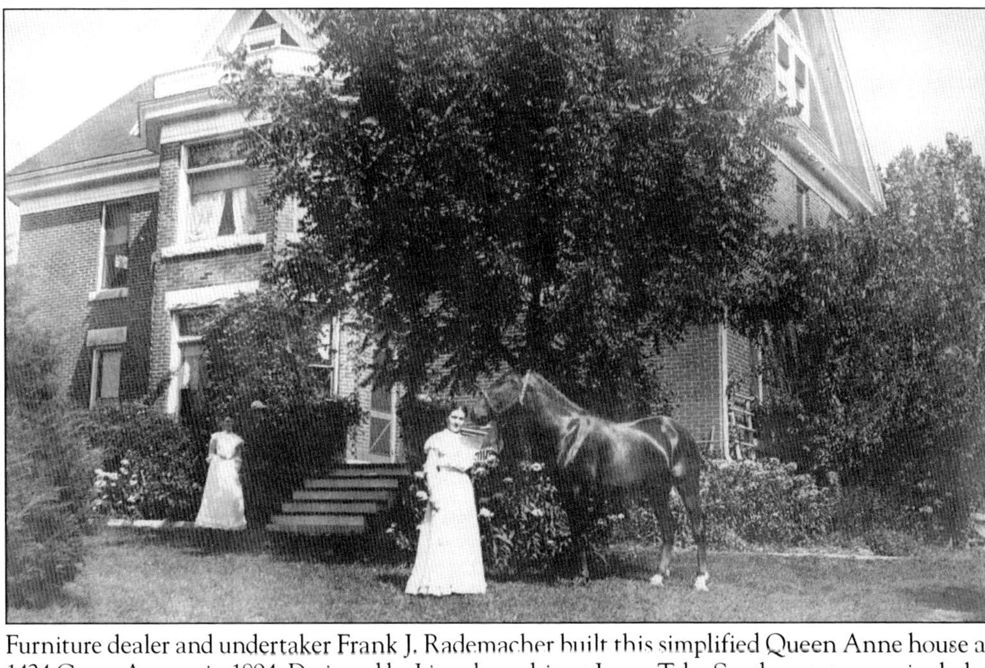

Furniture dealer and undertaker Frank J. Rademacher built this simplified Queen Anne house at 1424 Grove Avenue in 1894. Designed by Lincoln architect James Tyler Sr., the estate once included a hearse barn. Rademacher settled in Crete in 1870 and was an organizer of St. James Parish, a school board member, a Crete Savings and Loan Association officer, and a charter member of the Nebraska Funeral Directors Association. (Kersenbrock family collection.)

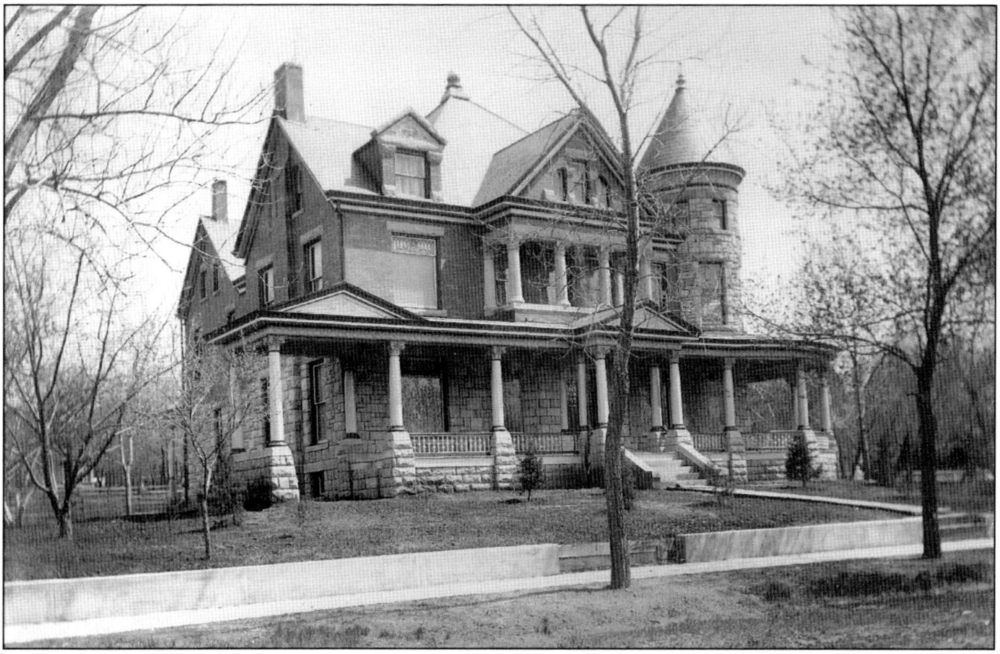

Entrepreneur Theodore H. Miller built this late–Queen Anne mansion at 1112 Grove Avenue in 1899. Constructed of brick and stone brought from Colorado, the estimated cost was between $16,000 and $20,000. The house, designed by Lincoln architect George W. Shaffer, features a corner tower and an expansive porch with a covered carriage entrance at its north end. The property originally had a carriage house and stable north of the house. (CHS, Jennie Chapman Stevens collection.)

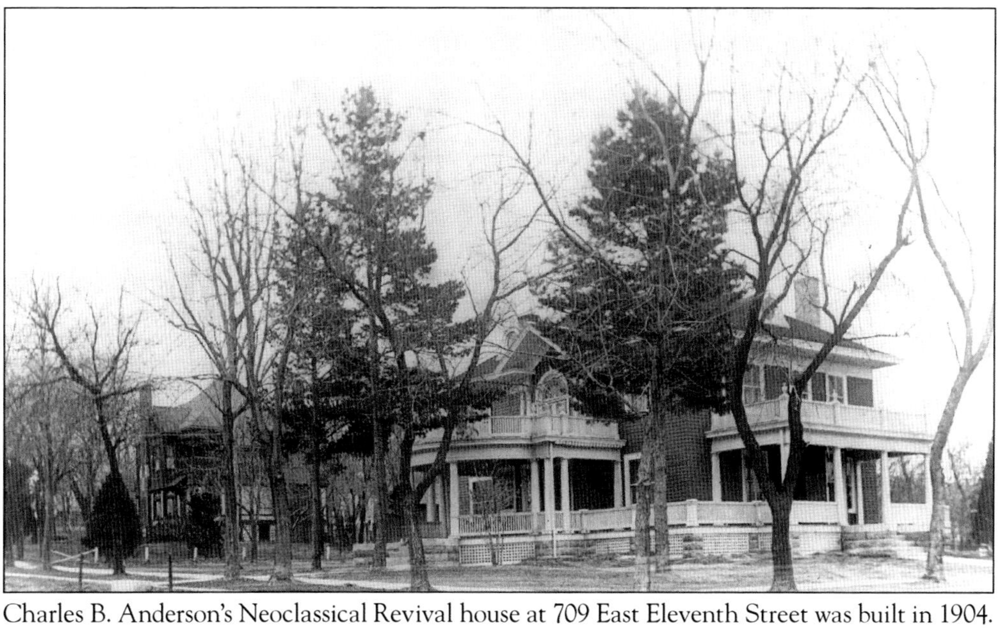

Charles B. Anderson's Neoclassical Revival house at 709 East Eleventh Street was built in 1904. Anderson, a banker and politician, was the son-in-law of T.H. Miller, who lived across the street to the north. The house features a fanlight window over the second-story balcony doorway and large porches with classical columns. A carriage house was also built on the property. The Judge Morris House is in the background. (Author's collection.)

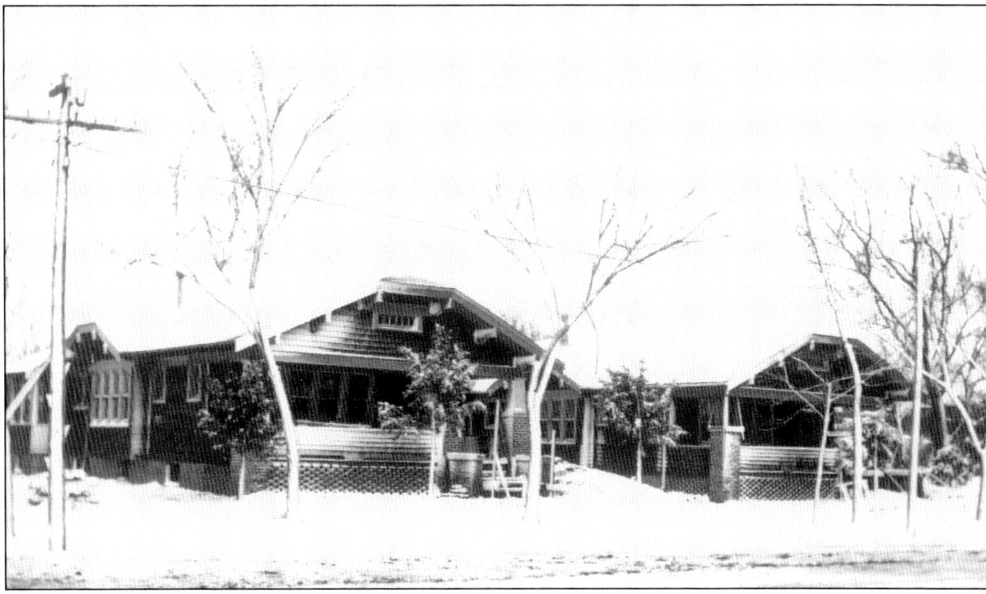

These small bungalows at 309 and 317 East Fourteenth Street were built by contractor Otto Feeken in the early 1920s. He discovered this "new" housing style while on a trip to California. The house on the left was built for Isis Theatre owner Arva Burrus, and the one on the right was for general store manager Andrew Barton. These houses were among the first bungalows in Crete. (Marilyn Feeken Reiss collection.)

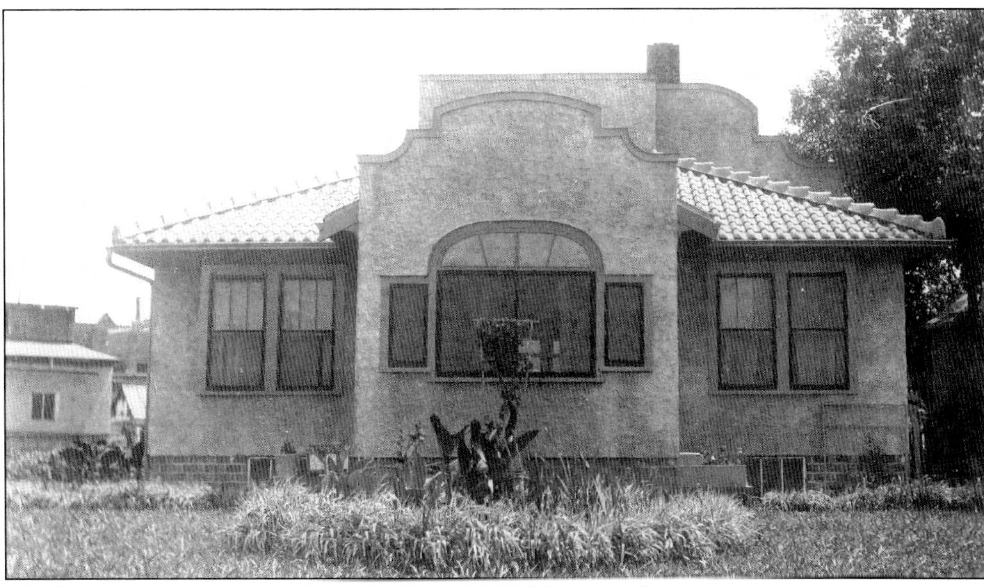

This Mission-style house on the southeast corner of Fourteenth Street and Norman Avenue was built by contractor Otto Feeken in 1920–1921 for his own family. Clad in stucco and covered by a red tile roof, the house is reminiscent of early Spanish missions on the West Coast. Feeken's carpenter shop was also on the property. (Marilyn Feeken Reiss collection.)

Six

Leisure, Social Life, and Recreation

While city fathers were busy establishing the economic and administrative structure of the city, citizens were also organizing social and leisure groups and entertainment venues. Crete residents have long had a wide variety of recreational and social opportunities. As early as 1872, the Masonic Lodge was organized in Crete, and soon after, other secret and fraternal organizations were established. Religious groups were organized during the 1870s settlement period, and numerous social gatherings were held.

Perhaps the most substantial vote of confidence in Crete's future as a "modern" and refined city was the completion of Band's Opera House in 1876 at the corner of Thirteenth Street and Maine Avenue, an intersection that evolved as the hub of the 14-square-block business district. Dr. Charles Band constructed the three-story brick building to house businesses on street level, his office and other professional offices on the second level, and a large hall on the third story that was purportedly as well designed and equipped as any opera house in Omaha or Lincoln.

By the 1880s, there were many social organizations in town, several affiliated with churches and Doane College and others that were organized by individuals. These included vocal and instrumental musical groups, Bible societies, the Women's Christian Temperance Union, various lodges, a Grand Army of the Republic post, Sokols, and sporting groups. Through the years, Crete had swimming pools and golf courses in various locations, ball games were popular, and the Nebraska Chautauqua Assembly was a major social event.

Much activity revolved around holidays and patriotic events. Crete often had parades, and the Saline County Fair has always been held here. The Big Blue River offered recreational opportunities, and a city park system provided sites for concerts and picnics.

The following photographs give examples of leisure activities that occupied Crete residents in the early days.

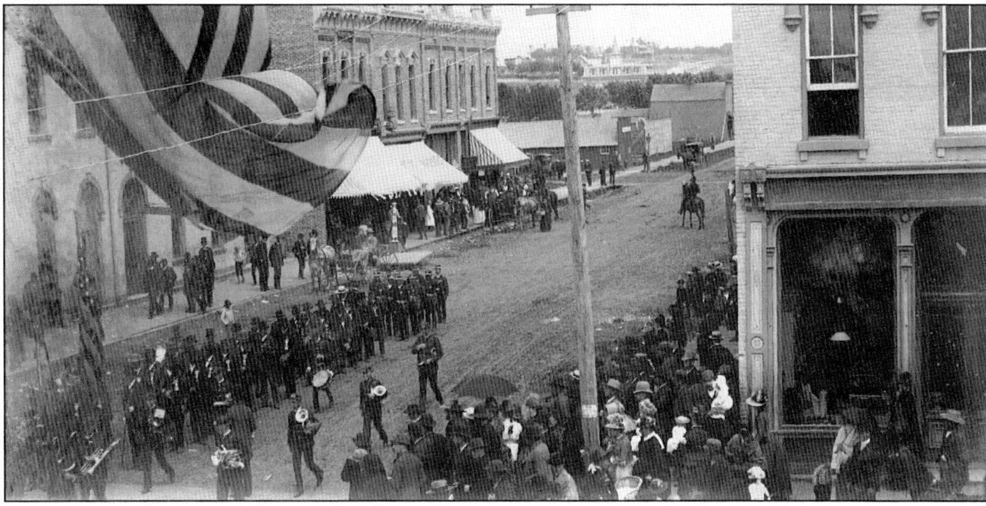

Memorial Day was celebrated in style each May. Organized by the Holland Post of the Grand Army of the Republic, the event included a procession to Riverside Cemetery from downtown Crete, orations, grave decorating, and sometimes a picnic supper. This 1890s photograph shows the procession, led by a marching band, at Thirteenth Street and Maine Avenue. (CHS, Jennie Chapman Stevens collection.)

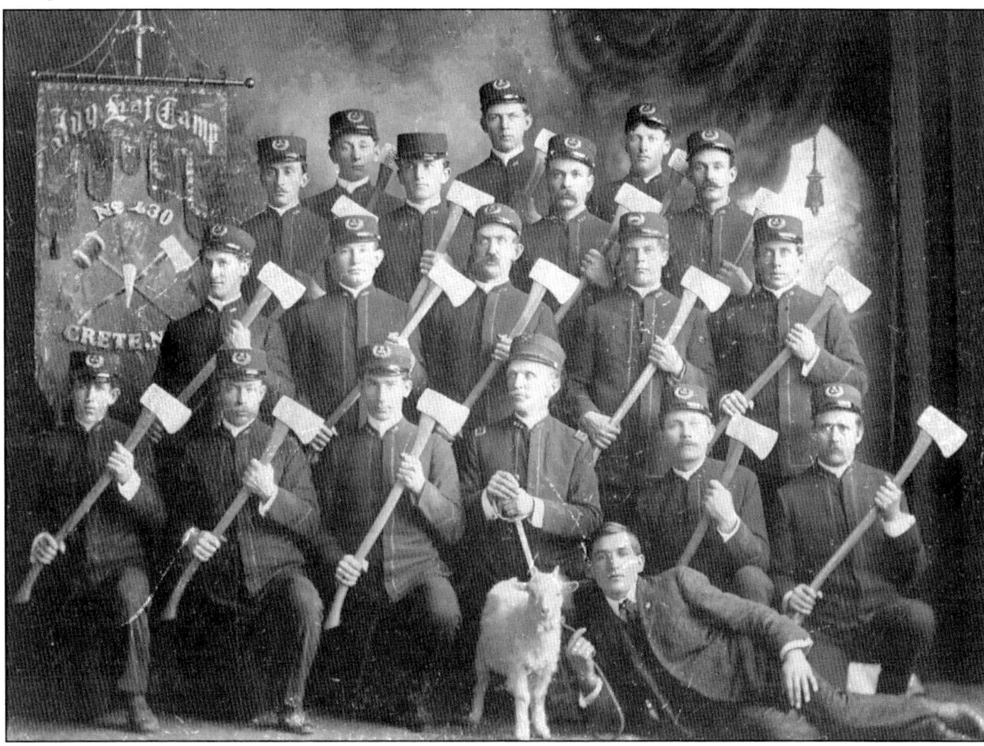

In 1887, the Modern Woodmen of America organized in Crete with 18 charter members. The purpose of this group was to assist families who lost a breadwinner and to host community building events. The name "woodmen" refers to foresters who cleared land to build communities. Membership was limited to rural residents in 12 Midwestern states and organized in "camps." Crete's Ivy Leaf Camp is seen here in full dress with their goat mascot. (CHS.)

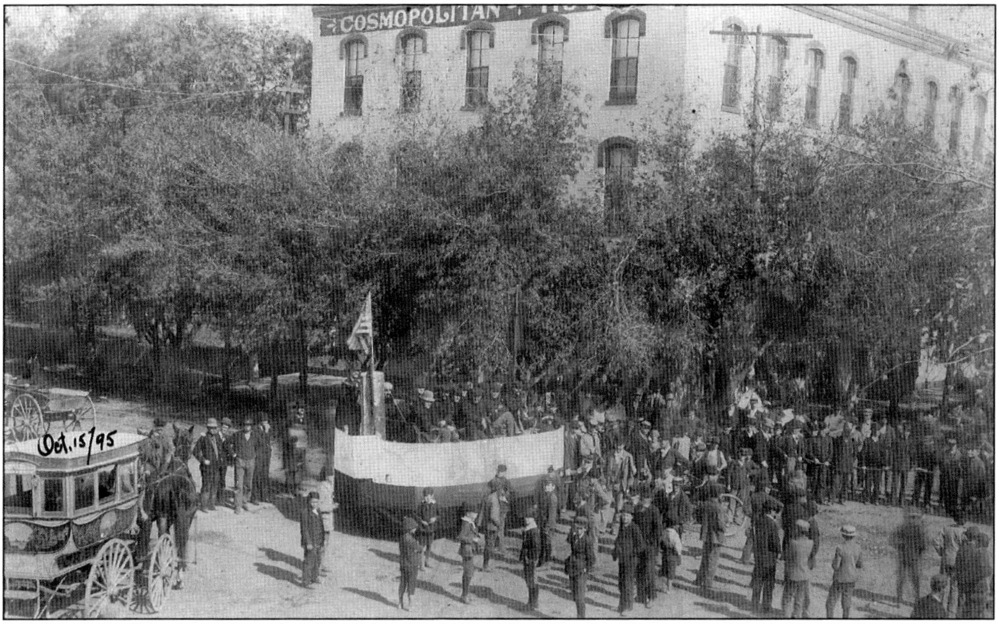

This celebration at the intersection of Fourteenth Street and Maine Avenue welcomed the Doane football team home on October 15, 1895. The team arrived on the train after they had defeated three Iowa teams during their five-day trip. Visible in the background is the Cosmopolitan Hotel, on the northeast corner of Fourteenth Street and Maine Avenue. (CHS.)

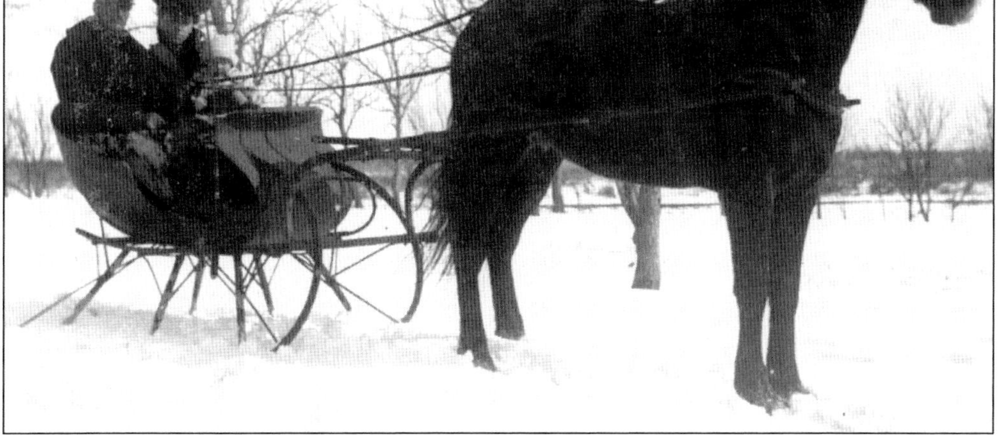

Fred and Minnie Wild Ball and their daughter Elvena have Royal Wilks hitched to their sleigh, or cutter, about 1902. The family farmed just northwest of Crete and used the sleigh for winter travel. Fred was a member of the Nebraska House of Representatives in the 1920s, an organizer of the Norris Public Power District, the secretary of the Saline County Fair board, and active in numerous civic causes in Crete. (Author's collection.)

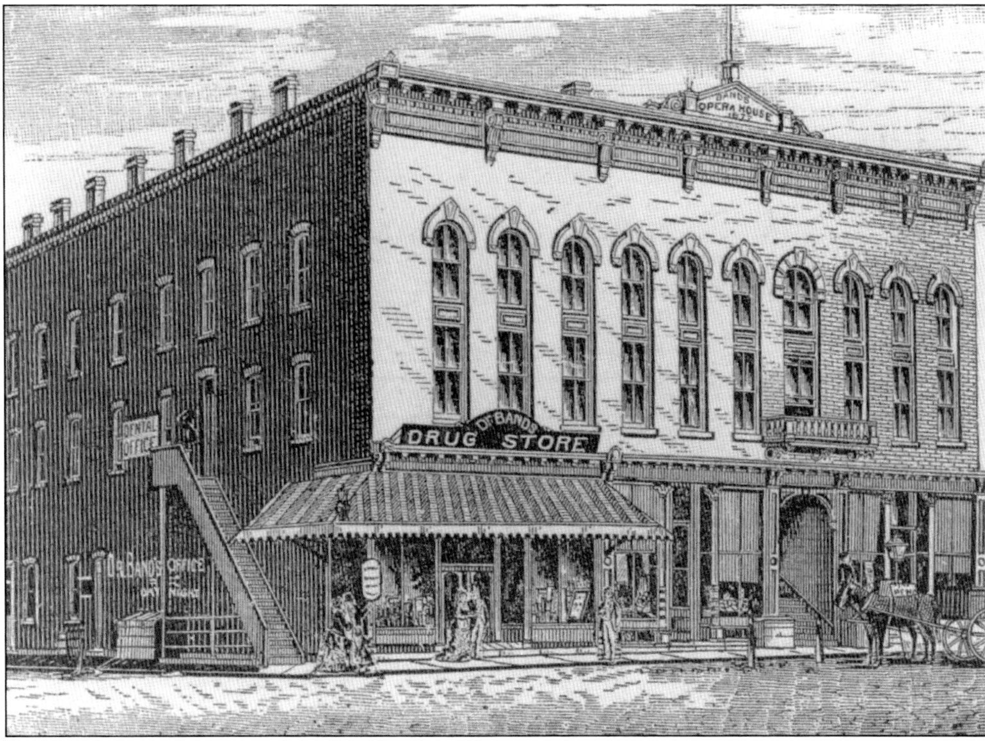

Band's Opera House, at the northwest corner of Thirteenth Street and Maine Avenue, was the first brick building constructed in downtown Crete. Constructed in 1876 with brick locally made by John Lanham, the hall was the inspiration of Dr. Charles Band, who had his medical practice and drugstore in the building. Major traveling acts performed regularly on the second-floor stage, and a baby elephant was even hoisted up from the alley for a show. The hall was the site of Crete High School graduations, community dances, Doane College events, and holiday functions. In the 1920s, the building was purchased and remodeled by Adolph and Elsa Rozanek and the opera house space became the Cinderella Ballroom, a popular dance venue. The building was razed in 1979 to make way for the construction of a bank. (Above, CHS; below, *Crete News* collection.)

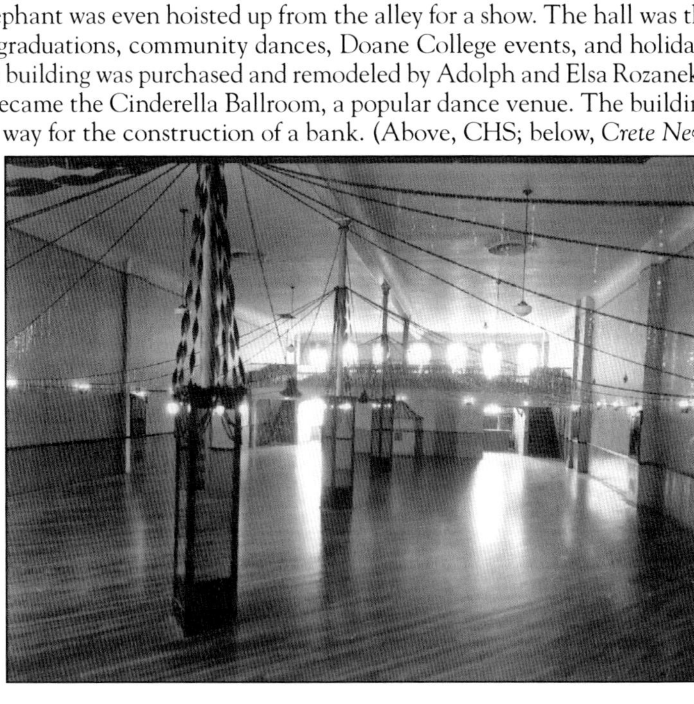

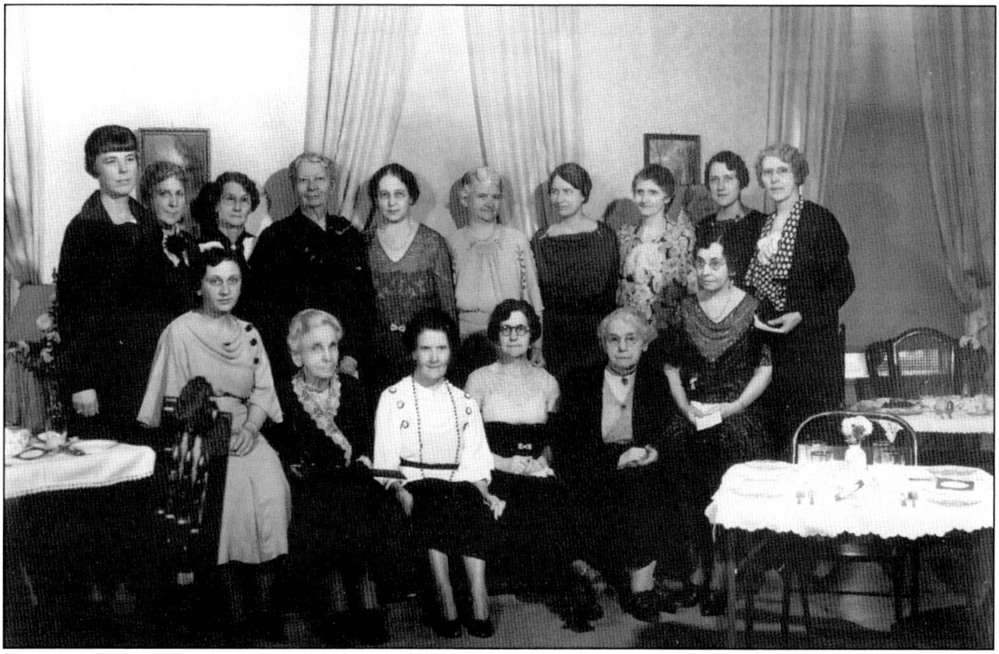

Crete's Wednesday Club is the oldest women's club in Nebraska. Organized in 1885, the ladies met every two weeks in members' homes to study history and American writers. The ladies presented results of their research and gave book reports. This 1935 photograph shows the Wednesdays ready to have dessert at tables elaborately set for the club's 50th anniversary. The club is still active. (CHS, Wednesday Club collection.)

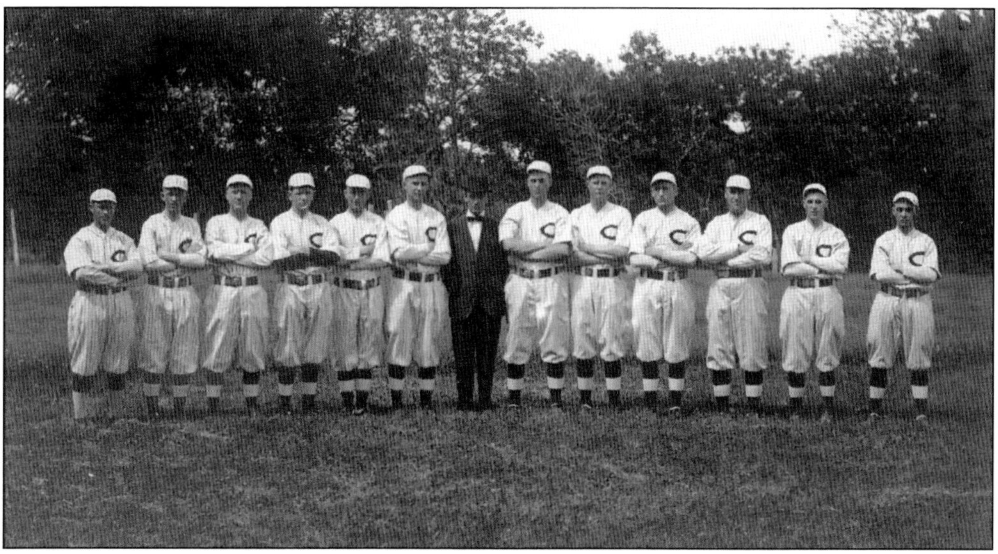

Organized sports were a major part of public school and college activities, but there were also several community sport clubs. There was a baseball club in Crete as early as 1885, playing teams from neighboring towns. This photograph shows the Crete Baseball Club in 1916. (CHS, Alyce Hokuf Collett collection.)

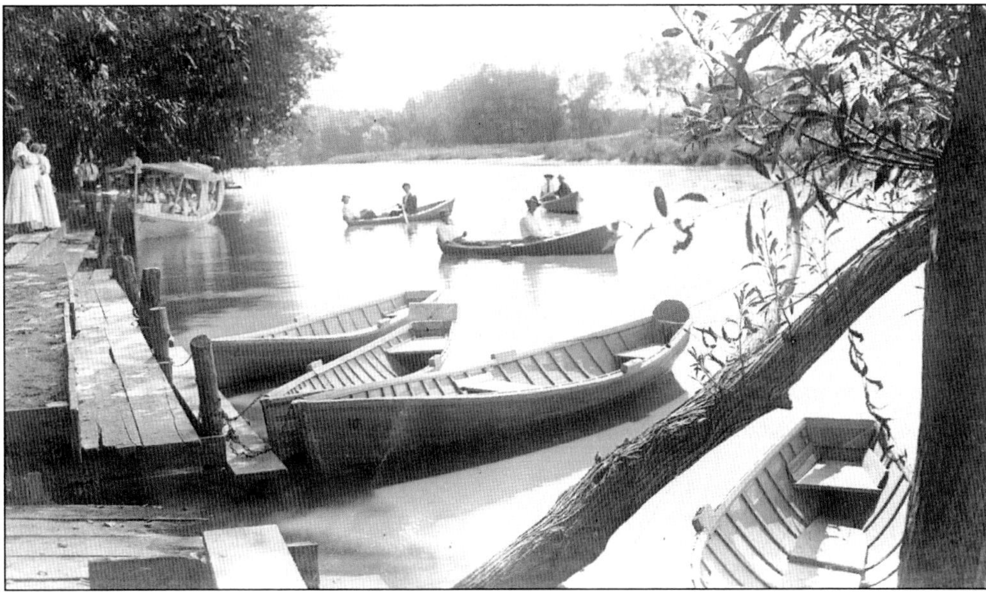

For decades, boating on the Big Blue River was a popular pastime. William H. Stone opened the Blue River Boat Company in 1904 and ran the operation for many years from his boat landing (shown above about 1909) at about Eighteenth Street and Oak Avenue above the north milldam. Rowboats and canoes could be rented and larger launches, including the *Elaine*, named after Stone's daughter, were available. Stone had several big boats, operated by a captain, that took large groups of passengers from Stone's boat landing to Chautauqua Park (later Tuxedo Park) and also upriver to Horky's Park (now Blue River Lodge). Below, *Elaine* is ready to push off from Stone's dock. *Elaine*'s horn was a familiar sound in Crete during boating season. (Above, Robert Sykes collection; below, CHS.)

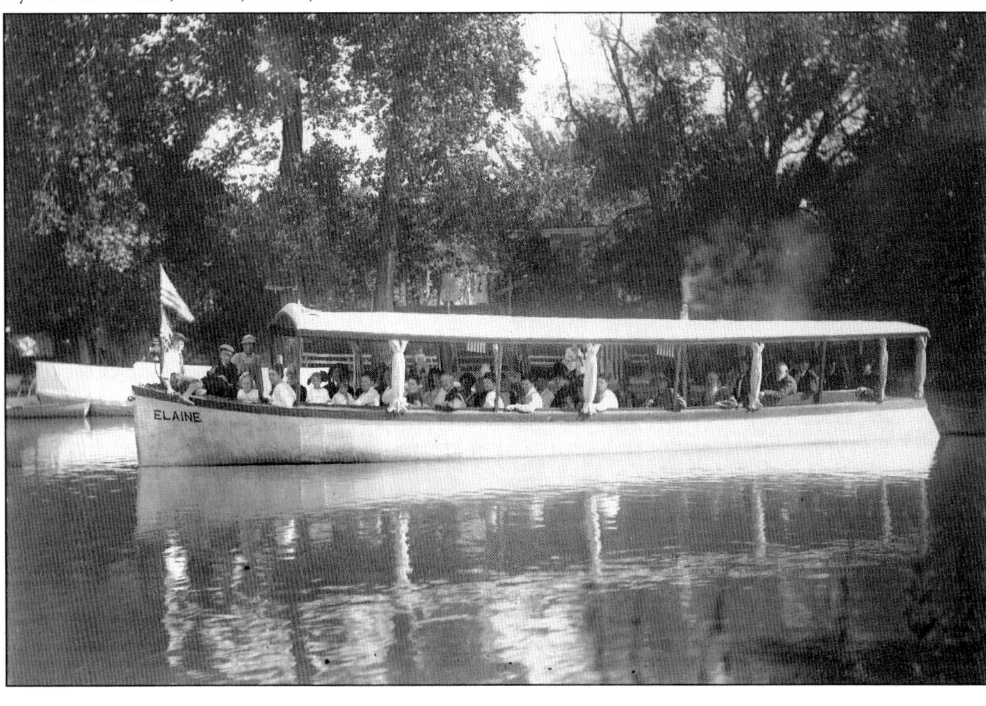

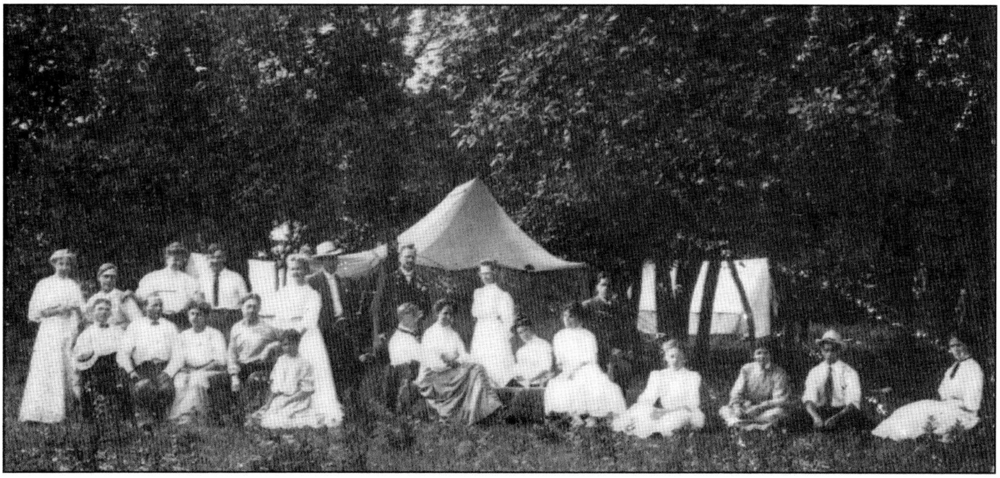

Areas along the banks of the Big Blue River above the north milldam were favorite spots for recreational activities. People picnicked and camped all along the river. This photograph is labeled "Camping on the Blue, Crete, Nebr." and shows a large group of well-dressed people posed near their tents about 1907. (Marti Ator Williams collection.)

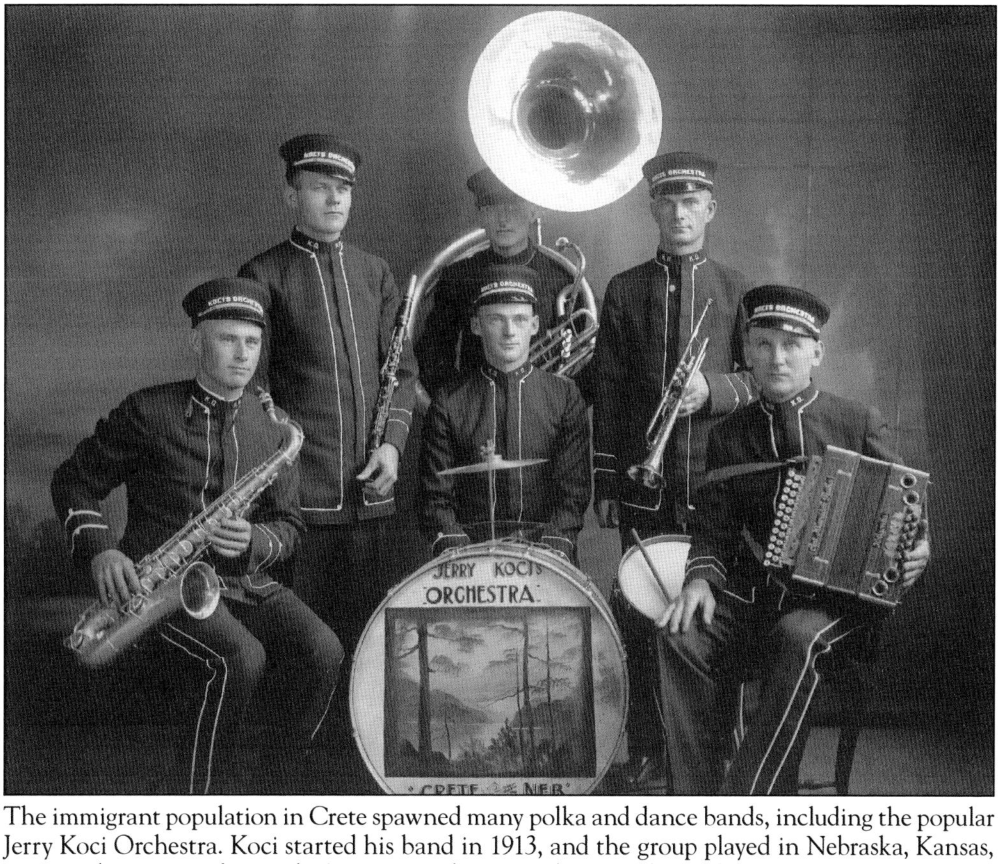

The immigrant population in Crete spawned many polka and dance bands, including the popular Jerry Koci Orchestra. Koci started his band in 1913, and the group played in Nebraska, Kansas, Iowa, and Wyoming for nearly 50 years. In this 1925 photograph are, from left to right, (first row) Jim Sinkule, Ed Keller, and Jerry Koci; (second row) Fred Chrastil, Axel Smith, and Fred Spinar. (CHS, Gladys Rahe collection.)

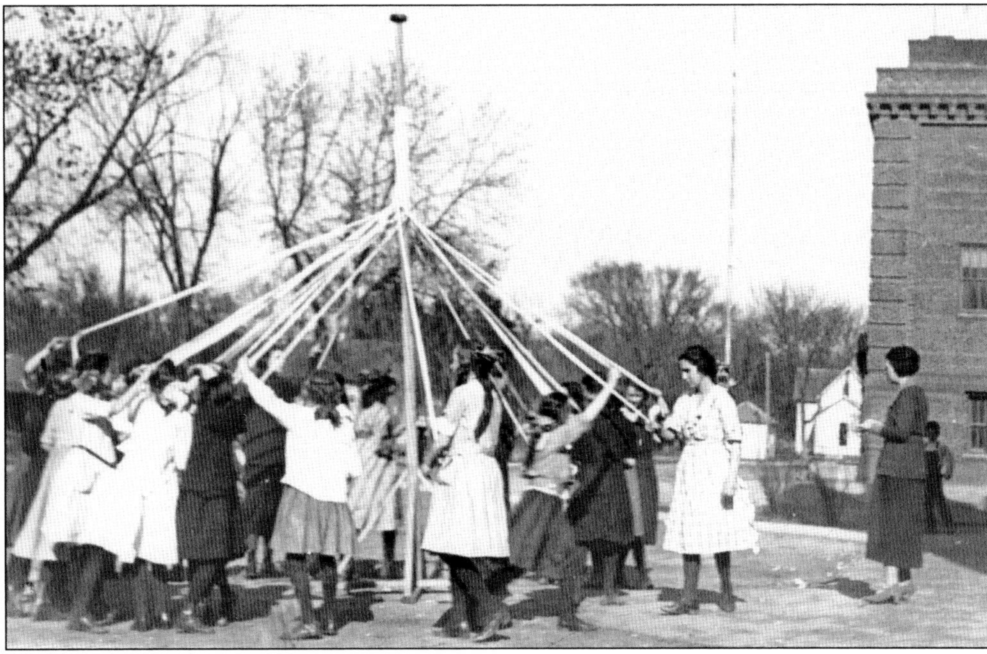

Several young ladies participated in May Day festivities on the Crete Public School grounds in this 1920s image. The students wove ribbons under the watchful eye of their teacher. The 1918 Crete High School building is on the right. Maypole dances were popular at the public school and also at Doane College, where an annual May Fete was held. (*Crete News* collection.)

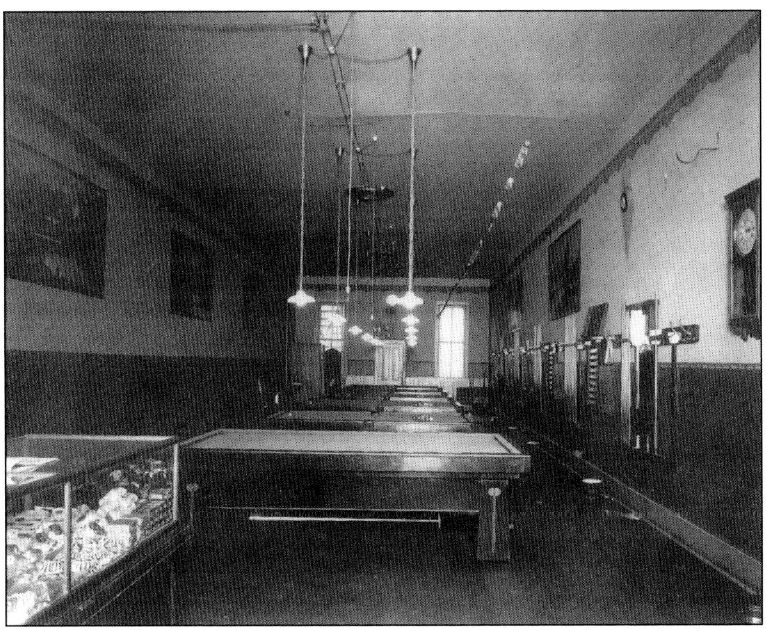

This photograph shows the south room of the pool hall at 1239–1241 Maine Avenue. Originally Wolf and Baltzley's general store, the pool hall opened in 1910. It was operated by Fred Kusy in the 1930s and 1940s and then by Cleo Wiebelhaus. The hall closed in 1982. (CHS, Terry Petracek collection.)

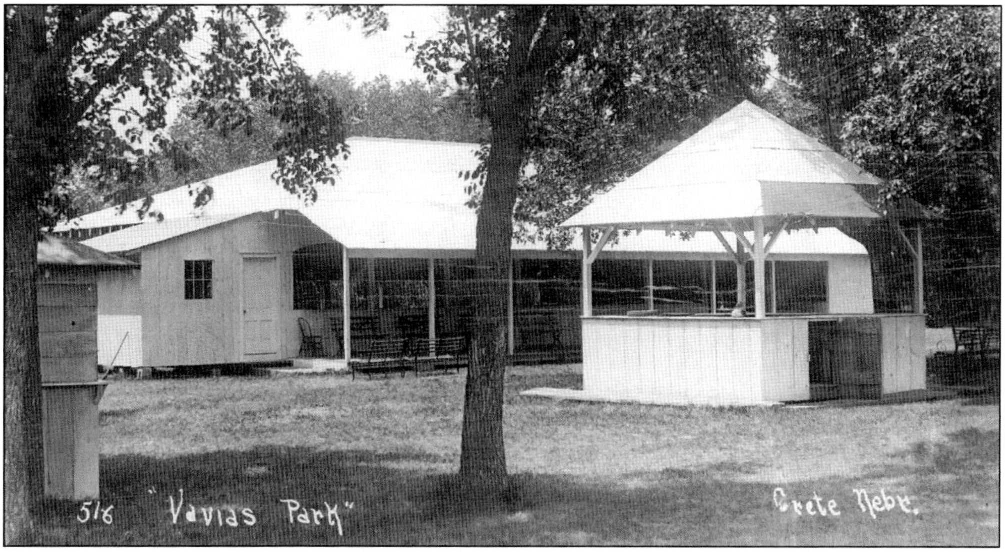

Anton Vavra bought the defunct Chautauqua grounds in west Crete in 1899 for $5,000. He operated the property as a rural park, sometimes called Riverside Park, and offered recreational spaces and exotic animals. Most original assembly buildings were sold and moved off the site, but Vavra retained several to use in the park. The city bought the property in 1926, and it became Tuxedo Park. (Larry and Terri Shestak collection.)

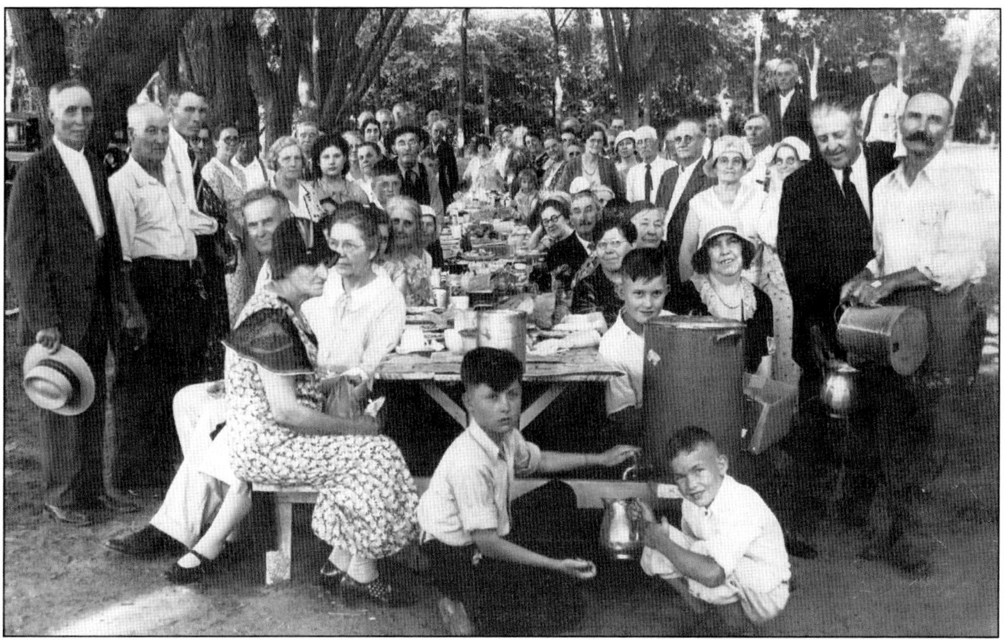

The Saline County Old Settlers Association met annually for a picnic in Tuxedo Park. This photograph shows the September 1935 Old Settlers Picnic. An Old Settlers Cabin was later constructed in the park. Built with donated material in 1938 by John Kerst, it was furnished with pioneer relics and provided a place for members and their families to gather and reminisce about old times. (CHS.)

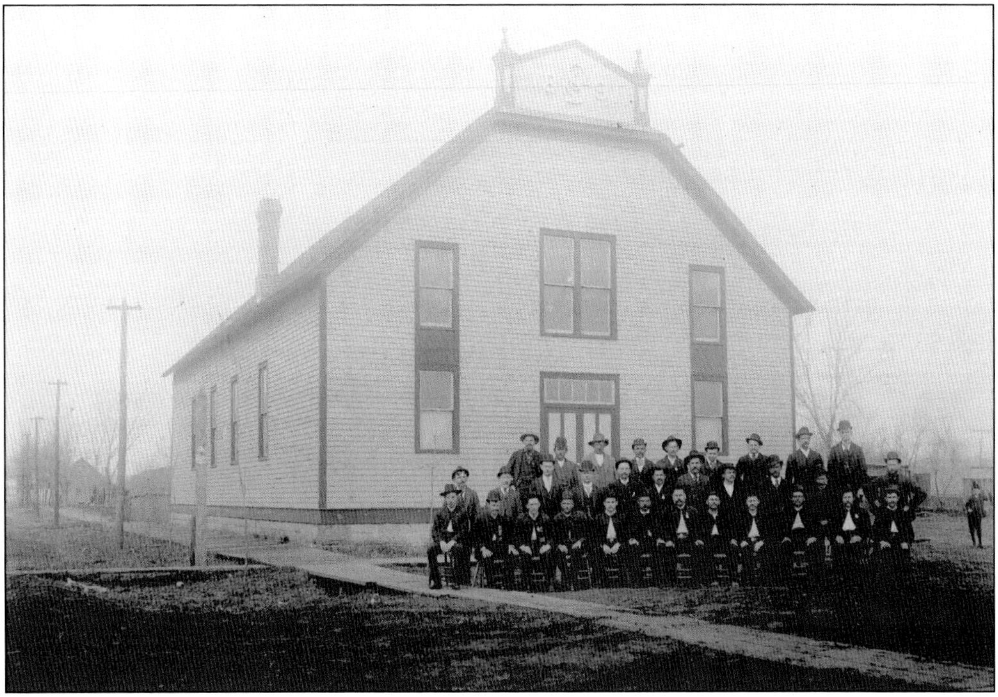

Crete's Telovicna Jednota Sokol gymnastic and fraternal organization (T.J. Sokol) was established in 1887 by Bohemian and Moravian immigrants. This 1891 hall, west of the business district, was the group's first home, but it was destroyed by fire in 1913. The Sokol movement, founded in 1862 in Prague, was brought to this country in 1865. The word *sokol* means "falcon" in Czech. (CHS.)

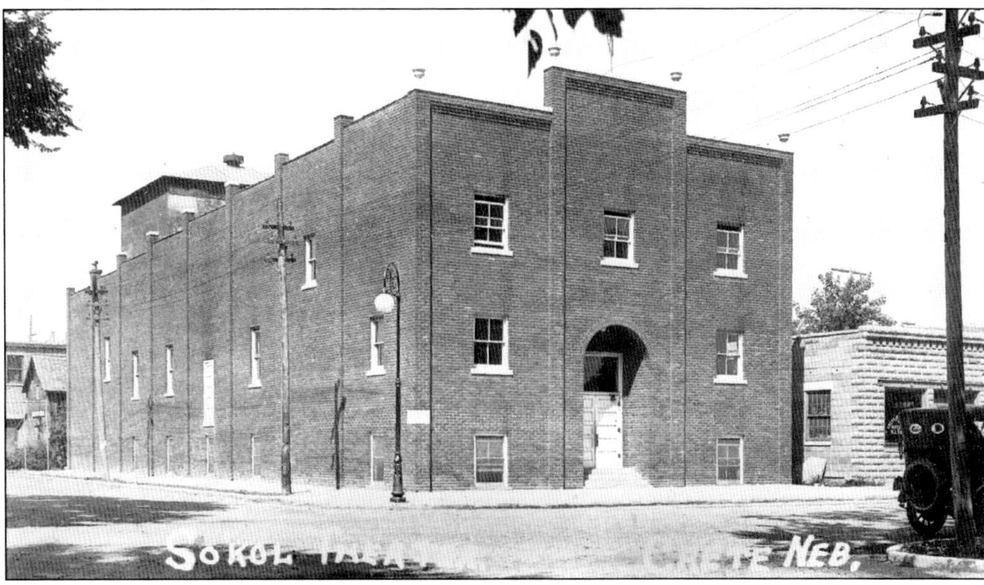

The present-day T.J. Sokol building, at Twelfth Street and Norman Avenue, was built by Moravian architect Anton Daniel. Completed in 1915, it featured a well-equipped stage and assorted scenery curtains painted by artist Jack Ballard. There is a head house above the stage, a gymnasium in the lower level, and a large auditorium space. Sokol Hall is listed in the National Register of Historic Places. (Marti Ator Williams collection.)

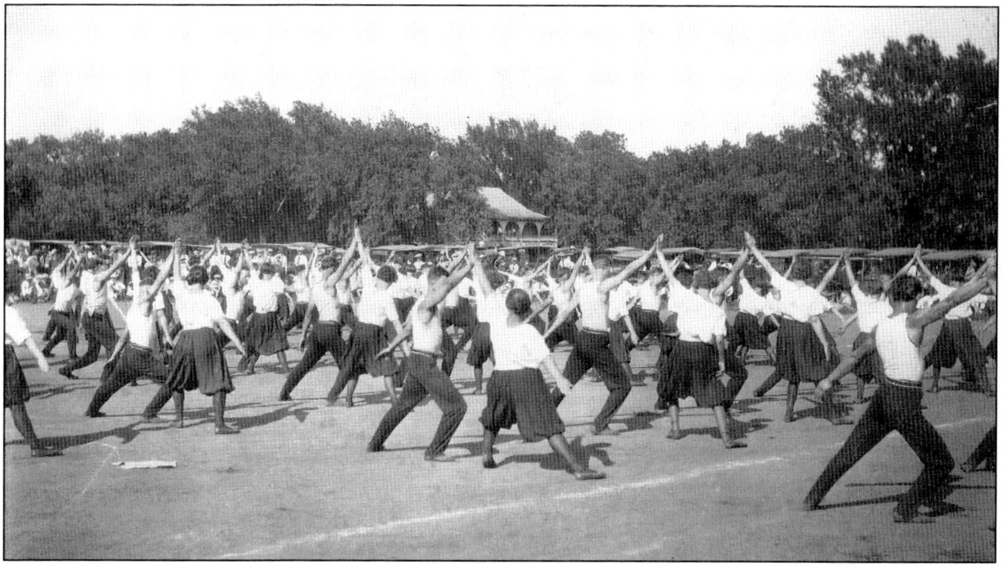

The Crete Sokol Drill Team practiced for a *slet*, or meet, in Vavra's Park in 1916. Sokol routines involve manipulating batons, hoops, and flags in precise formation. Many original routines continue today, as members adhere to the Sokol motto, "A sound mind in a sound body." This organization provided a sense of community and cultural preservation for immigrants in the new world and is still active. (CHS.)

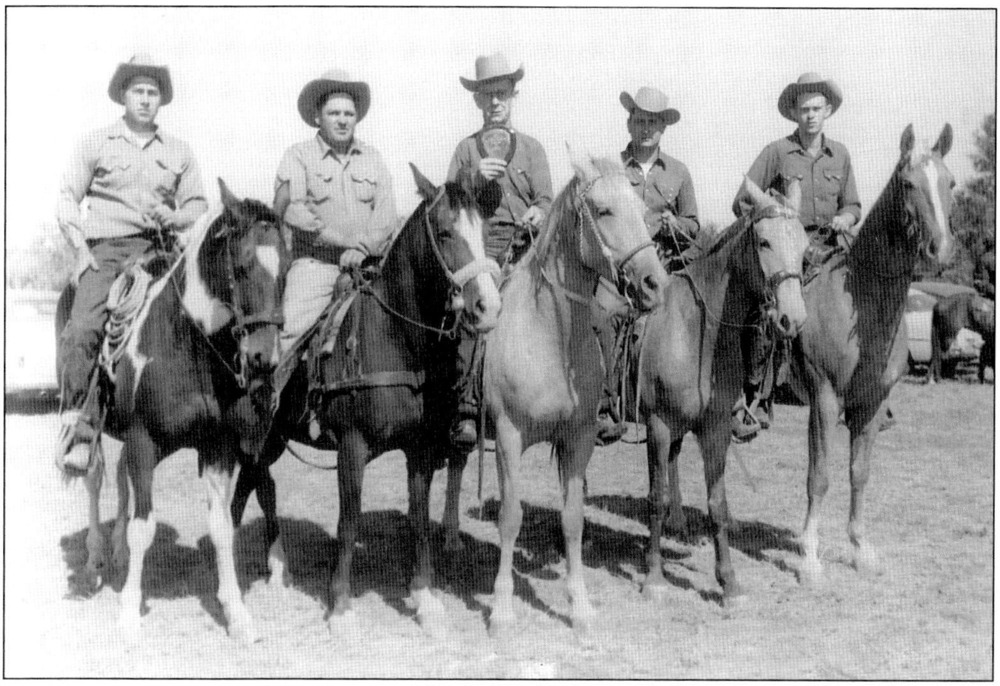

Local horsemen organized the Crete Saddle Club in the early 1950s. Victor Nespory, a local shoe-repair shop owner, experienced horse trainer, and trick rider, was an advisor. Other towns also had clubs, and weekend horse shows provided competition in many games on horseback. Posing at a 1952 event are, from left to right, Henry Hollman, Elvin Vergith, Arius Markle, Don Jeffries, and Terry Krull. (Bernice Jeffries collection.)

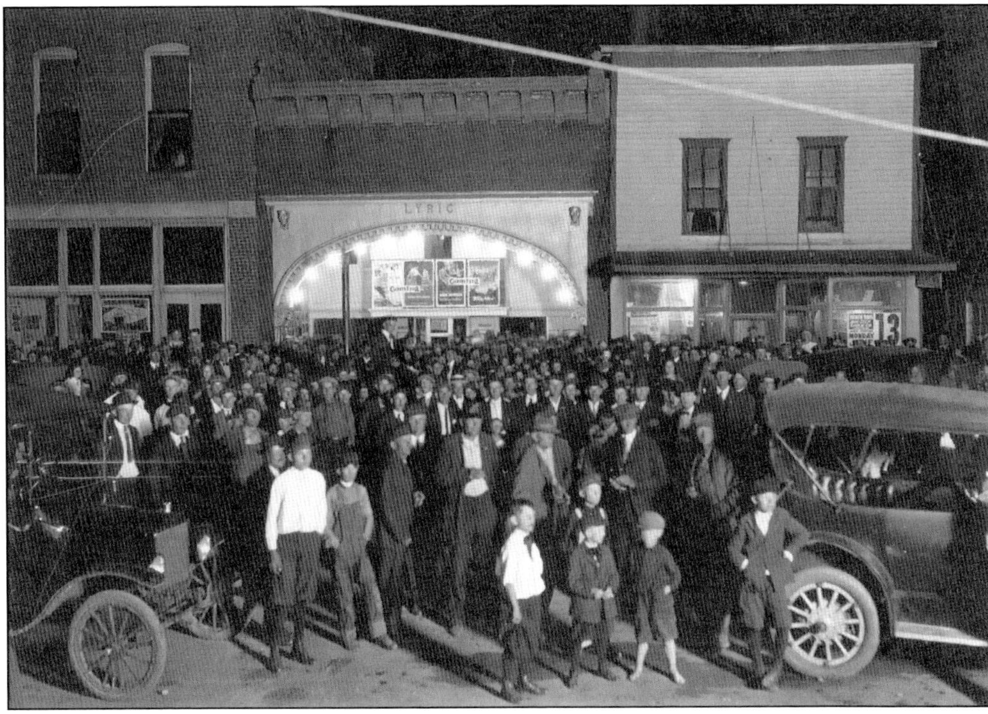

The Lyric Theatre opened on August 20, 1915, with live vocalists; a five-reel, silent feature picture, *Alone in New York*; and a Charley Chaplain comic strip. The Lyric occupied the west wing of the present VFW Club. Later owned by Arva Burrus, it closed a few years after the opening of the modern Isis Theatre. This photograph of the Lyric shows people admiring the new Isis across the street. (SCHS.)

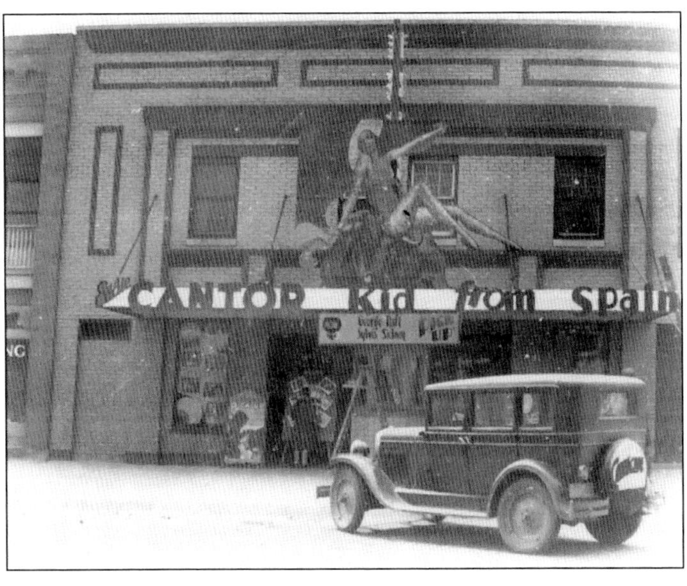

Completed in February 1926, the Isis Theatre was state of the art. Owner Arva Burrus hired Otto Feeken to design and build the theater on West Thirteenth Street. Feeken had been to California, where he met actor Lionel Barrymore and learned the latest in movie house design. The Isis featured components for the new "talking" pictures, a pipe organ, 437 seats, and an innovative cooling and heating system. (Thomas Reeves collection.)

Seven

CHAUTAUQUA DAYS

"The Nebraska Chautauqua Assembly is one of the most promising offshoots of that grand, majestic institution at Chautauqua, New York," read the 1888 *Nebraska Chautauqua Assembly Programme, Crete, Nebraska.*

This proclamation described the seven-year-old Crete assembly in an 1888 booklet, published by the Nebraska Sunday School Assembly, advertising the upcoming weeklong summer event. Crete's program was patterned after the national Chautauqua movement created at Lake Chautauqua, New York, in 1874 to educate Sunday school teachers and encourage moral and spiritual instruction rather than blatant entertainment. Crete's assembly was, for a time, second in size only to the mother Chautauqua in New York. The annual event generated thousands of visitors and many nationally known speakers and performers.

The Nebraska Sunday School Assembly was created in 1882 soon after a small summer gathering was held at Crete's First Congregational Church. After a successful second assembly, a large tract of land along the Big Blue River near the railroad line in west Crete was platted as a permanent Chautauqua park and first used in 1884.

By the late 1880s, Crete's Chautauqua Park, designed by Frank and William Hunt, who created the original Chautauqua grounds in New York, boasted more than 20 permanent buildings and cottages constructed by special interest groups and private citizens. Hundreds of participants, including local residents, kept house in tents and cottages during assembly week, and the railroad annually operated a temporary depot nearby for the convenience of Chautauqua attendees.

Crete's assembly included lectures, workshops, sermons, games, boating and swimming in the river, and religious and patriotic musical performances. Famous Nebraskans, including William Jennings Bryan and Willa Cather, participated in the Crete Chautauqua.

Crete's Chautauqua attendance waned in the late 1890s, purportedly because leaders were reluctant to diverge from the emphasis on instruction and moral edification, while other regional assemblies included more entertainment. The movement diminished nationwide when entertainment such as vaudeville, movies, radio, and later automobile travel became preferred leisure activities. Crete's Chautauqua Park was sold, became Vavra's Park, and later was named Tuxedo Park in 1926. Only the original eight-sided Chautauqua office building remains on the site.

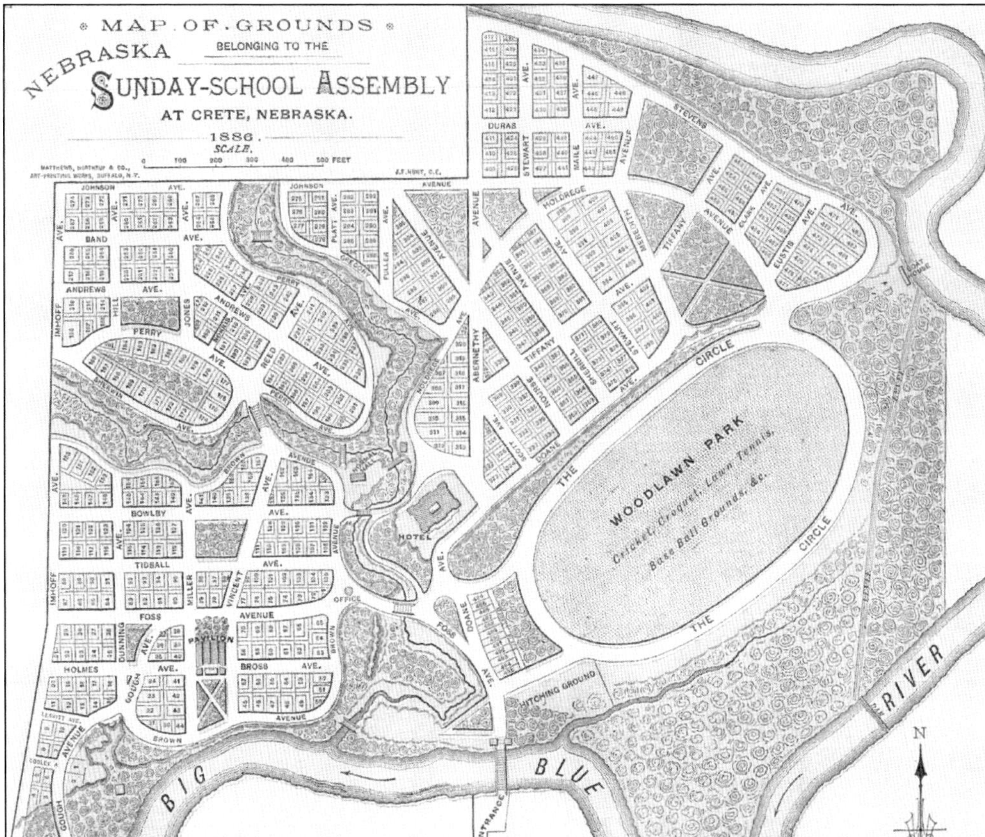

NEBRASKA
Sunday-School Assembly
THE CHAUTAUQUA OF NEBRASKA.
CAPITAL STOCK, - - $50,000.
EXTENSIVE GROUNDS ON THE BLUE RIVER, NEAR CRETE.
AMPLE BUILDINGS.
Able Lecturers and Teachers in Normal and Musical Courses.
DEPARTMENTS OPEN TO ALL DENOMINATIONS.
$2,500 APPROPRIATED FOR PROGRAMME OF 1886.

TO THOSE INTERESTED IN THE SUNDAY-SCHOOLS OF NEBRASKA.

The unequalled rapidity of material development, the high position attained by our State in educational interests, the many churches and philanthropic institutions arising everywhere within our borders, are sufficient guarantees of the deep interest taken in every worthy enterprise.

It is within the present century, and almost in the last decade, that the first provisions were made to mitigate the loss of early opportunities by the establishment of Reading Circles and Assemblies at pleasant summer resorts, where talent comprehending the needs was employed as lecturers and teachers.

THE LOCATION OF OUR CHAUTAUQUA.

Chautauqua is loved by thousands of our citizens for the advantages it has given them. Its locality is far from us; very few at this distance can ever enter its choice retreats, but its principles are capable of being made known and taught at the Chautauqua of the West—the Nebraska Sunday-School Assembly grounds, located on the banks of the Big Blue River, near Crete.

These grounds contain 109½ acres, especially adapted by Nature for one of the finest summer resorts in all the West.

Natural scenery, enhanced by the power of wealth, art and religion, has made the original Chautauqua what it is, and will make ours the favorite retreat for the people of Nebraska.

THE PRESENT DEVELOPMENT OF OUR CHAUTAUQUA.

$10,000 has already been raised and used in beautifying and improving these grounds and erecting a Pavilion, Normal Hall, *Auditorium*, Head-quarters, Dormitory and Dining Hall—all connected by plank walks.

ITS FUTURE DEVELOPMENT.

The grounds have been surveyed, platted and laid out by one of the most skillful and experienced landscape architects in the country—J. F. Hunt, who has charge of the Chautauqua grounds, and whose skill has so greatly developed and improved that magnificent place. There are already a number of applicants for lots, who will soon erect cottages thereon.

THE CO-OPERATION AND THE MANAGEMENT.

Perfect catholicity of spirit has existed among the different denominations with reference to all pertaining to these grounds.

Several denominations have already decided to erect at an early date *denominational head-quarters* on lots set apart for that purpose.

The management rests in a board of twenty-one trustees, selected from the different denominations, nominated by the stockholders and confirmed by the board.

THE PROGRAMME.

In 1885 $1,200 was expended on the programme, and $2,500 has been voted for the year 1886.

Rev. A. E. Dunning of Boston, Mass., who has had large experience in connection with eastern assemblies, has been appointed manager. Such talent as John B. Gough, John A. Logan and other eminent lecturers, teachers and divines, will be employed by him.

ITS FINANCIAL PROVISIONS AND NEEDS.

The capital stock is $50,000, divided into shares of $10 each. It is the earnest desire of the management to place this stock in the hands of the many and not in the hands of a few. An effort will be made to distribute these shares in every town in the State, and your assistance to this end is solicited. Only ten per cent. of the stock must be paid down, and not more than thirty-five per cent. can be assessed in any one year, though paid-up stock is preferred. Will you kindly act with us in this good work? Money and names for stock can be sent to the Treasurer, A. W. Jones, of Crete, Neb., who will at once forward certificate therefor.

F. I. FOSS, President, CRETE, NEB.
C. H. ABERNETHY, Secretary, FAIRMONT, NEB.
A. W. JONES, Treasurer, CRETE, NEB.

This 1886 plat of the Crete Chautauqua grounds was used for promotion and to lease building lots to organizations desiring a permanent headquarters on the site. Private individuals could also choose rental spaces for tent camping and lease lots upon which to build permanent cottages. The original map is colorized, giving it an attractive, easy-to-read appearance. (Author's collection.)

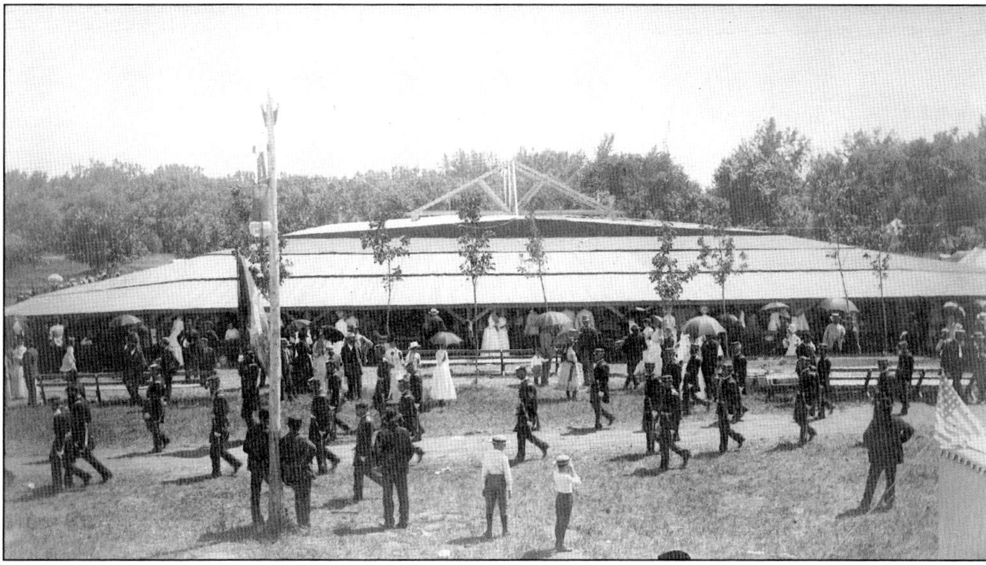

This open-air pavilion, erected in 1884, served as the main gathering place during summer assemblies. Capable of sheltering about 1,000 people, it was the largest facility in the park. It was situated on a north-south axis at the south end of the park near the river, about where a later roller-skating rink and dance hall stood until recent years. (CHS, F.I. Foss collection.)

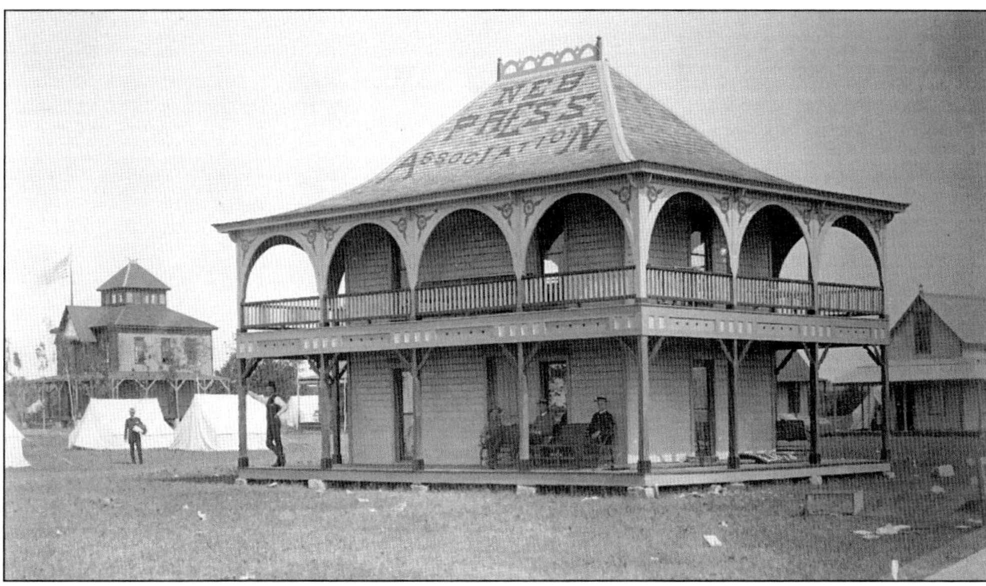

The Nebraska Press Association built this permanent headquarters on the Crete assembly grounds for newspaper editors and publishers. Commonly known as Editors Hall, it cost $679 to build in 1887. During the 1894 assembly, Willa Cather taught classes in practical newspaper work there. It was home to the Anton Vavra family from 1899 to 1926, when they owned the park, and was razed in 1962. (CHS, F.I. Foss collection.)

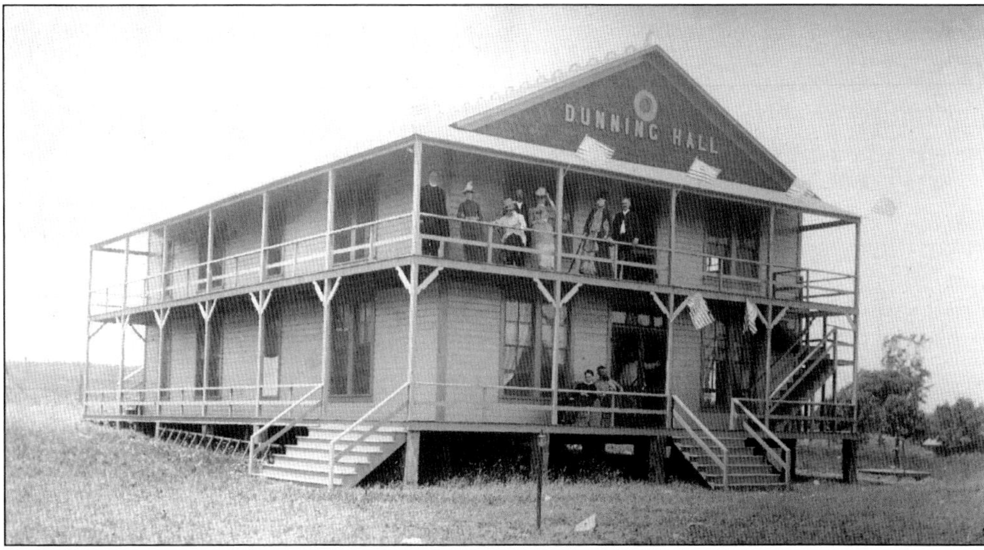

Dunning Hall, built in 1888, was named for Rev. A.E. Dunning of Boston, the superintendent of instruction for the Crete Assembly. It was used as a lodge for Chautauqua speakers. Willa Cather stayed there during the July 1894 session and claimed in a *Lincoln Evening News* article that it was the "most audible building it has ever been my misfortune to dwell in." (CHS, F.I. Foss collection.)

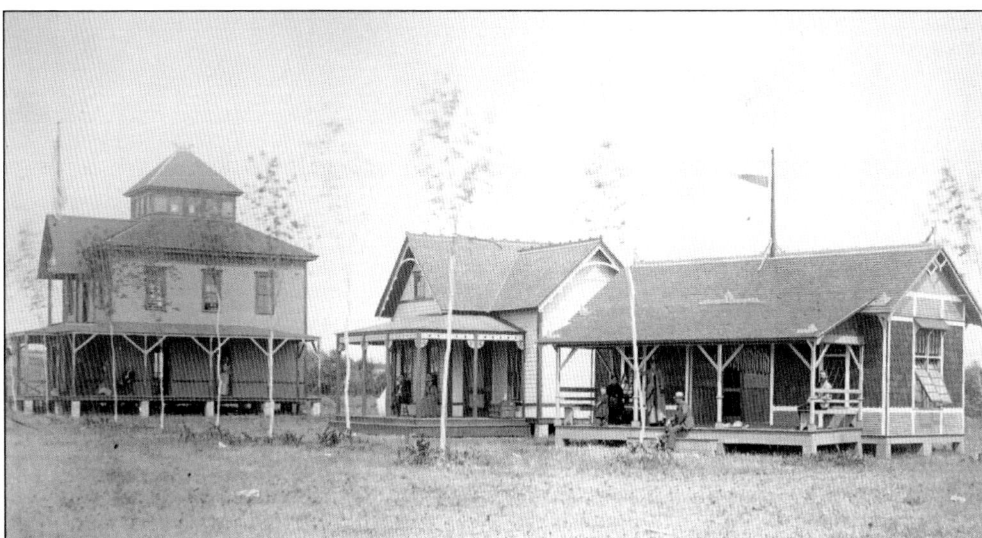
This view of the assembly grounds shows the Lawyers Union (at left) and two smaller cottages. Many cottages were built by people from other cities and states who wanted a permanent place to stay during the assemblies. Building lots were leased by individuals who then owned their cottages. (CHS, F.I. Foss collection.)

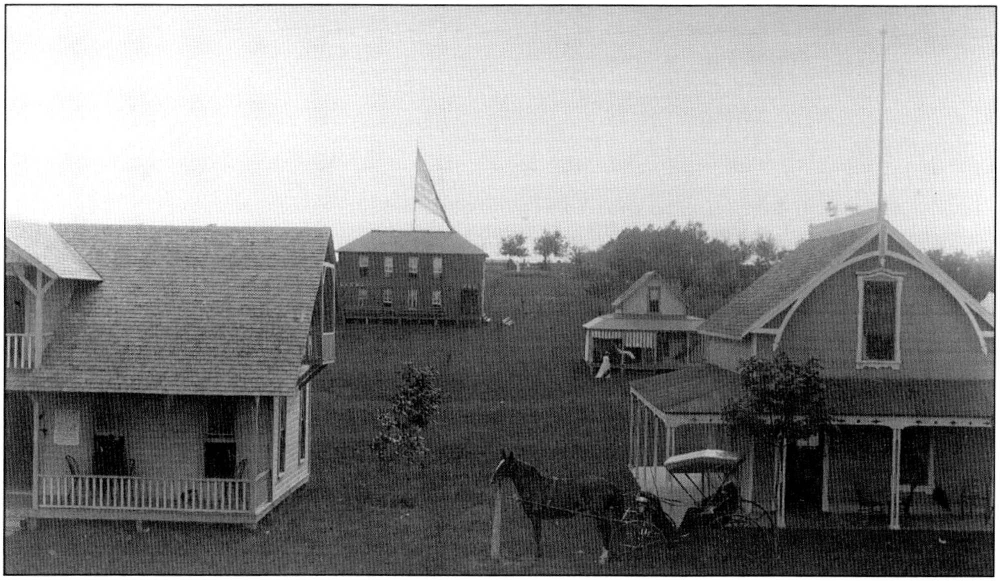

The cottages and buildings on the assembly grounds were often rather whimsical in design and were painted in a variety of colors. Floor plans included large porches that encouraged outdoor living. (CHS, F.I. Foss collection.)

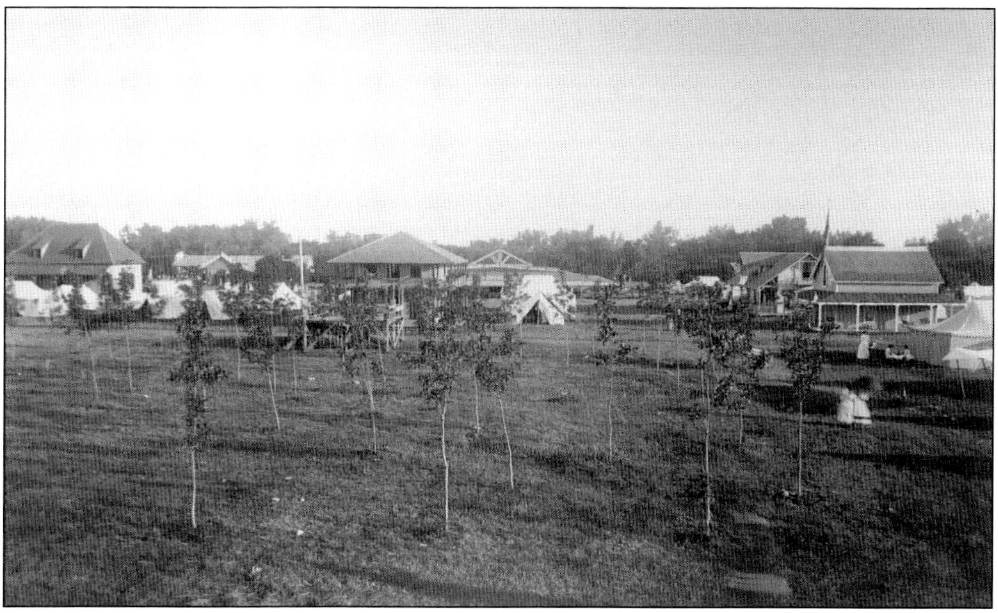

This photograph of the grounds was taken looking south toward the Big Blue River. The triangular roof structure of the pavilion is visible in the tree line. Tents were pitched among the cottages and buildings. Chautauqua officials had an ongoing landscape design program during the 1880s; note the small grove of newly planted trees in the foreground. (CHS, F.I. Foss collection.)

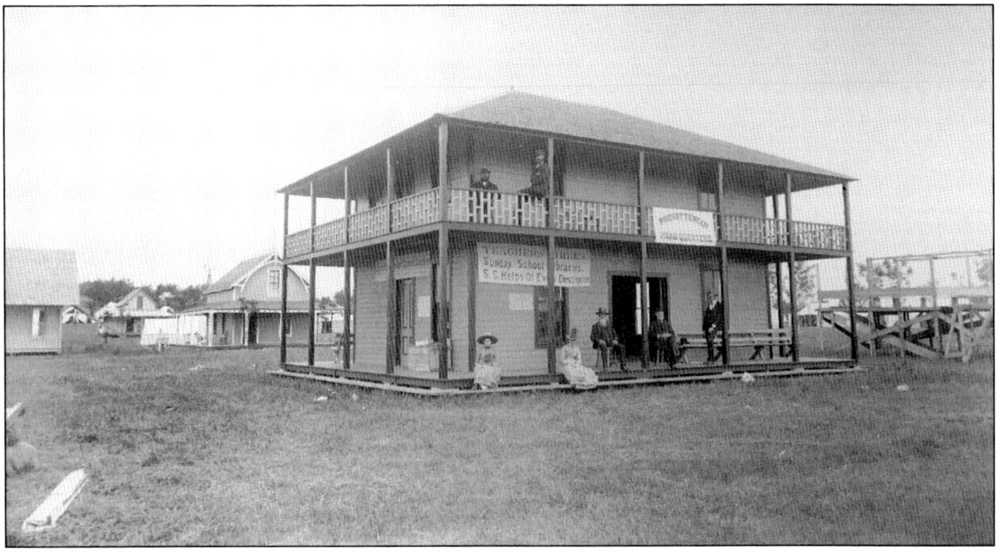

The Presbyterian headquarters building was completed in 1888. As with all permanent buildings constructed for special interest groups, fundraising for this structure was widespread, and not just a local effort. This structure featured a porch on each level surrounding all four facades. (CHS, F.I. Foss collection.)

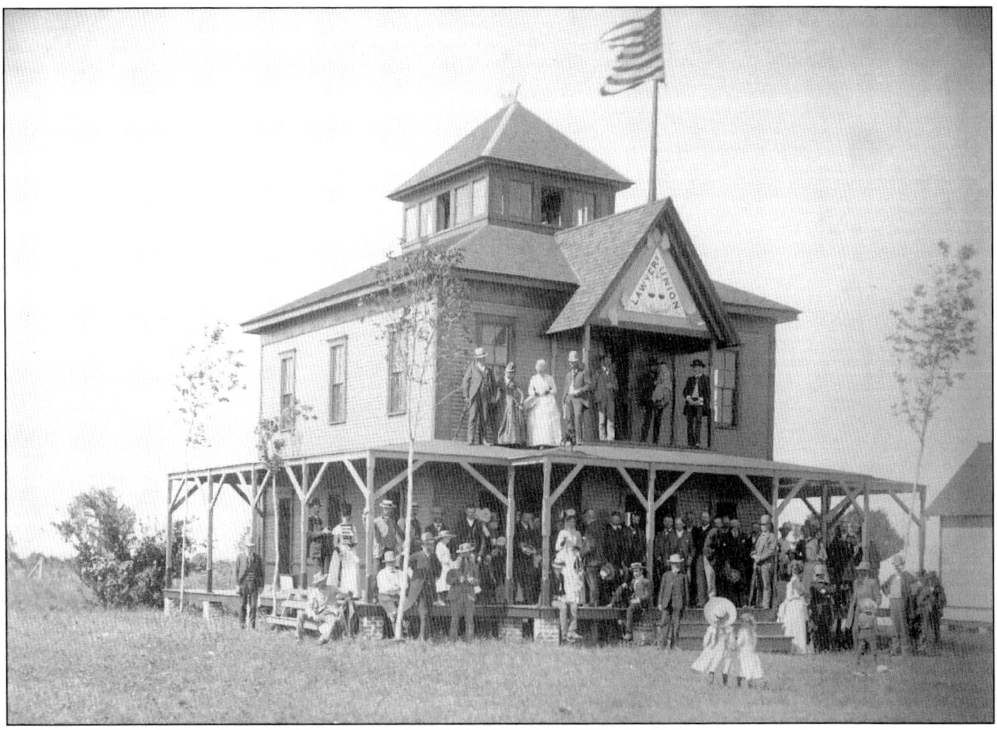

Nebraska lawyers paid for the construction of this building, known as Lawyers Union or Blackstone Hall. It was one of the largest structures on the grounds. All lawyers attending Chautauqua were welcome. Other organizations that constructed permanent buildings were the Congregationalists, Methodists, Episcopalians, the GAR, the YMCA, and the Women's Christian Temperance Union. (CHS, F.I. Foss collection.)

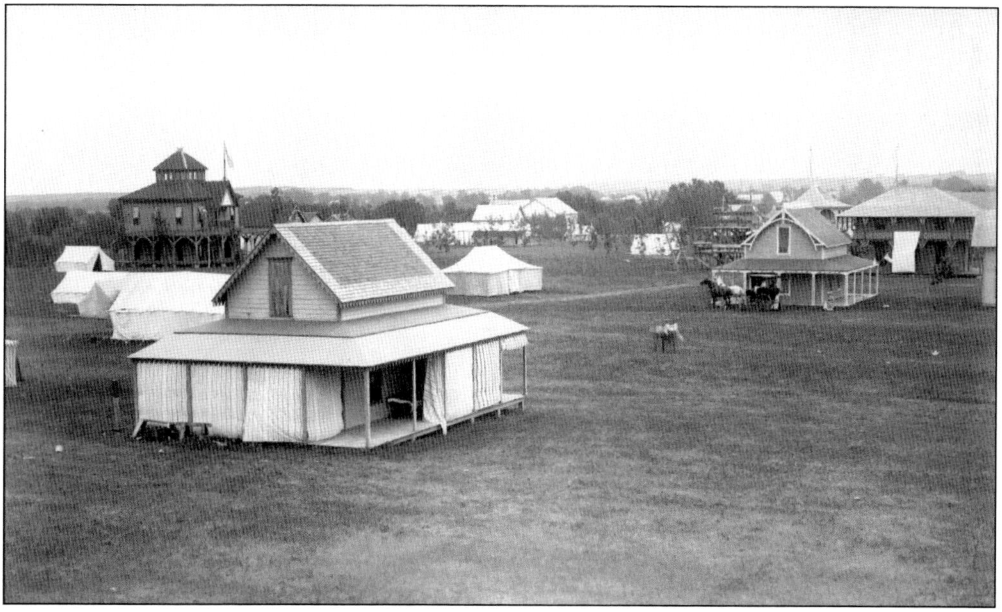

This view of the grounds shows an array of cottages and tents. The Lawyers Union is in the upper left, and the Presbyterian headquarters is on the right. Most porches were equipped with curtains as protection from the elements. On June 7, 1888, the *Globe* newspaper reported that 200 tent sites had been reserved. (CHS, F.I. Foss collection.)

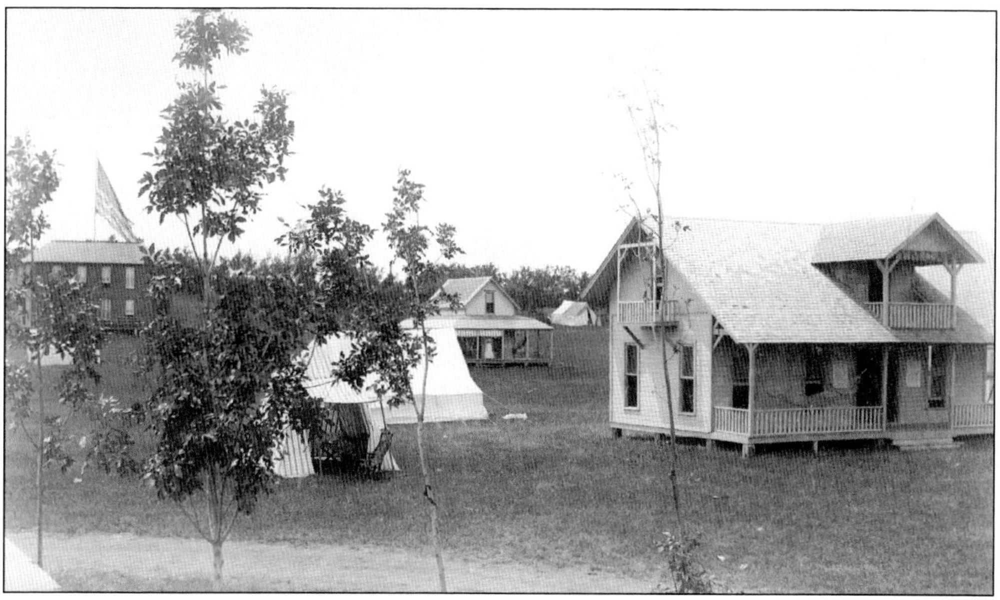

Most Chautauqua attendees could not afford to build permanent cottages, so they either brought their tents and camping gear or rented those items from local merchants. The Burlington Missouri River Railroad shipped camping equipment at no charge for out-of-towners attending the assemblies, making it easier to set up housekeeping. (CHS, F.I. Foss collection.)

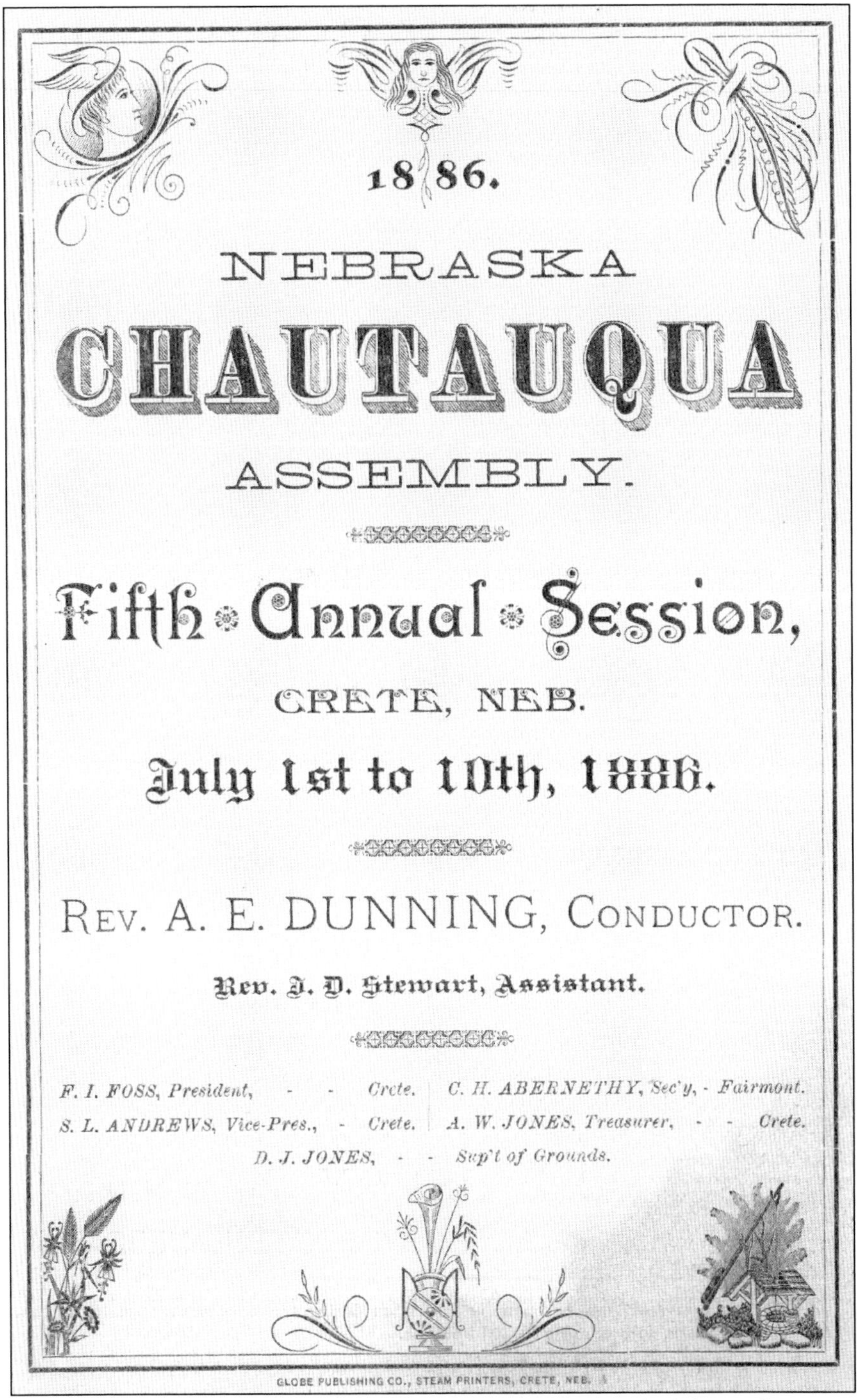

1886.

NEBRASKA

CHAUTAUQUA

ASSEMBLY.

Fifth Annual Session,

CRETE, NEB.

July 1st to 10th, 1886.

REV. A. E. DUNNING, CONDUCTOR.

Rev. J. D. Stewart, Assistant.

F. I. FOSS, President, - - *Crete.* | *C. H. ABERNETHY, Sec'y,* - *Fairmont.*
S. L. ANDREWS, Vice-Pres., - *Crete.* | *A. W. JONES, Treasurer,* - - *Crete.*
D. J. JONES, - - *Sup't of Grounds.*

GLOBE PUBLISHING CO., STEAM PRINTERS, CRETE, NEB.

Each year, elaborate, detailed programs were printed with daily schedules, information about speakers and classes, and advertisements by local merchants. These booklets were used as guides during the assembly and were also widely distributed across the state and region well in advance of the event to encourage attendance. This 1886 program was produced by the local *Globe* newspaper print shop. (DCA.)

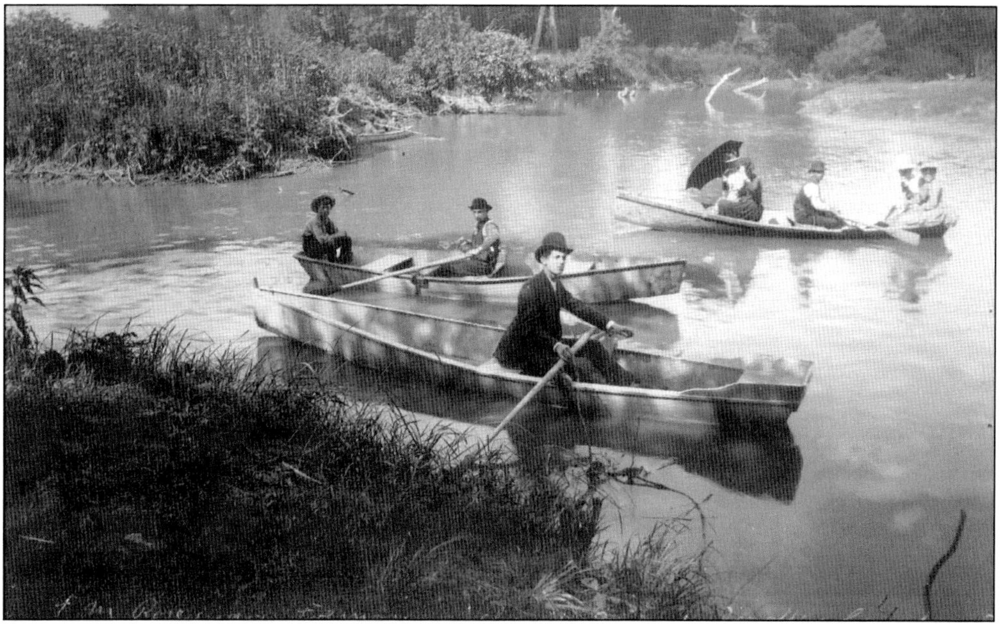

Recreational activities were also part of the Chautauqua experience. Boating on the Big Blue River and lawn games were popular leisure diversions from the more serious lectures and workshops. Note that the participants were quite dressed up during these activities. (Both, F.I. Foss collection.)

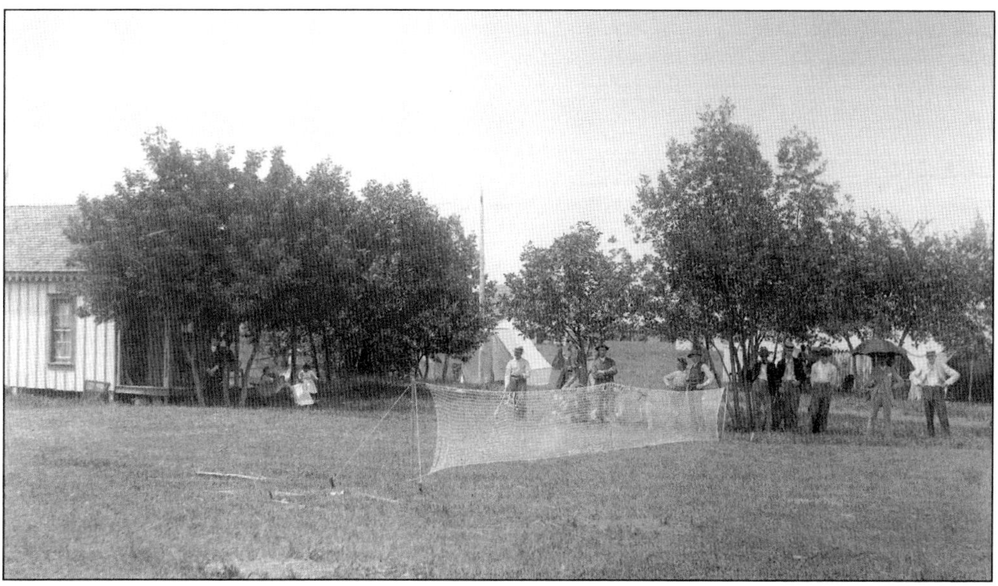

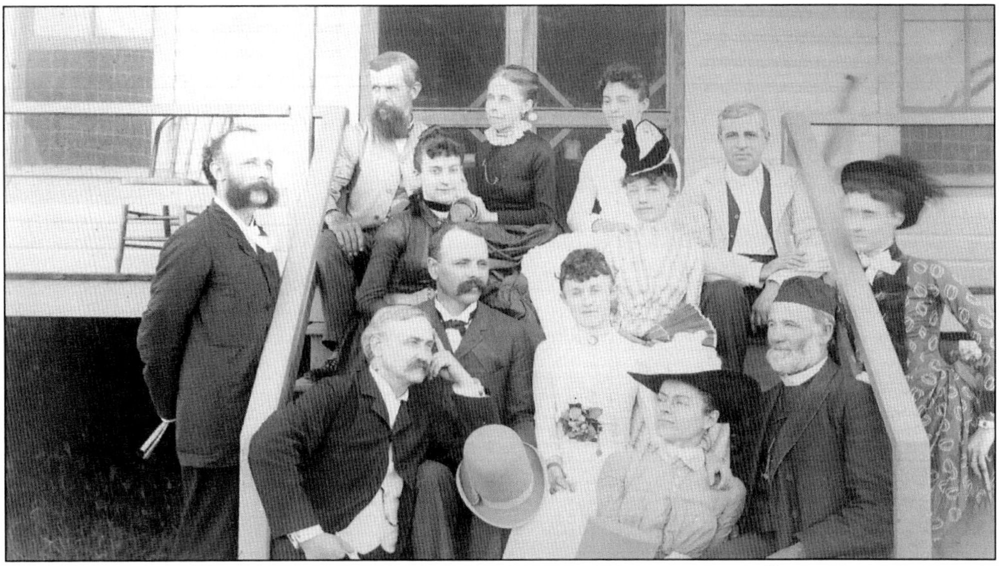

A group of Chautauqua participants poses on the steps of Dunning Hall in 1888. Horace M. Wells, a Crete newspaper editor, is seated at lower left. (CHS, F.I. Foss collection.)

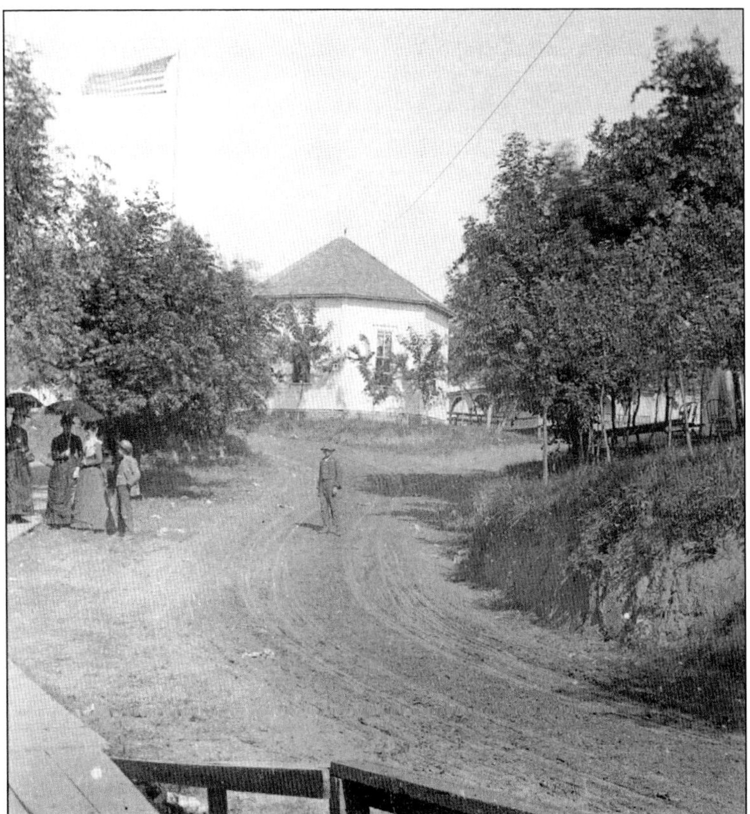

This eight-sided building was the office and information booth during assemblies and was situated just inside the grounds. In later years, after the Saline County Fair moved to the park, this structure was again used as an office and fair headquarters. The building still stands in Tuxedo Park but in a new location. It is the last remnant of the Nebraska Chautauqua. (CHS, F.I. Foss collection.)

Eight

Personalities

Community building on the 19th-century frontier created social and economic challenges, and the diverse backgrounds of early town founders made life interesting. In Crete, the mix of German and Bohemian immigrant customs with the New England culture of the Doane College founders made for a fascinating blend. The unshaped social structure of the new community put most residents on even ground as they worked to build Crete, and a class system was not particularly relevant. Anyone who worked hard could rise to a position of leadership and become a commercial entrepreneur, city administrator, or other community leader.

Activities at Doane College brought assorted educated people to town, some of whom stayed and made Crete their permanent residence. The Nebraska Chautauqua Assembly also brought many prominent state and national religious leaders, scholars, and businessmen to Crete each year prior to and during the 10-day assemblies. Chautauqua visitors—often wealthy, urban individuals—integrated with the local citizens to work toward the success of the event. In many cases, these people became lifelong friends of Crete residents.

In Crete, language barriers were prevalent for the first several years, but citizens worked to remedy that issue. Doane College president David Brainerd Perry taught himself German and Bohemian to communicate with, and recruit, children of local settlers to attend Doane. Edward Steidl, a local druggist of Czech descent, bought a cash register that printed receipts in English, German, and Bohemian. Prominent civil engineer Thomas Doane of Boston worked side by side with local immigrant laborers and businessmen to construct the railroad and several campus buildings, create a bank, and nourish the local Congregational Church.

The following pages will introduce the reader to several of Crete's influential citizens, many of whom were here already in the late 1860s and early 1870s, when Crete was a rough frontier town. The choice to include these specific people does not diminish the significance of other Crete leaders not shown in this work.

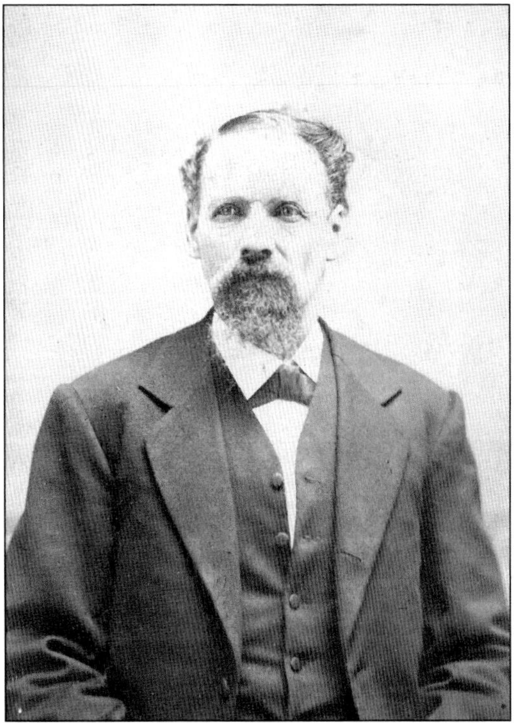

Jesse C. Bickle homesteaded on land that became part of Crete. He and his family came from Ohio in 1863 and first lived in a dugout on the banks of the Big Blue River. The next year he built a log cabin, and soon after he was named postmaster of the new town. He was a farmer, stock raiser, and energetic community builder. (CHS.)

Elizabeth Hunt Bickle was Jesse Bickle's second wife and stepmother to his four children. She also helped in the post office in their cabin. The Bickle farm in west Crete became a gathering place that gained some notoriety. An early Fourth of July party purportedly drew hundreds of visitors from a 40-mile radius and included much eating, imbibing, and dancing. (CHS.)

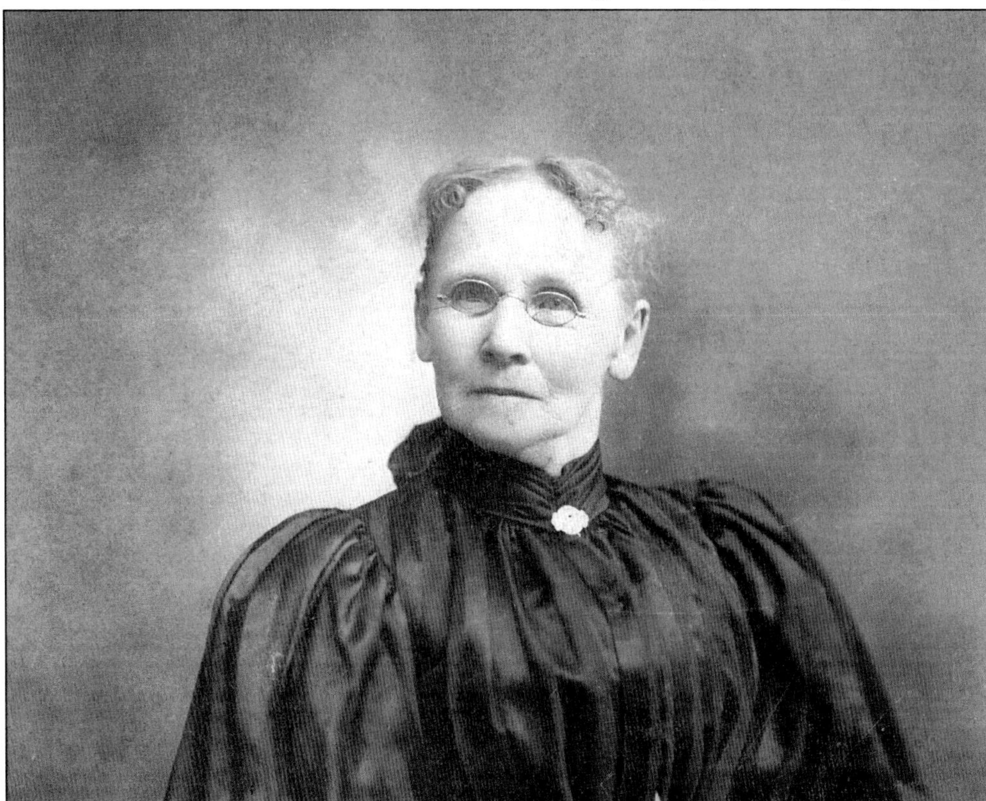

Joseph Francl, the first documented Bohemian immigrant to enter Nebraska, came through Crete in 1854 en route to the California Gold Rush. His mining was unsuccessful, so he homesteaded near Crete in 1870 and opened a trading post at Twelfth Street and Maine Avenue. Francl left again in 1874 to search for riches but unfortunately died in 1875 in Oregon. His great-grandson was longtime Crete resident James Francl Krebs. (CHS.)

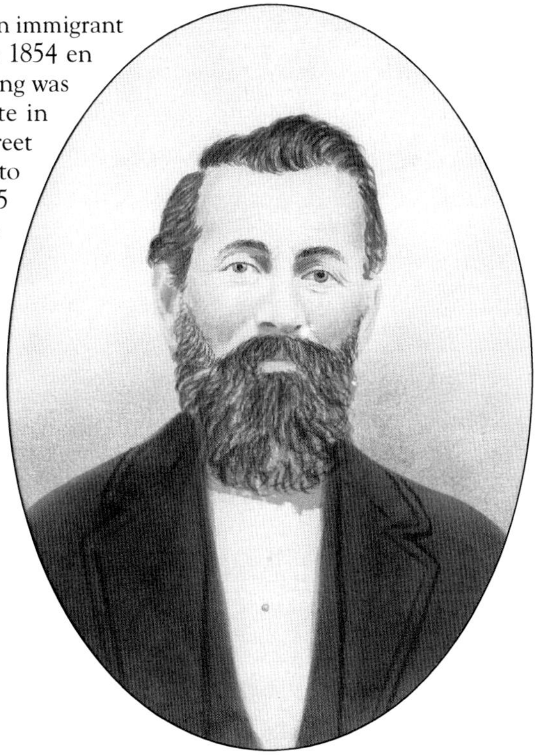

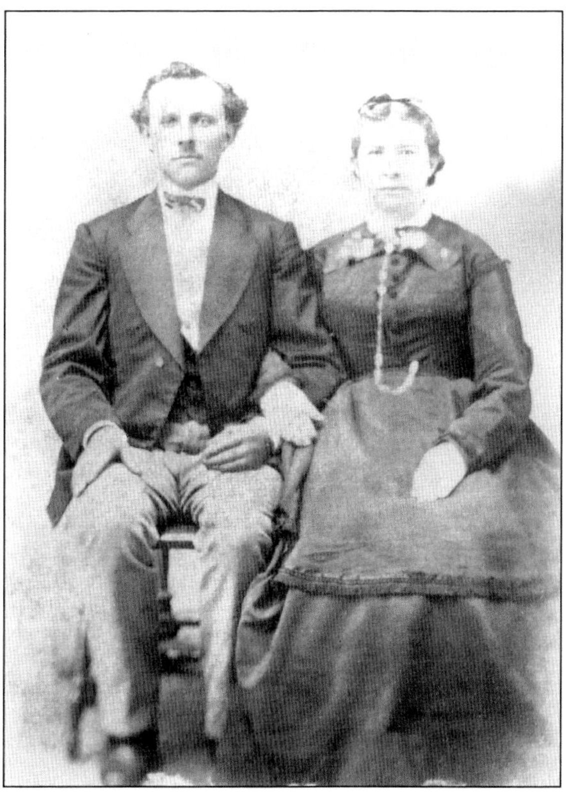

Theodore H. and Mary George Miller were early town founders. The town of Crete, east of Maine Avenue and south of Thirteenth Street, was platted on Mary's homestead. Theodore Miller came to Crete in 1871 and was a farmer, ran a general store, served as mayor, dealt in real estate, and was a generous philanthropist. He cofounded the Crete State Bank in 1897. The Millers were members of Bethlehem Lutheran Church. (Miller family collection.)

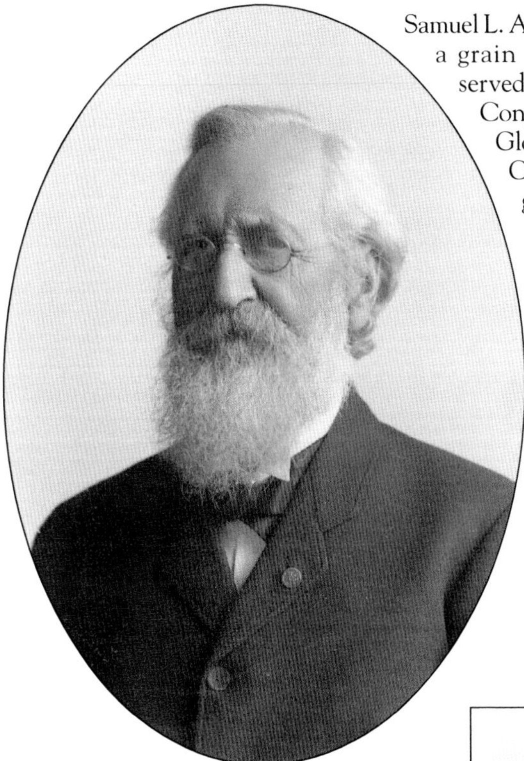

Samuel L. Andrews settled in Crete in 1877 and established a grain business. A Civil War veteran, Andrews served as mayor of Crete and was postmaster, a First Congregational Church member, and president of Globe Publishing Company. He was also a Doane College trustee and chairman of the building and grounds committee as well as an officer of the Nebraska Chautauqua Assembly. He and his wife, Frances, had four children. (DCA.)

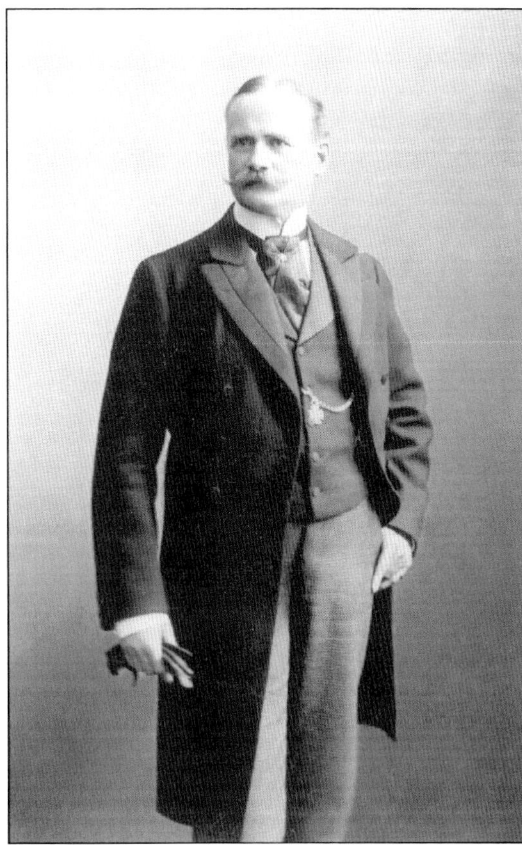

Dr. Arthur Conrad emigrated from Germany in 1876 and attended medical school in St. Louis. En route to California in 1880, his trip was stalled by a train wreck in Crete. Dr. Conrad assisted the injured and was persuaded to stay in town, where he set up a medical practice, married Dora Broz of Wilber, and raised a family. The Conrads resided at 1126 Hawthorne Avenue. (Carol Casteel Ator collection.)

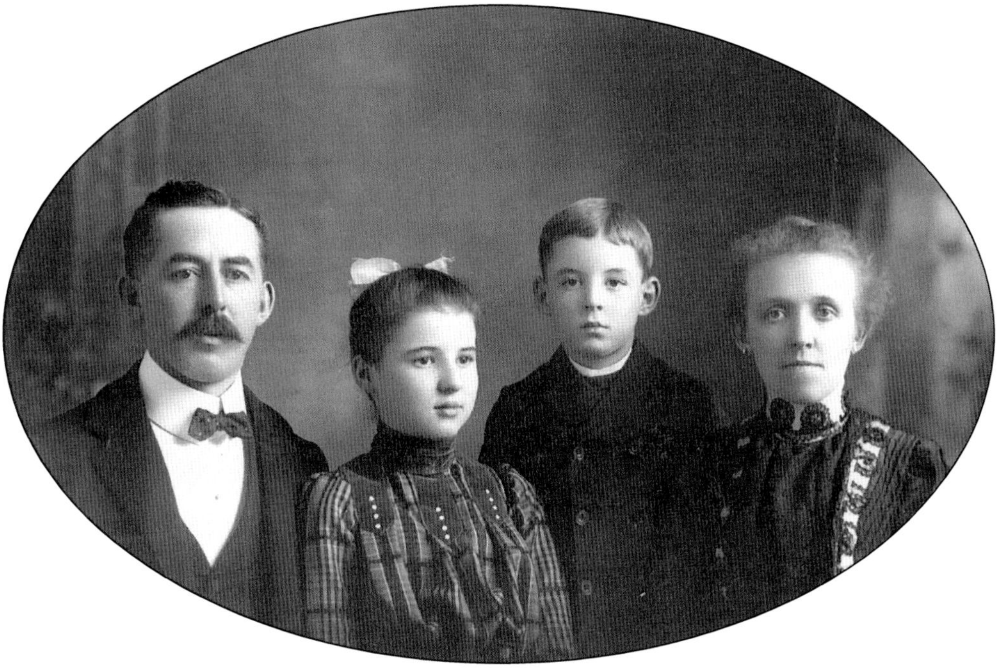

Charles B. Anderson was a Crete banker, a three-term state legislator, a University of Nebraska regent, and a state insurance commissioner. He and his father-in-law, T.H. Miller, organized Crete State Bank. Before that, Anderson had been in the banking business in DeWitt, Nebraska. He and his wife, Mathilda, had six children, including Olsie (second from left) and DeLos, shown here with their parents. The family home still stands at 709 East Eleventh Street. (CHS.)

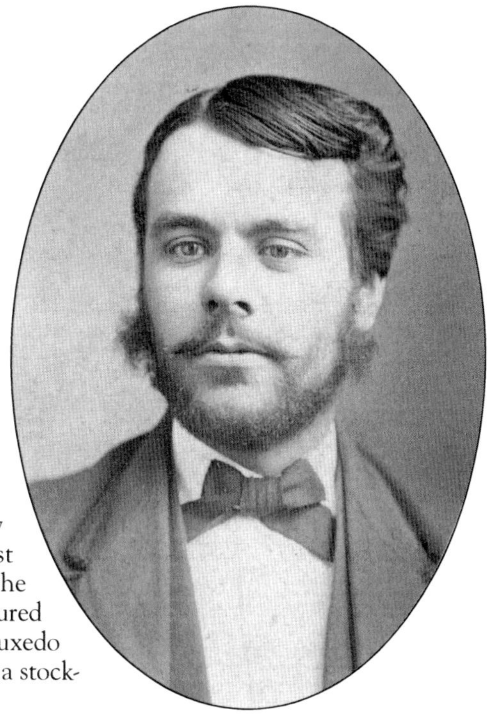

Fayette Ingersoll Foss was admitted to the bar in Vermont in 1878 and came to Crete soon afterward. He practiced law, was a community developer, was active in politics and the First Congregational Church, and was president of the Chautauqua Assembly for several years. Foss secured the land that became Chautauqua Park (now Tuxedo Park). He was also John R. Johnston's partner in a stock-raising business. (CHS.)

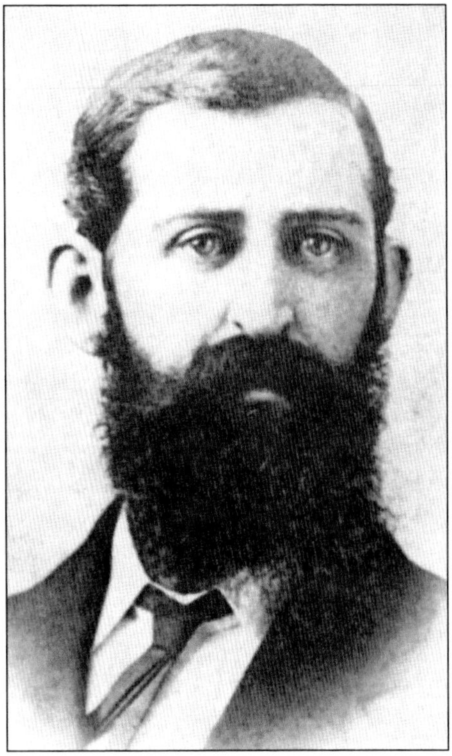

Two-term Nebraska governor James W. Dawes was a Crete attorney and businessman who originally came to Crete in 1871 and opened a mercantile store. Later, he established a law practice, became a state senator, and began his first term as governor in 1883. Dawes returned to Crete in 1887, resumed his law practice, and also dealt in real estate. He resided at 941 Grove Avenue. (Author's collection.)

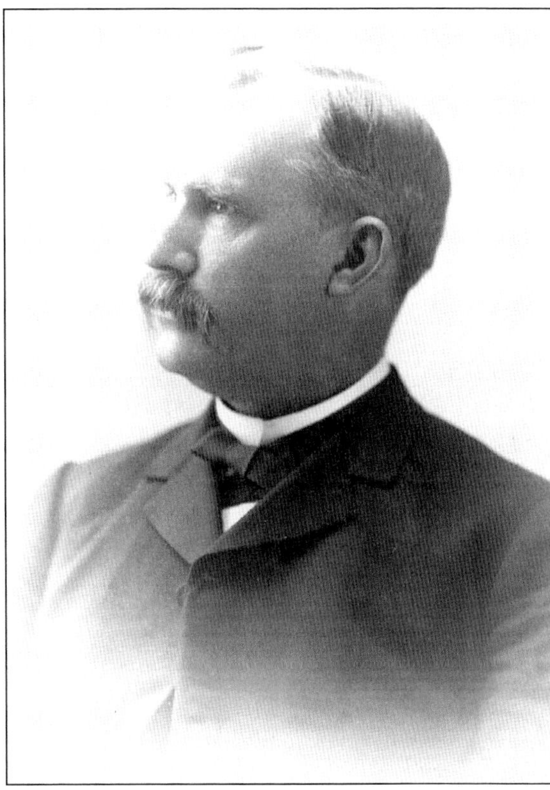

Judge William Morris came to Crete in 1872 and became a significant figure in state and local government. He practiced law and was a district attorney and district court judge. Morris also served as mayor of Crete for several years. The Morrises were members of Trinity Memorial Episcopal Church and often hosted social events at their home at 1039 Forest Avenue. They retired to California in 1898. (CHS, Wallace collection.)

Editor and lawyer Horace M. Wells arrived in Crete in 1873. He and a partner bought the *Saline County Post* newspaper and developed it into the *Crete Vidette*. Wells was Crete's first fire chief, mayor, state senator, state bank examiner, and postmaster. Wells married Harriet Code, the daughter of hotel proprietor Henry Code, and the Wells family lived in the Code mansion at 1120 East Thirteenth Street. (Author's collection.)

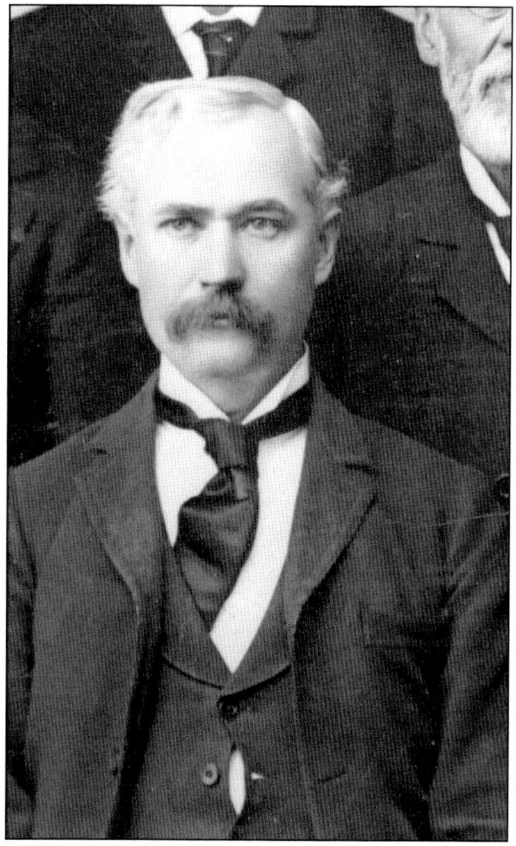

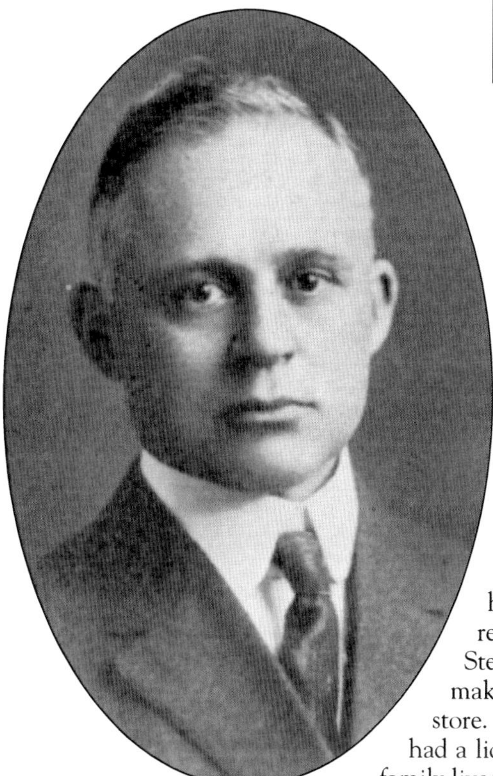

Edward J. Steidl, a Bohemian druggist, received his pharmacy degree in Philadelphia in 1886 and returned to his native Crete to open Steidl Drug. Steidl was known for innovative marketing, frequently making improvements and adding new signage to his store. He created a perfume, Steidl's Clarene, and also had a liquor license for medicinal purposes. He and his family lived at 1242 Hawthorne Avenue. (CHS.)

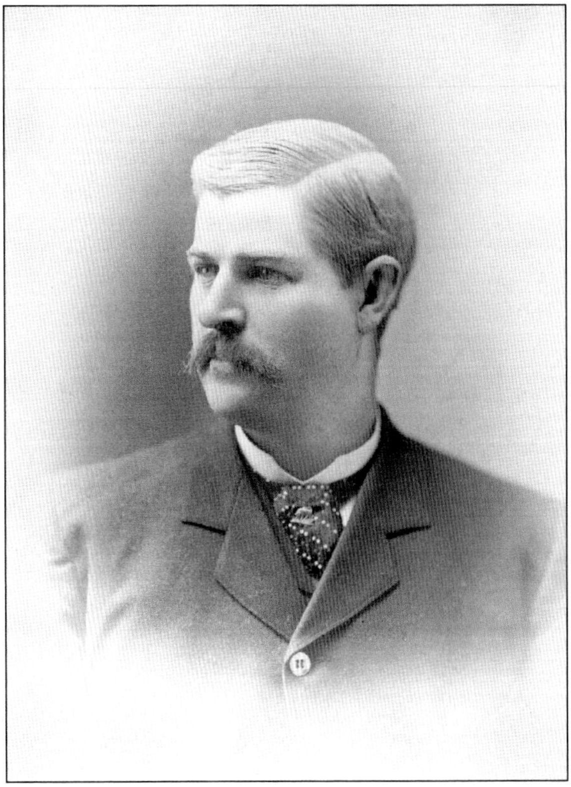

John R. Johnston homesteaded near Crete in 1870 and became an enthusiastic town builder. He was an early postmaster, stock-raiser, and speculator and owned the Crete Mills with his father-in-law, George W. Bridges. In 1885, Johnston purchased interest in the State Bank of Nebraska and became president. He and a partner, George Stevens, built the waterworks system. Johnston retired to California in 1894 after a bank scandal. (CHS.)

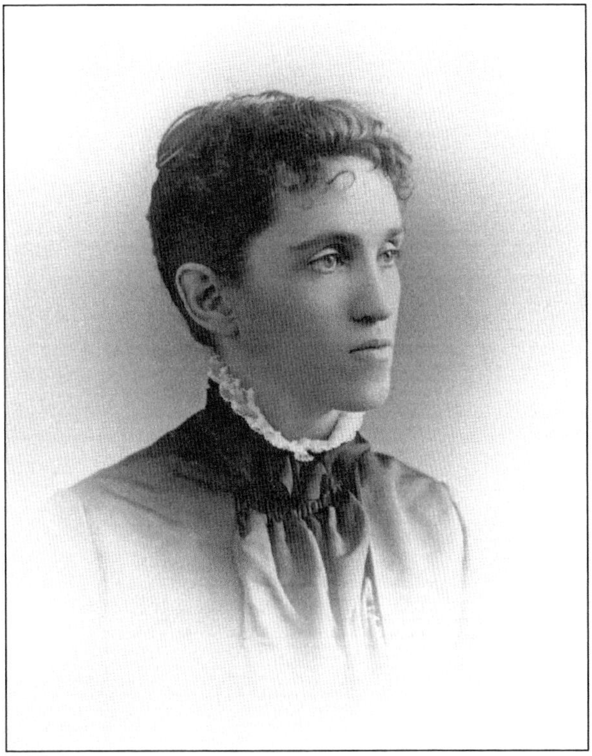

Ida Bridges Johnston was the daughter of Crete Mills founder George W. Bridges. The Bridges family lived near the lower milldam at Fifth Street and Norman Avenue. Ida Bridges and John R. Johnston married in 1873. The couple belonged to Trinity Memorial Episcopal Church and often hosted church dignitaries and other visitors at their grand home at 1422 Boswell Avenue on Prospect Hill. (Author's collection.)

John L. Tidball came to Crete in 1870 from Pennsylvania. He was a longtime merchant who first had a general store and then went into the lumber business. Tidball was president of the First National Bank, a Doane College trustee, and a school board member. Tidball and his family resided in a brick Italianate house at 1112 Forest Avenue on College Hill, which he built in 1880. (CHS.)

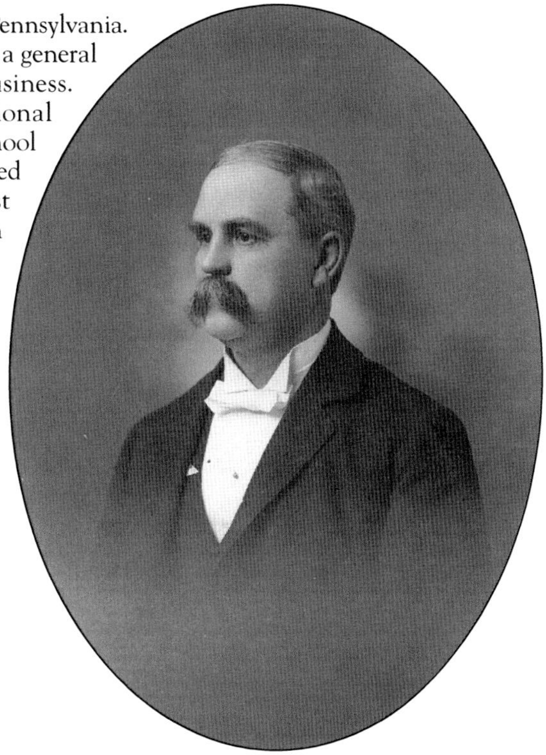

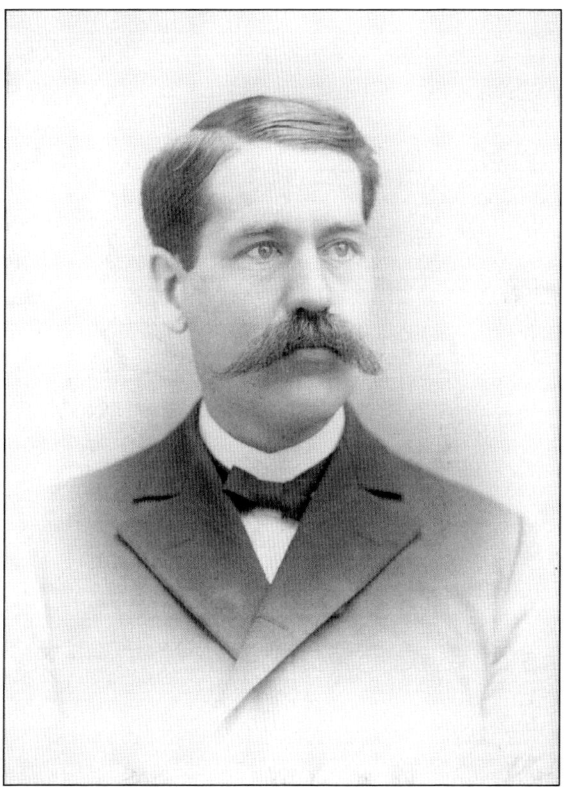

George A. Gregory served as a teacher and school administrator in various places before joining the Crete school system. He was superintendent from 1900 to 1909 and then became the state normal training inspector. An advocate of manual training, Gregory created the Crete Plan in Domestic Science in 1909, which was adopted statewide. He also organized the Crete Boy Scout troop in 1911. (DCA.)

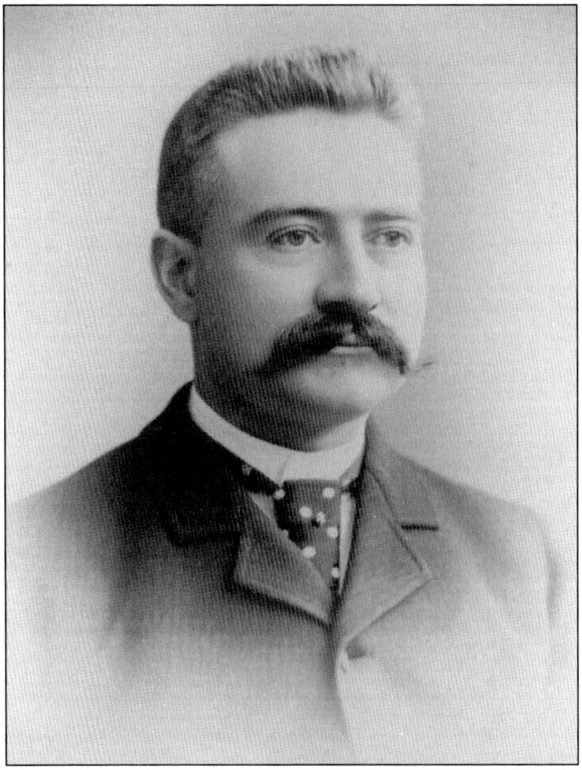

Vermont native George D. Stevens moved to Crete in 1879 and became cashier of the State Bank of Nebraska. The Stevens family was active socially, and George was a talented vocalist. In 1892, Stevens disappeared while on a business trip. The State Bank crashed and evidence suggested that his partner, John R. Johnston, perhaps positioned him to take the fall for the struggling bank. George Stevens was never found. (Author's collection.)

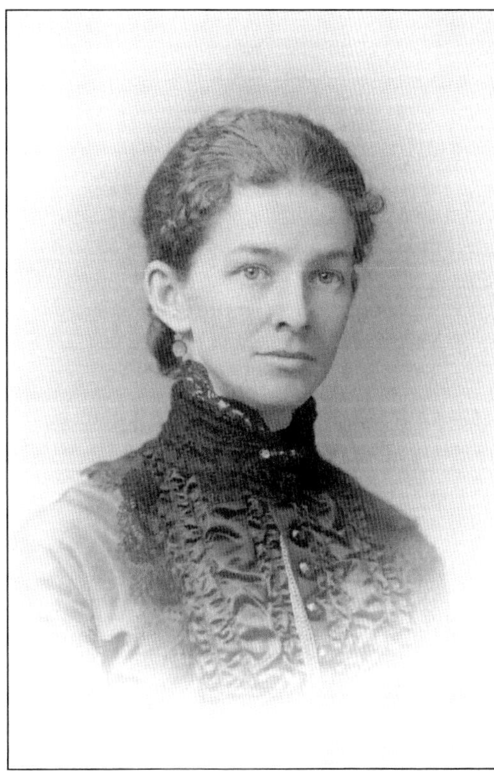

Jennie Chapman Stevens, George's wife, was a member of the First Congregational Church and a charter member of Wednesday Club. Called "the songbird," she was church choir director and performed as a soloist and in vocal ensembles for church and community events. Several photographs in this book are from an album she created as a Christmas gift for her Vermont relatives in 1900. (CHS, Wednesday Club collection.)

Michigan native Frank Osborn came to Geneva, Nebraska, in the late 1870s and worked in hotels before coming to Crete to be a porter in the new Cosmopolitan Hotel. In 1883, he bought the local hack company and launched a 40-year career meeting trains and hauling merchandise and passengers to destinations in town. Osborn's dog, Beauty, pictured at right, was killed after being run over by a dray wagon in 1899. The *Crete Vidette* printed an obituary for the dog that described Beauty as a great dog with unusual coloring. Osborn died in 1923 at the age of 68 and is buried in Riverside Cemetery. (Right, CHS; below, *Crete News* collection.)

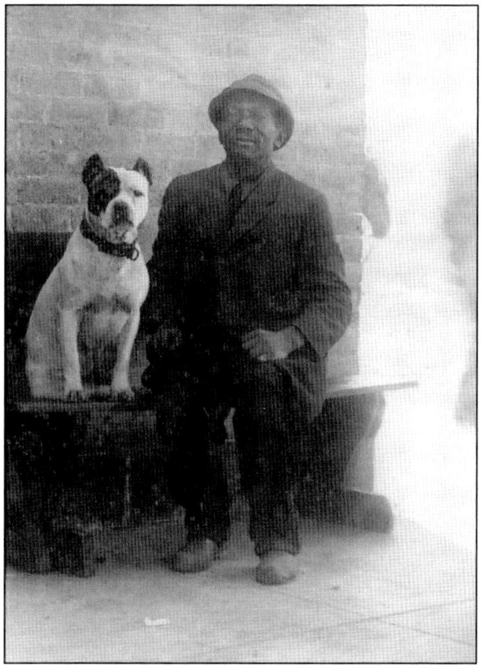

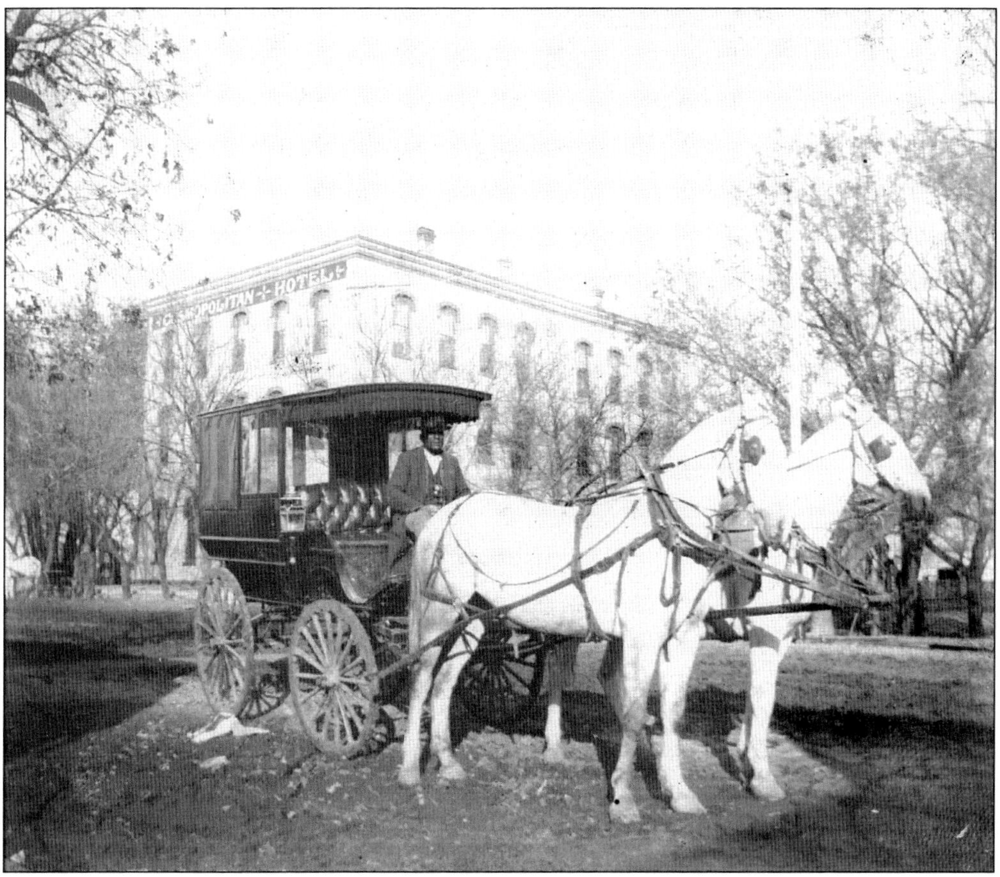

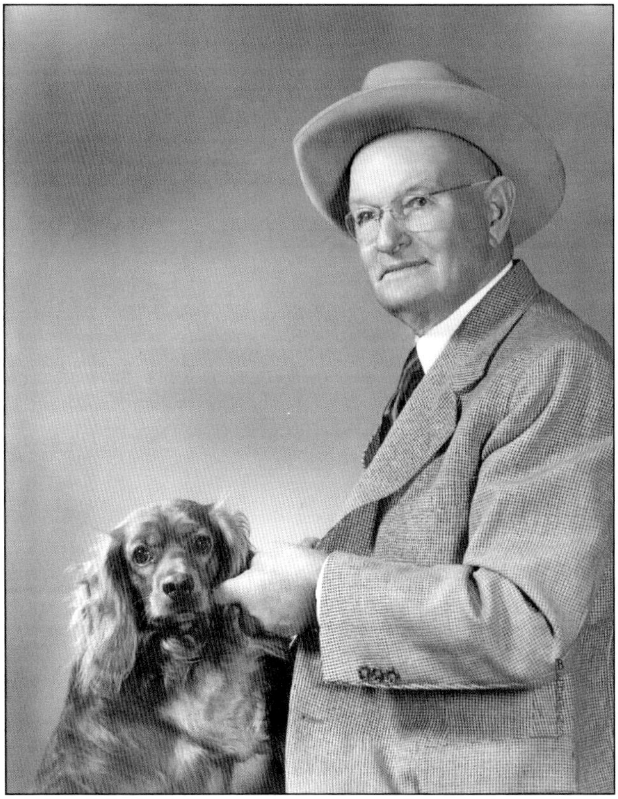

Milton O. Smith bought the original Bickle farmstead in 1923. His family lived in the Bickle house, raised livestock, built a barn for butchering, and sold meat and groceries at the Maples Market on Thirteenth Street at the south end of his driveway. Smith also offered outdoor dances and other amusements on the property. Smith is seen here with his dog, Bimbo, in 1955. His land is now owned by the Crete Heritage Society. (CHS.)

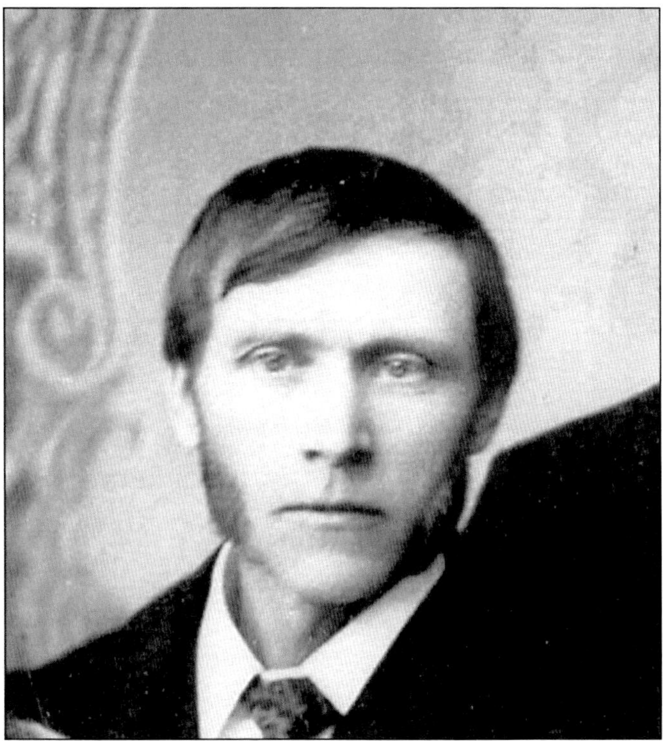

Andrew Smith, an immigrant from Denmark, was the foremost photographer in town in the 19th century. Most of the photographs in this book were taken by Smith. His studio was on the southwest corner of Maine Avenue and Fourteenth Street, but much of his work was done on location. His son Axel followed his father's profession, and both men used "A. Smith" in their official identification stamp. (CHS.)

Nine

A Few More Memories

Through the years, Crete achieved regional and national notoriety for many situations and activities. Some were unfortunate, heartbreaking events, and others gave reason to celebrate. The interesting combination of personalities in the town, the eclectic cultural component of the city, and Crete's location near Nebraska's urban areas provided opportunities for people to make significant achievements to make the town proud. In contrast, Crete's proximity to the Big Blue River and a major rail line, while of vital importance for the town's development, caused many challenges for residents.

The Big Blue River and its tributary, Walnut Creek, have flooded the north part of Crete and parts of downtown several times. Basements were filled with water and, in some instances, the first floors of houses were inundated. Residents were evacuated in boats by the fire department and other volunteers.

The grade of the Burlington railroad tracks served as a levy between the worst of the flooding and the remainder of town; however, the water sometimes flowed all the way to the Kingwood Avenue and Eleventh Street area via an old Walnut Creek channel. The flooding was exasperated by the two dams at the Crete Mills. When the dams were eliminated and other water control systems were built, the threat of flooding, while not completely removed, became manageable.

The rail lines that crisscross the town have also caused distress. They have been the site of serious and fatal car-train accidents and train derailments, including the ammonia disaster of 1969.

Several creative, talented Crete residents brought recognition to Crete through their work with local improvements and community and artistic projects. The Anderson-Rawlings Company brought the unique Lustron house to town; clubwoman Florence Hazen Miller put Crete on the map with her varied civic endeavors, including the design of the Nebraska state flag; and Vincent Prucha made a showplace of his yard with his remarkable topiary trees.

On the following pages, a mixture of disheartening events and extraordinary accomplishments that help to define Crete are presented.

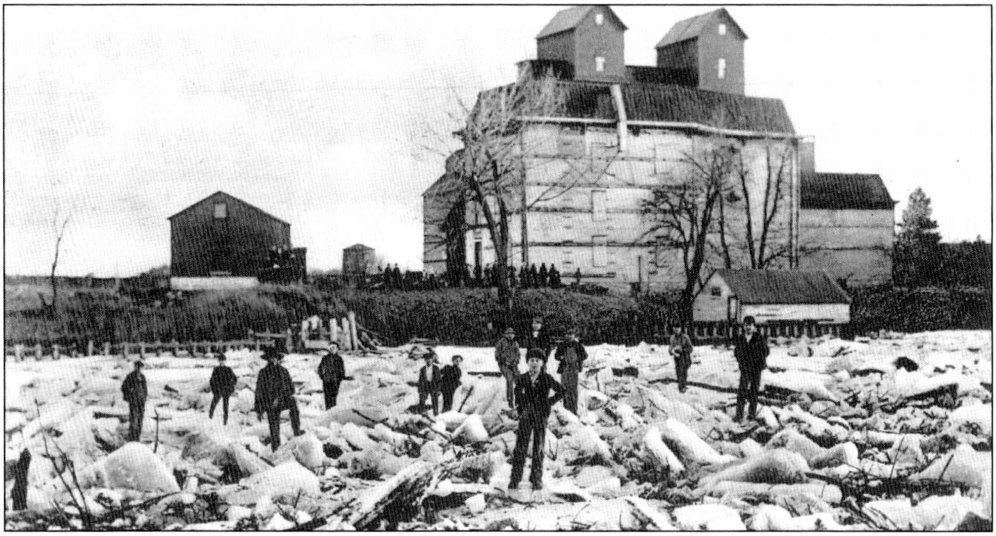

In February 1905, melting ice on the Big Blue River broke, moved, and refroze, creating a phenomenal ice gorge. These men and boys felt the ice was stable enough for them to venture onto the gorge and pose for this photograph. In the background are the roller mills at the upper dam. (Marti Ator Williams collection.)

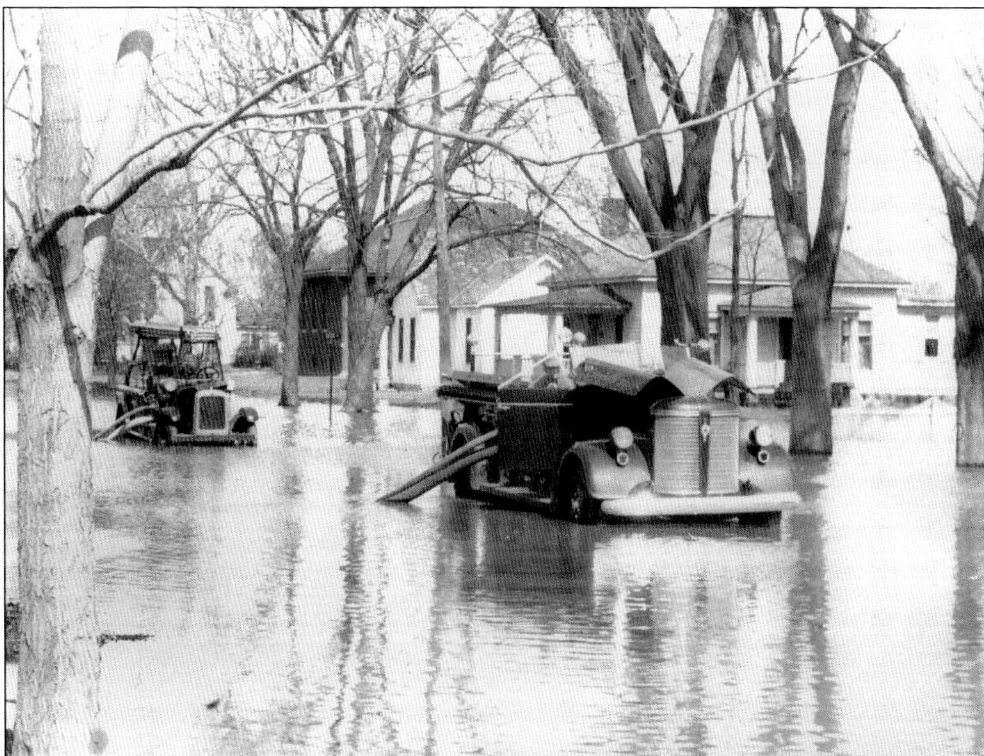

Crete Volunteer Fire Department trucks drove through deep water on North Maine Avenue during the spring 1948 flood. The truck in front is a 1946 LaFrance pumper, and the rear tuck is a 1928 GMC pumper. This view looks north-northwest at Nineteenth Street and Maine Avenue. North Ward School is behind the houses. (CHS, Krebs collection.)

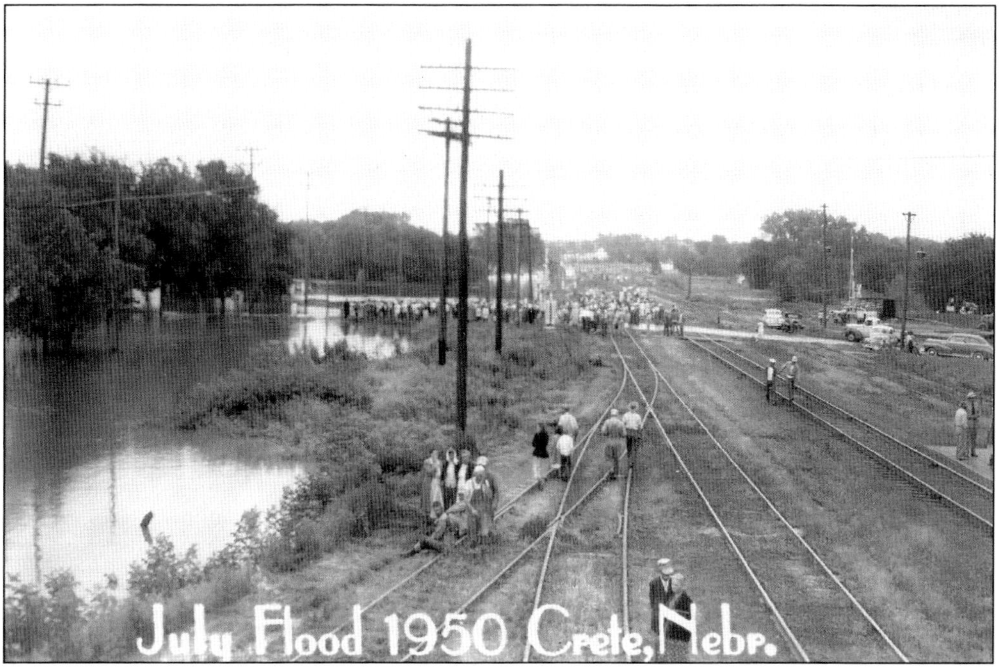

People gathered at the railroad tracks on Maine Avenue during the July 1950 flood, concerned about friends and loved ones in the north part of town. This flood covered nearly 75 city blocks. Many people and pets were evacuated by boat, while some waited out the flood by moving to the second stories of buildings. (CHS, Krebs collection.)

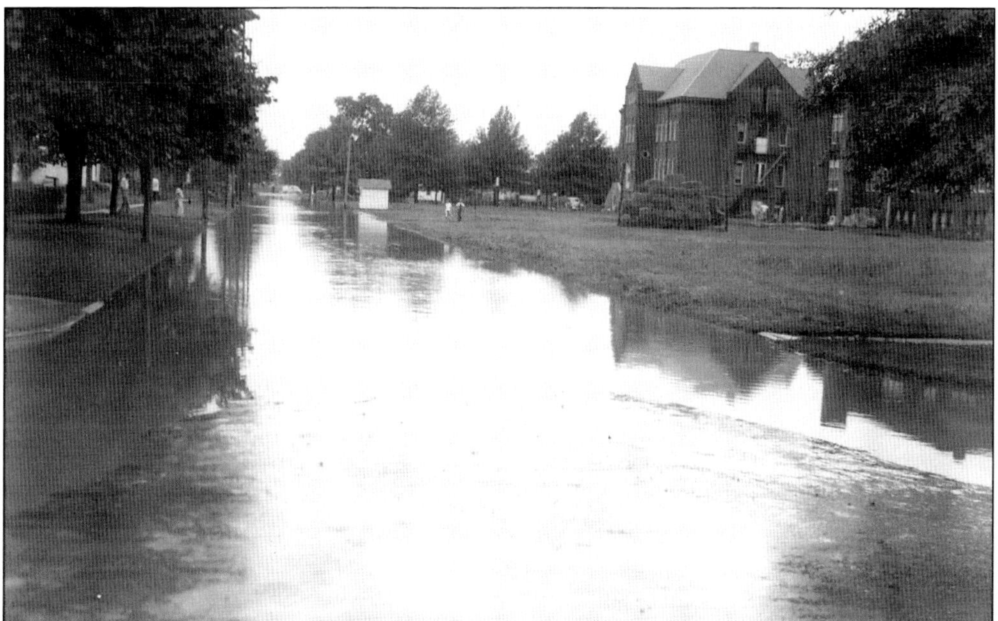

The July 1950 floodwaters moved south in an old Walnut Creek channel from the Burlington railroad tracks, south along Kingwood Avenue, past the library, through the city park, and onto the public school property at Eleventh Street and Kingwood and Linden Avenues. Crete's high school, "Old '88," is on the right. (CHS, Krebs collection.)

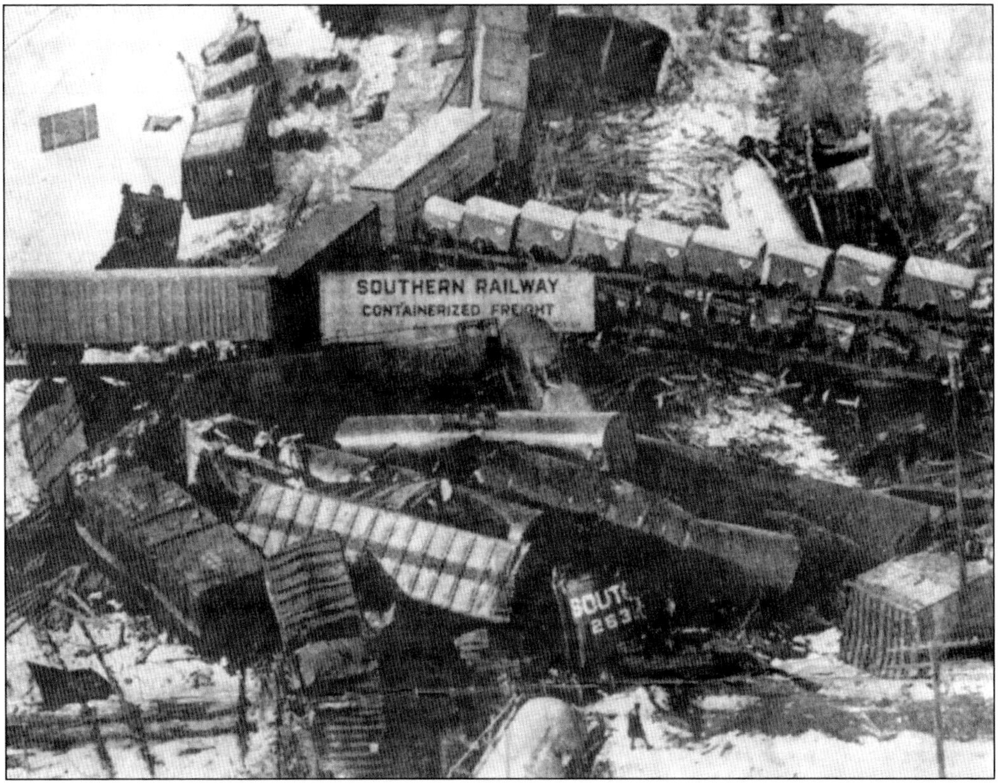

At 6:30 a.m. on February 18, 1969, the town of Crete was stunned by a 25-car train derailment that caused three tankers of anhydrous ammonia to explode, spreading deadly gas into snow-covered residential neighborhoods. Thermometers read zero, and there was no wind, allowing the gas to hover over the city. Eight people died, and 25 were seriously injured. The Crete Volunteer Fire Department, Doane College students, and others rallied to evacuate residents. (CHS.)

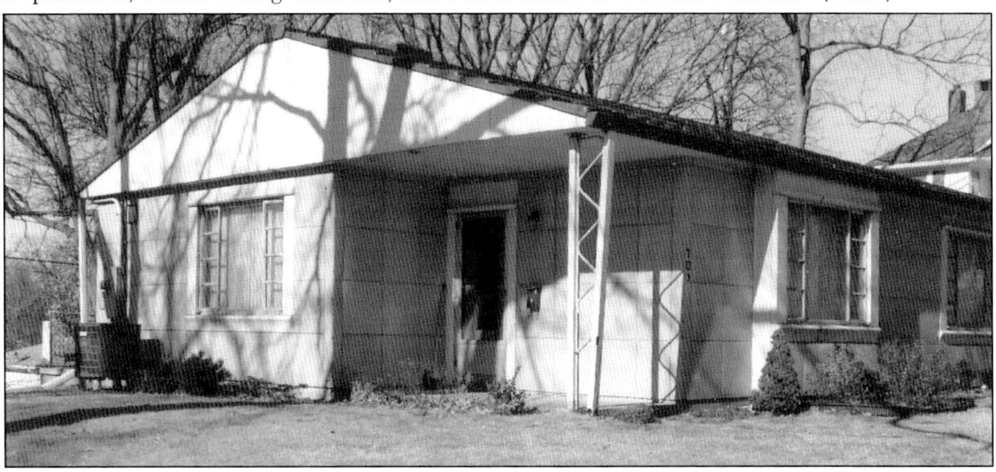

This prefabricated steel house at 707 Boswell Avenue was made in Ohio by the Lustron Corporation. Components were factory-made and shipped to Crete by truck. Crete's Anderson-Rawlings Company, led by Philip C. Anderson, assembled this home in 1949 for Gustav W. Lindberg, a business professor at Doane College. The Lustron Corporation lasted about two years, and only about 2,500 houses were made. Just a few were built in Nebraska. (Author's collection.)

Florence Hazen Miller moved to Crete in 1911 with her husband, Benjamin G. Miller, the local telephone company manager, and became involved in numerous civic activities. In 1923, she created the concept of the living Christmas tree, which was recognized by Pres. Calvin Coolidge. Crete's living Christmas tree was located in front of the library. Florence Miller wrote song lyrics about the Christmas tree and Nebraska and also funded the redesign of a prominent Doane College water feature, since known as Miller Pond. Her philanthropic efforts benefited Grace Methodist Church and the city itself. She donated the five acres upon which the National Guard Armory was built. Her most visible and long-lasting contribution to Nebraska was the design of the state flag, which was adopted in 1925. (Right, CHS; below, Office of the Nebraska Secretary of State.)

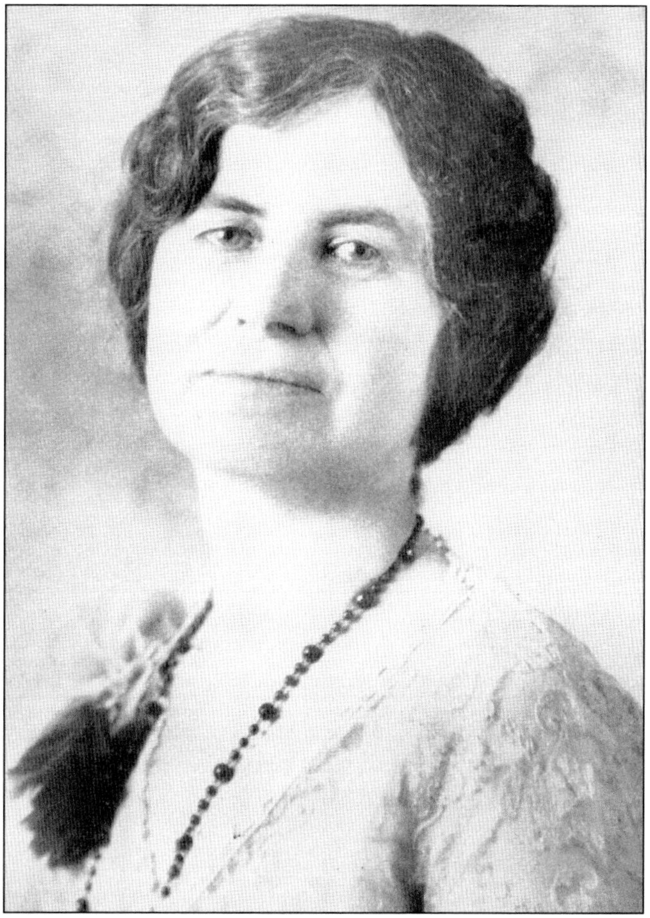

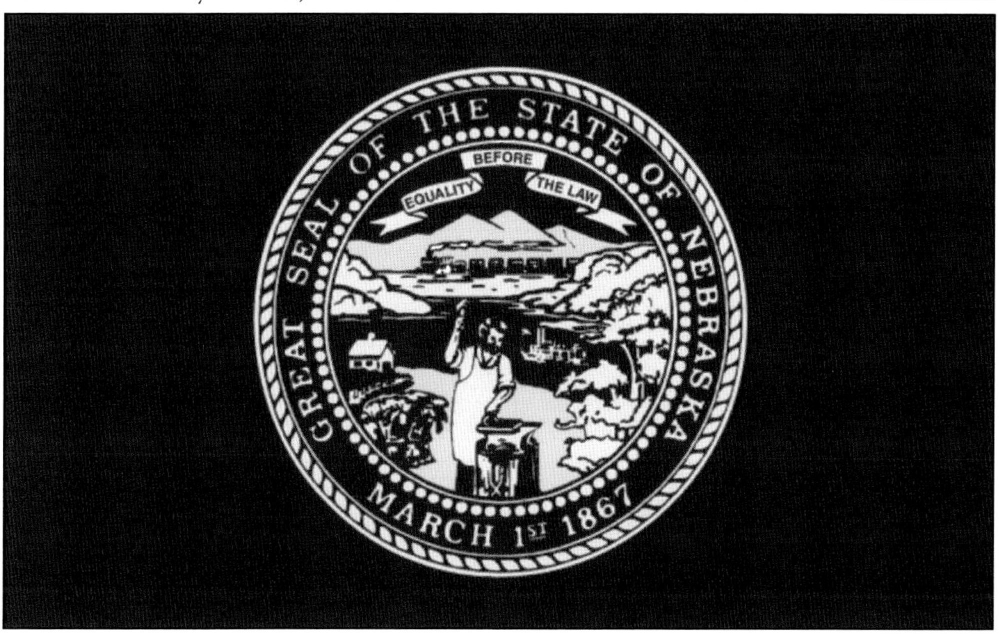

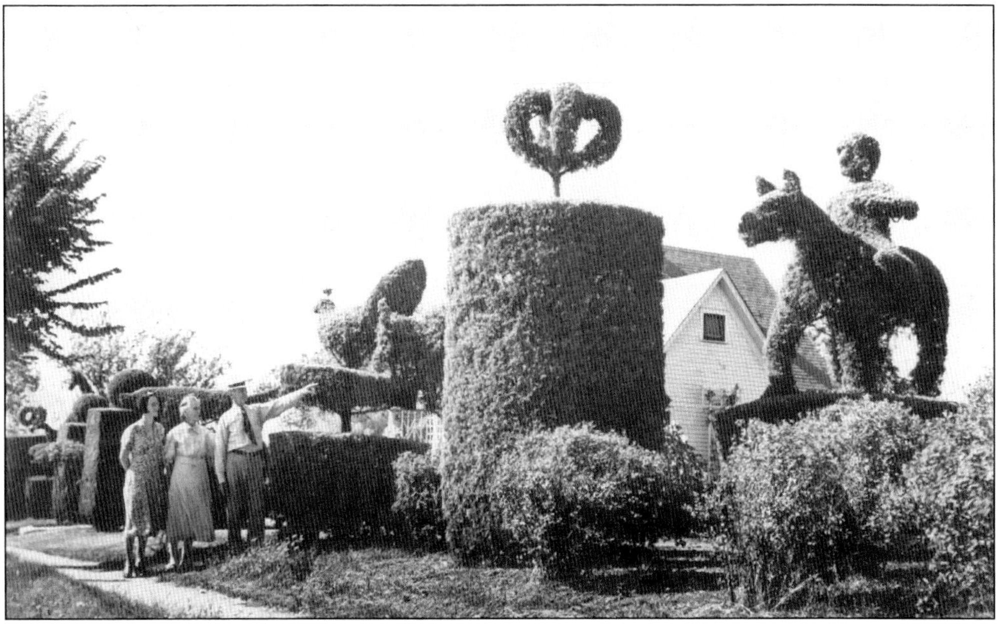

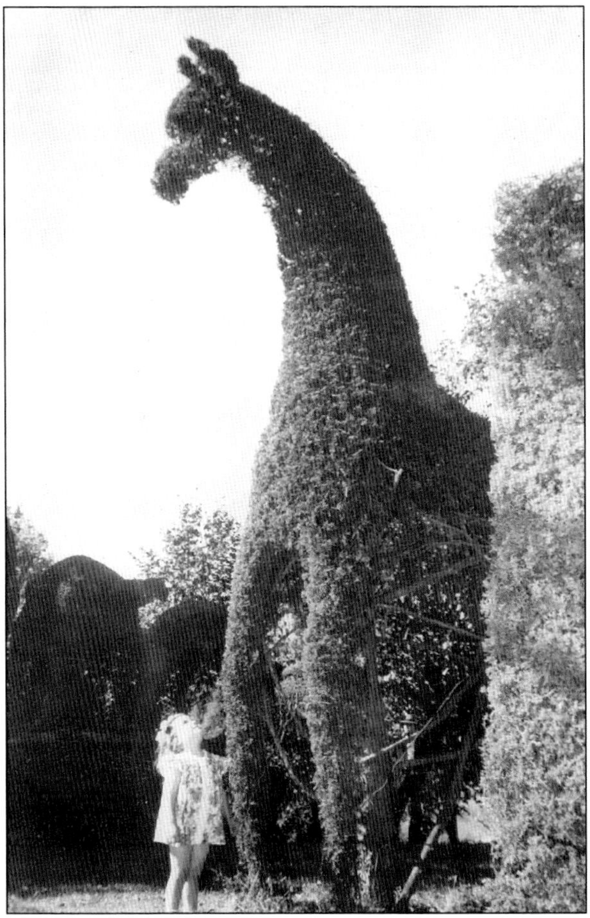

When Vincent J. Prucha built his house at 930 East Thirteenth Street in the 1910s, he planted cedar trees in the yard. As the trees matured, they blocked the breeze and sunshine to the house, so Prucha, a tobacco salesman and artist, trimmed them into topiary sculptures. He lived on the main automobile route through Crete, and his yard soon became a tourist attraction called Prucha's Cedar Zoo. (CHS.)

The trees were fashioned into animals, including a camel, a giraffe, a buffalo, a pointer dog, several birds, and an elephant. Prucha even made a life-sized sculpture of Gen. Ulysses S. Grant astride his horse. He also created a living tree house made from bending four young cedars over to form a canopy. Other trees were carved into geometric shapes. (CHS.)

Prucha tended to his "zoo" daily, using a tall stepladder and handsaw. He even offered postcards of his creations in the 1930s. Visitors came from all over the country to see Cedar Zoo, particularly after an article about the attraction appeared in *Life* magazine on September 22, 1947. (Ann Howard collection.)

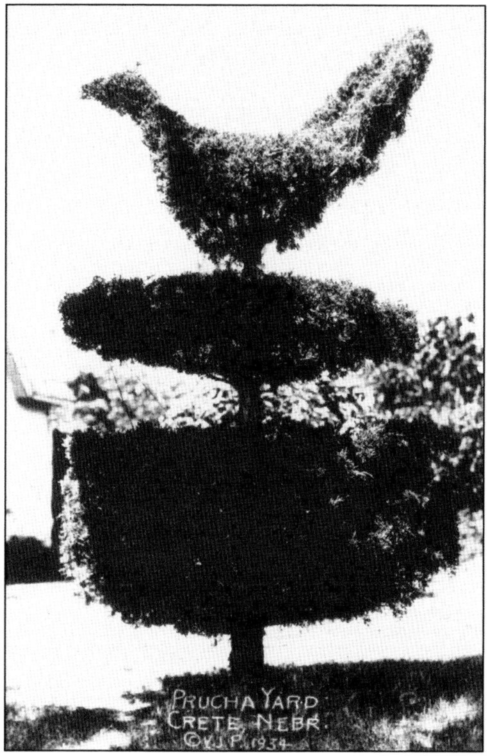

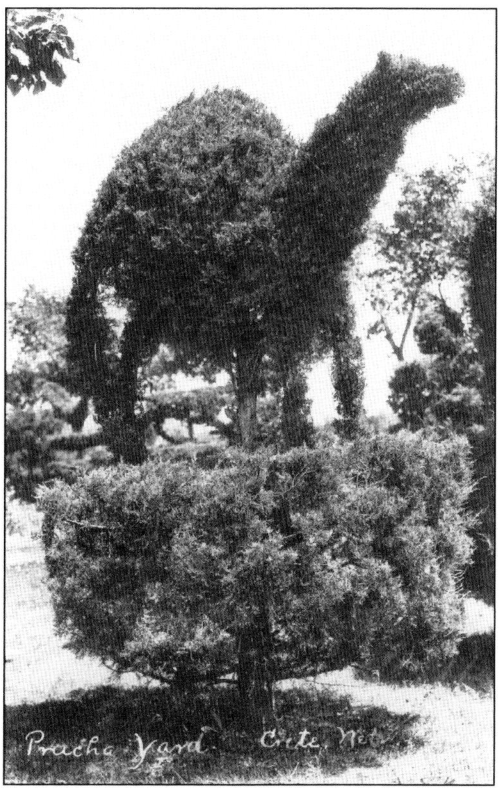

When Prucha died in 1953, his son Otto tended to the yard, but allergies prevented him from properly maintaining the living artwork. The sculptures then disappeared as the trees filled out in natural fashion. Prucha's house still stands on the site, but a modern duplex now occupies the "zoo" lot. (CHS.)

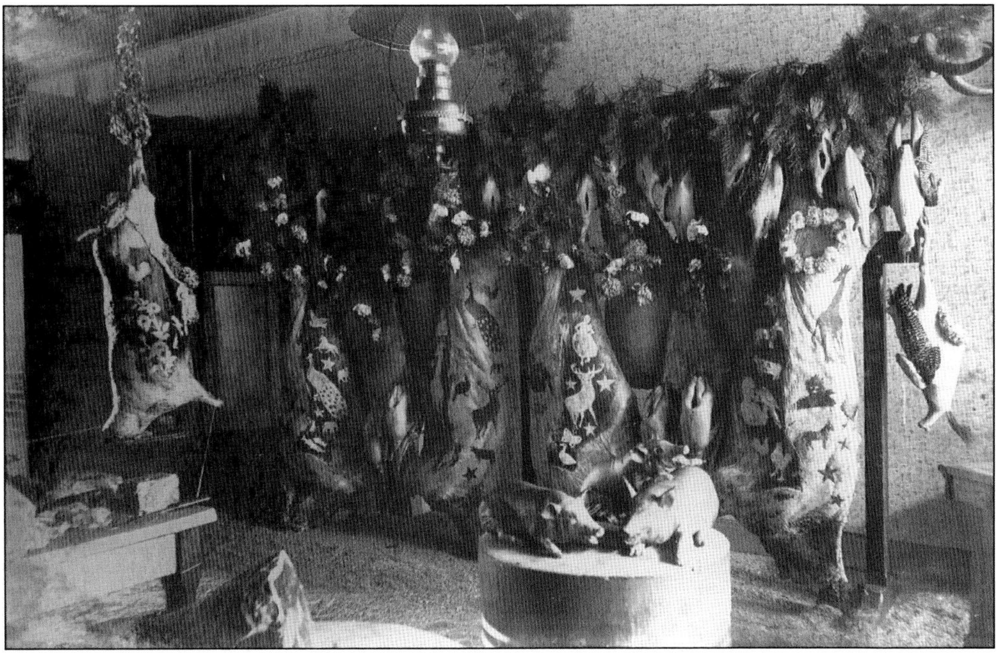

Crete's early meat markets created holiday displays using their products as "canvas." Butchers showed off their artistic talents by carving designs onto the sides of all meats. As Christmas Day approached, newspapers urged Crete citizens not to miss the meat market displays downtown. On December 27, 1888, the *State Vidette* printed the following: "D.J.F. Reed's meat market was handsomely decorated on Christmas. Beef, veal, mutton, turkey, chicken, fish, etc. were placed on exhibition and adorned with artificial flowers and artistic decorations by the butcher's knife." These two photographs from the 1890s show just how fancy these meat displays became. The above image, from Jennie Chapman Stevens's album, features elaborate designs on nearly every piece of meat in the shop. Below, the City Meat Market had meat slabs arranged with Christmas garland. (Above, CHS, Jennie Chapman Stevens collection; below, author's collection.)

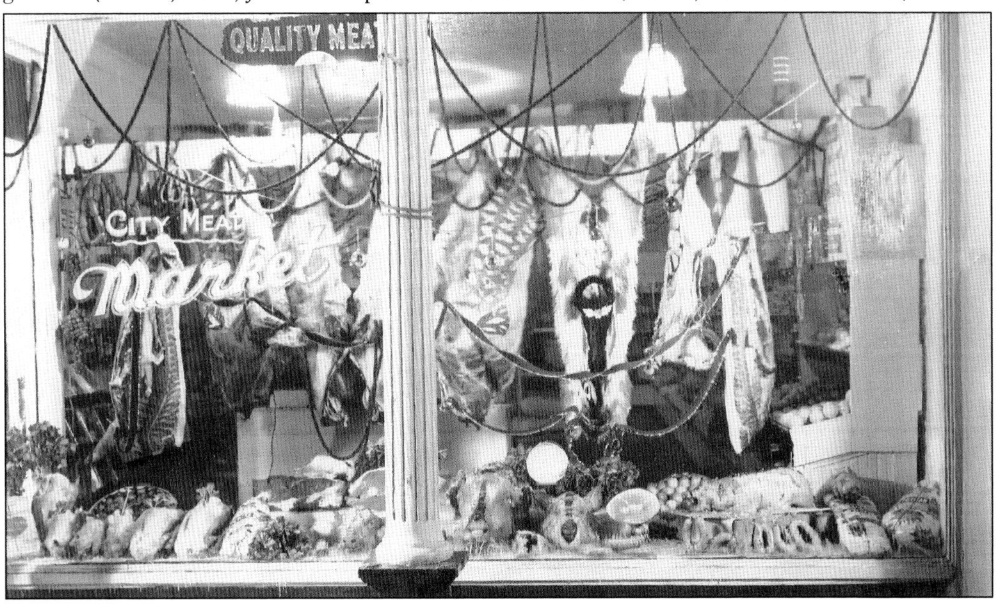

Bibliography

Andreas, A.T. *History of the State of Nebraska*. Chicago: Western Historical Company, 1882.

Breitkreutz, Sandra J., ed. *Saline County Roots*. Crete, NE: Saline County Genealogical Society, 1997.

Eckman, James P. "Respectable Leisure: The Crete Chautauqua, 1882–1897." *Nebraska History*, Vol. 69, No. 1, 1988.

Gregory, Annadora F. *Pioneer Days in Crete, Nebraska, 1870–1888*. Lincoln, NE: State Journal Printing Company, 1937.

Jeffries, Janet L. *Gentility on the Prairie: Refinement and Urbanization in Crete, Nebraska, 1871–1891*. Unpublished master's thesis, University of Nebraska-Lincoln, 1996.

Jeffries, Janet L. and David R. Murphy. "Jesse C. Bickle Farmstead." National Register of Historic Places Inventory-Nomination Form, Historic Preservation Office, Nebraska State Historical Society and National Park Service, Department of the Interior, 1977.

Murphy, David R. "Doane College Historic District." National Register of Historic Places Inventory-Nomination Form, Historic Preservation Office, Nebraska State Historical Society and National Park Service, Department of the Interior, 1977.

Perry, Thomas Doane, ed. *History of Doane College 1872–1912*. Crete, NE: Doane College, 1957.

Rosicky, Rose. *A History of Czechs (Bohemians) in Nebraska*. Omaha, NE: Czech Historical Society of America, 1929.

Saline County, Nebraska Federal Census. City of Crete, 1870, 1880, 1900, 1910, 1920.

[Spencer], Janet Jeffries. "College Hill Historic District." National Register of Historic Places Inventory-Nomination Form, Historic Preservation Office, Nebraska State Historical Society and National Park Service, Department of the Interior, 1980.

———. "Meet Thomas Doane." Doane Family Association of America 1994 Report of Proceedings, 1995.

———. "To Make a Good Product Better: The Fairmont Creamery Company, 1884–1984." *Nebraska History*, fall 1984.

Ziegler, Donald J. *A College on a Hill: Life at Doane College, 1872–1987*. Lincoln, NE: Media Publishing, 2007.